The Heart of the Yoginī

THE HEART OF THE YOGINĪ

The Yoginīhṛdaya, *a Sanskrit Tantric Treatise*

Introduction, translation, and commentary

by

ANDRÉ PADOUX

with

ROGER-ORPHÉ JEANTY

OXFORD
UNIVERSITY PRESS

OXFORD
UNIVERSITY PRESS

Oxford University Press is a department of the University of Oxford.
It furthers the University's objective of excellence in research, scholarship,
and education by publishing worldwide.

Oxford New York
Auckland Cape Town Dar es Salaam Hong Kong Karachi
Kuala Lumpur Madrid Melbourne Mexico City Nairobi
New Delhi Shanghai Taipei Toronto

With offices in
Argentina Austria Brazil Chile Czech Republic France Greece
Guatemala Hungary Italy Japan Poland Portugal Singapore
South Korea Switzerland Thailand Turkey Ukraine Vietnam

Published in the United States of America by
Oxford University Press
198 Madison Avenue, New York, NY 10016

Library of Congress Cataloging-in-Publication Data
Padoux, André.
The heart of the yoginī : The Yoginīhrdaya, a Sanskrit tantric treatise /
Introduction, translation, and commentary by Andre Padoux with
Roger–Orphé Jeanty.
pages cm
Includes bibliographical references and index.
ISBN 978–0–19–998232–5 (hardcover : alk. paper)—ISBN 978–0–19–998233–2
(pbk. : alk. paper)—ISBN 978–0–19–998234–9 (ebook) 1. Tantras.
Yoginihrdaya—Criticism, interpretation, etc. 2. Tripurasundari (Hindu
deity)—Cult. 3. Srividya (Sect) 4. Tantrism. 5. Hinduism—Rituals.
I. Jeanty, Roger-Orphe. II. Tantras. Yoginihrdaya. English. III. Title.
BL1142.6.Y656P33 2013
294.5'95—dc23
2013003295

1 3 5 7 9 8 6 4 2
Printed in the United States of America
on acid-free paper

To the memory of Professor Vraj Vallabha Dvivedi and of Pandit R. N. Bhatt

Contents

Preface

THIS BOOK ORIGINATES in a French translation of the *Yoginīhṛdaya* from Sanskrit by André Padoux, published in 1994 in Paris by the Collège de France. It was printed by Editions de Boccard as an annotated translation with transliterated Sanskrit of the three chapters of the *Yoginīhṛdaya* and of its commentary by Amṛtānanda, meant for an academic readership.

Pursuant to his interest in the Śrī Vidyā tradition, this book was read by Roger-Orphé Jeanty, living in the United States. Assuming that the *Yoginīhṛdaya* would be of considerable interest to a larger English-speaking readership, he proceeded in 2003 to translate its three chapters into English, working with his colleague Sarah Caldwell, using Padoux's French translation and a Sanskrit *devanāgari* edition. This was published informally in English with the original Sanskrit both in the Indian *devanāgari* script and in transliteration. It was designed for use by readers interested in or practicing within contemporary Śrī Vidyā communities.

Some time after completion, Jeanty sent a copy of this effort to Padoux, in recognition of the considerable effort required for the original published French version. In fact, Padoux had already considered the possibility of such a translation and began writing an English introduction to the text and attempted a translation of the first chapter. But he found translating Sanskrit into English very difficult and the attempted translation very awkward and unsatisfactory, and he therefore abandoned it.

Upon receiving a copy of this English translation, Padoux found it quite satisfactory, while admiring the beautiful *devanāgari* text that accompanied it. He thought it a pity that such useful work should be known and made use of by only a few people, and he suggested that they take up the job together.

Padoux emended Jeanty's translation when needed to make it more true to the original Sanskrit text, and Jeanty corrected Padoux's English (in the introduction and the notes and in the translation) whenever necessary to make it more grammatically correct, more fluent, and conforming to American usage.

It is sincerely hoped that this conjoined effort will make this important text much more widely known and distributed within an English-speaking readership.

Note on the Transcription and Pronunciation of Sanskrit

THE SANSKRIT ALPHABET has forty-nine letters, which are transcribed in this book when necessary using diacritical signs according to a common international system.

The vowels are pronounced very much like Spanish or French vowels.

The short *a*, however, is pronounced like the *u* in "but," and the long *ā* is pronounced like the *a* in "fast."

As for the consonants, *g* is pronounced as in "guest," *c* as *ch* in "church," and *j* as in "jungle." The aspirated consonants (*tha, dha, pha, bha*) are pronounced marking the aspiration, as in "top hat," for instance. And *ṛ* is a vowel pronounced more or less like "ri."

The Heart of the Yoginī

Introduction

IN SPITE OF its modest size, the *Yoginīhṛdaya* (abbreviated as YH hereafter), whose title may be translated as "The Heart of the Yoginī," rates among the principal works of Tantric Hinduism. For the lay reader who is not a scholar, this text may be surprising or disconcerting because of its language, its obscurities, and its challenging concepts. We have made every effort in our comments and annotations to clarify these difficulties in the text and have used extensively the commentary by Amṛtānanda called the *Dīpikā* ("The Lamp").

Some help to the reader would first consist in placing the YH in its context, which is Tantric Hinduism, the world of Hindu Tantra. This, naturally, cannot be done satisfactorily within the limits of this introduction. A few points, however, may be made to situate the YH in the historical development of Indian Hindu culture and, in that culture, within the Tantric phenomenon.[1]

THIS PARTICULAR ASPECT of Hinduism, as far as we can say, seems to have appeared around the fifth century of our era (we do not know exactly where), as cults arose of mostly feminine, often fearsome deities whose worship included having the officiants become "possessed" by the deity, occasional sexual rites, and having the adepts follow particular observances (*vrata*). In contrast with mainstream orthodox Hinduism, the religious doctrines of these groups were not traced back to the Veda by their followers but attributed to deities, a male god, most often an aspect of Śiva/Bhairava or of Viṣṇu, or a goddess, usually Kālī. The religious beliefs of these ascetic groups were deemed to have been revealed by these deities. The texts upholding them are usually called Tantra but also Āgama (tradition) or Saṃhitā (collection). They were composed in Sanskrit by brahmins, which demonstrates that these traditions did appear within the socioreligious Hindu fold. The Tantric traditions, in effect, did not reject entirely the Vedic fund of doctrines and practices. They considered it only as socially valid but unable to give liberation, which could only be attained through the complementary and higher teachings of the Tantras.

First limited to small esoteric transgressive groups of ascetics, this teaching progressively spread to larger groups, being adopted by (externally) orthodox Hindu householders who, from a certain time (perhaps the seventh or eighth century) onward, formed the vast majority of Tantric believers. This was in spite of the fact that Tantric teachings are esoteric and in principle meant only for initiates, initiation (*dīkṣā*) being theoretically the necessary first step toward liberation—a liberation giving both *mukti* (liberation) and *bhukti* (the enjoyment of mundane or supramundane rewards or supernatural powers) and, of course, to be enjoyed while still living: a *jīvanmukti*. The Tantric *jīvanmukta*, the liberated in this life, is not only free from this world, but he also dominates it magically.

In the course of time, Tantric traditions developed, expanded, and diversified. As they spread, their notions and ritual practices progressively permeated the whole Hindu world, so much so that for the last thousand years, there has been practically no Hindu tradition entirely devoid of Tantric elements. The Hindu worship, the *pūjā*, for instance, is Tantric in its conception and ritual process, the principles of Hindu temple building and iconography are Tantric, and so on. The Tantric domain penetrated also the social and political field. It spread to the whole Indian subcontinent and South Asia. Its textually most active period was (approximately) from the eighth to the fourteenth centuries. One of its main centers in the Indian subcontinent was in Kashmir, where several important Śaiva traditions appeared, such as the Spanda, Krama, Pratyabhijñā, or Trika. Abhinavagupta, one of the most remarkable and brilliant Indian philosophers and mystics, the master of the Trika, was from Kashmir (fl. c. 975–1025).

Among the Kashmiri nondualist systems and forming one of the four "transmissions" (*āmnāya*) of the Kula is the Śrīvidyā, whose main deity is Tripurasundarī, the supreme goddess of the YH.

THE YH is a very typical text of Tantric Hinduism and embodies archetypal characteristics. As is often the case in such works, its esoteric teaching is expounded in a dialogue between two deities, the Goddess Tripurasundarī (or Mahātripurasundarī), "The Beautiful [Mistress] of the Three Cities" (or "Fortresses")—of the three worlds,[2] that is—who questions, and the god Bhairava, a fearsome form of Śiva, who answers her in the form of these teachings.

Tripurasundarī, a beautiful, auspicious (and erotic) form of the great Hindu Goddess, is the main deity of an important Tantric Śaiva tradition, often called *śrīvidyā* because such is the name of her main or root mantra (*mūlamantra*).[3] The term *śrīvidyā*, however, is not usual in ancient works and has come to be used mainly to refer to a modern form of this tradition, which (as we shall see) is still active in India today. It is therefore better to call this system the tradition of Tripurā (*traipuradarśana* or *traipurasaṃpradāya*,[4] in Sanskrit, the doctrine or tradition of Tripurā), as is done in most texts. We shall do this here. It is also sometimes referred to as *saubhāgyasampradāya*, the *śrīvidyā* being sometimes called *saubhāgyavidyā*. *Saubhāgya* means good fortune, happiness, and success, in addition to beauty and charm; all of these terms evoke an important aspect of this goddess and therefore of this tradition.

The name Tripurasundarī is often explained as referring to that goddess's character as "Mother"[5] of various triads—all the more so when the exegetes of the system interpret it in the spirit of the Kashmirian Śaiva nondualist system of the Trika, the "Triad" (which happens to be the case of Amṛtānanda, whose commentary on the YH we follow here when trying to elucidate this sometimes obscure text). She is also Kāmeśvarī, associated with Kāmeśvara as the Mistress and the Master of Love.[6] Tripurasundarī is sometimes called Lalitā. She is also considered as one of the ten Mahāvidyāṣ, or Nityās,[7] in which case she is sometimes named Ṣoḍaśī ("Sixteenth") or even Śrīvidyā. There exist, too, such aspects of her as Tripurabhairavī or Balatripurasundarī. Indian deities commonly have many aspects, corresponding to different characters or aspects of the deity, auspicious or fearsome, receiving different types of worship. In the auspicious form that she has in the YH, she is usually shown as a beautiful shining woman, three-eyed, with the waxing moon on her forehead, wearing a red garment, seated on a lotus, holding in her four hands goad and arrow, bow and noose.

There are very few stone images of Tripurasundarī, but there are many paintings. Her worship is done using the *śrīcakra*, and no concrete image is used, but during the ritual, she is to be visualized by the officiating adept as described in the texts.

AS IS FREQUENT in India, next to nothing is known of the origins of the tradition of Tripurā. It goes back probably to the tenth or eleventh century a.d. It has survived until our day and has produced important and interesting works well into the modern period. As far as we know, its two oldest and most basic texts are the *Vāmakeśvara/Vāmakeśvarīmata* Tantra (VM), also known as the *Nityāṣodaśkārṇava* (NṢA) and the YH. These works may date from the tenth or eleventh century. It seems that a passage of the VM was quoted by Abhinavagupta (11th c.) in two of his works, the *Parātrīśikavivaraṇa* and the *Mālinīvijayavārttika*; and Jayaratha, who lived in the twelfth century and wrote a commentary on the VM, mentions several earlier commentators on this Tantra, one of whom may have lived as far back as the ninth century. But there is no proof of this.

There also does not seem to exist any iconographical evidence of Tripurā's worship before the tenth or eleventh century. It has indeed been suggested that an allusion to the *śrīvidyā* and perhaps to the *śrīcakra* is to be found in the South Indian Tamil work *Tirumantiram*, which some scholars date as far back as the seventh or eighth century. This, however, remains to be proved. There is also a belief in the modern Śrīvidyā tradition that a *śrīcakra* was installed in Sṛṅgeri, together with an image of the goddess Śāradā, by Śaṅkarācārya (8th c.). But this is mere imagining.

THE TRADITION OF Tripurā is one of the four "transmissions" (*āmnāya*) of the vast Kula (or Kaula) ensemble of Tantric Śaiva systems that developed from the earlier Śaiva fund of beliefs and practices based on the so-called *kāpālika* form of practice, on traditions in which the fearsome Bhairava was the main deity, the basic form of observance (*vrata*) was that of the skull (*kāpālavrata*),[8] and the worship was carried out in cremation grounds (*śmaśāna*). These cults may have originated in northern India, perhaps in Kashmir. They were visionary transgressive cults whose adepts were possessed by the deity and in which the main deity, male or female, was surrounded by secondary deities reflecting his or her power and pervading the cosmos with their (usually fearsome) energy. These secondary female deities, the Yoginīs, were considered to be grouped in lineages (*gotra*), clans, or families (*kula*), hence the name Kula given to this religious ensemble. In the course of time, the earlier transgressive practices tended to be replaced by more staid ones, the main adepts being henceforth usually householders of pure castes rather than skull-bearing ascetics. The ancient Tantras, their terminology, and their deities were, however, retained but tended to be symbolically interpreted. The actual performance of the most "Tantric" rites (the sexual ones in particular) was now limited to a few religious "virtuosi," and possession (*āveśa*) by the deity was replaced by mystical union or fusion (*samāveśa*, although the term *āveśa* continued to be used) of the adept's consciousness with the divine Absolute. This combination of Tantric visionary elements with an intellectual and mystical approach is clearly visible in the YH and still more in its commentaries and also in other texts of the Tripurā tradition (or in other Kula systems).

THE KULA ENSEMBLE of traditions is traditionally divided into four "transmissions" (*āmnāya*), named according to the points of the compass: eastern (*pūrva*), northern (*uttara*), western (*paścima*), and southern (*dakṣiṇa*).[9]

The *pūrvāmnāya* (*pūrva* being understood both as eastern and as primary or earlier) was perhaps the original *kula* system. It includes a number of elements (*pīṭhas*,[10] lineages, coded language, rituals, etc.), which are found in all four transmissions; we shall see some of them here. The worship included sexual rites. The Trika system, the Kashmirian and best known of the Śaiva nondualist traditions, seems to have developed mainly from this *āmnāya*. So does the Spanda, "Vibration." The Trika has long since disappeared as a living religious tradition but has survived to this day as the Kashmirian main form of nondualist shaivism.

The *uttarāmnāya*, the Northern transmission, is that of the Kālī cults. It included three traditions. One is the Mata (the "Doctrine"), of which very little is known and which has disappeared. Another is the Krama (the "Sequence"), so called because its pantheon and its worship are organized in sequences or phases (*krama*). In it, the Goddess dominates Bhairava. A number of Krama texts have survived; some are edited. Abhinavagupta included *krama* elements in his Trika, as did many Śaiva authors, including commentators on the YH. The third tradition is that of the worship of the fearsome goddess Guhyakālī, which survives in Nepal as the worship of Guhyeśvarī.

The *paścimāmnāya*, the Western transmission, has as its main deity the hunchbacked goddess Kubjikā, with the beautiful mantra god Navātman as consort. Its main text is the *Kubjikāmatatantra* (which is edited). Here, too, the goddess is placed above her consort.

Finally, the *dakṣiṇāmnāya*, the Southern transmission, is the one to which the YH belongs. Its chief deity is Kāmeśvarī, goddess of erotic pleasure (with Kāmeśvara as consort), or Tripurasundarī (with Bhairava). It is (or was) in many respects a cult of erotic magic, as appears notably in the VM/NṢA. Its main characteristic is the use in ritual and meditation of a particular diagram, the *śrīcakra*, and of a particular mantra, the *śrīvidyā*. It is probably the most recent of the four *āmnāyas*. It has lasted until today, producing several interesting works. It does not seem to have divided into different schools. There are, however, at least since the thirteenth century, two different lineages, with two different forms of the *śrīvidyā* (as we shall see). Variants also appeared. There is in particular a modern South Indian Śrīvidyā, based in Sṛṅgeri, very largely "vedantized" and "de-Tantricized," which is, however, not socially unimportant since it has been adopted by the Śaṅkarācāryas.[11]

AS WE HAVE seen, the four *āmnāyas* have different main deities, different pantheons and mantras, and so on; however, because of their common Śaiva *kāpālika* origin, they have, if not exactly a common esoteric core, at least a common fund of metaphysical (and sometimes theological) notions or doctrines, or ritual or spiritual practices, expressed by using a common vocabulary, such as the use of the term *kula* and its derivatives (*akula, kaula, kaulika*). Some mantras, too, are common to different *āmnāyas*.

ALTHOUGH IT IS still the most active tradition of the Kula, the Tripurā tradition is little known outside India. There is, as far as we know, no complete and systematic study of its vast literature.[12] This includes, among earlier authors, such people as Puṇyānanda, who was the master of Amṛtānanda, who often refers to his *Kāmakalāvilāsa*,[13] and Śivānanda or Vidyānanda, both of whom commented on the YH but also wrote various ritual, theological, or philosophical works. Later came Lakṣmīdhara (16th c.) and the polymath Bhāskararāya (c. a.d. 1700), who wrote a commentary on the YH to which we sometimes refer here; Kaśināthabhaṭṭa is also worth mentioning.

The tradition includes such works as the vast mythical and speculative *Tripurārahasya*, a number of Tantras or Tantric compilations such as the *Gandharvatantra*, the *Tantrarāja*, the *Tripurārṇava*, the *Śaktisaṅgama*, the *Vidyārṇava*, and so on. There are Upaniṣads, too, such as the *Tripurā*, the *Tripurāttāpinī*, or the *Bhāvanopaṇiṣad*. Very important from the ritual point of view is the *Paraśurāmakalpasūtra* (where the goddess is Lalitā), commented on by Umānanda in the *Nityotsava* (1745) and then by Rameśvara in 1831. A number of other works—digests, ritual manuals, hymns, and so on—would deserve mentioning.[14] Of these, we only refer to one of the best known, the *Saundaryalaharī*, traditionally attributed to Śaṅkarācārya.

NO PRECISE INFORMATION can be given on the origin of the YH or on that of its parent text, the VM/NṢA. No ancient manuscript has been found. Abhinavagupta (c. 975–1025) does not mention its name, nor does

Jayaratha (12th c.) in his commentary on the *Tantrāloka* (TĀ). It is not one of the sixty-four Bhairavatantras listed by him when commenting on TĀ 1.18, nor is it quoted or alluded to in other lists of the Śaiva canon. A *Yoginīhṛdaya* is indeed mentioned in a Nepalese manuscript of the eleventh century, but we do not know if this text is the same as the one we have now; it is probably not. Amṛtānanda, who lived probably in the thirteenth or fourteenth century, says in his commentary on the YH, the *Dīpikā* (Dī), that his was the first one made on that work. But surely, if the YH were by then an ancient work, other commentaries would have existed. All of this makes it very unlikely that the date of the YH is earlier than the eleventh century, and it might well be later.

There are many reasons for believing that the Tripurā tradition originated in northwestern India, more specifically in Kashmir. Jayaratha, who was certainly a Kashmiri, mentions in his commentary on the VM two masters as having introduced this *darśana* into Kashmir, and he appears to believe that there was a long tradition of local exegesis. Śivānanda, the thirteenth- or fourteenth-century commentator on the same text, explains certain peculiarities of the *śrīvidyā* as being a result of the Kashmirian origin of the tradition. Of course, the fact that Jayaratha mentions the tradition as having been brought down into Kashmir (*kaśmireṣu avatārakam*) may mean that it came from elsewhere, and some scholars believe it originated farther northwest, not far from Kashmir, in Uḍḍiyāna, the valley of Swat (now in Pakistan), a region often, but perhaps rather mythically, quoted as the place of origin of several Śaiva Tantric practices or traditions. Central India, too, has sometimes been named as the birthplace of this tradition.[15] All of this is possible. The metaphysics and the vocabulary of the YH, however, are so close to those of the postscriptural Śaiva texts, and especially to those of the later Pratyabhijñā[16] as expounded by Kṣemarāja, that its Kashmirian origin seems very likely. (But since a number of authors on the tradition, such as Puṇyānanda, Śivānanda, and Vidyānanda, were from the south, a South Indian origin of the YH, however unlikely, cannot be entirely ruled out.)

The Tripurā cult was certainly present at a comparatively early date in the North Indian Himalayan area. There seem to be ancient traces of it in Nepal. Even if it began in the north, Tripurā's cult appears to have soon spread to the south, as shown by works of such authors as those noted above. A large number of Śrīvidyā works come from the south, and the many manuscripts mostly in South Indian scripts that are found nowadays in libraries all over India testify to the comparatively early and widespread popularity of the Tripurā cult. This fact is also interesting in that it shows the vitality and importance, from ancient times, of intellectual contacts between different parts of the Indian subcontinent.

THERE ARE TWO important commentaries on the YH. The earlier one is the *Dīpikā* ("The Lamp") by Amṛtānanda, which we often refer to here (abbreviating it as Dī) since it is used as the basis of our explanation of the YH. The other one is the *Setubandha* by Bhāskararāya, who lived in Mysore and Varanasi at the end of the seventeenth and the beginning of the eighteenth centuries. It is a commentary on both the VM/NṢA and the YH, treating them as one and the same work. Amṛtānanda's Dī interprets the YH in the spirit of the later Pratyabhijñā as developed by Kṣemarāja, which shows that even if Amṛtānanda was South Indian, he was nevertheless steeped in the Kashmirian Śaiva nondualist tradition. Bhāskararāya's *Setubandha*, on the other hand, which was finished, we are told, on the Śivaratri day of Śaka 1655 (a.d. 1733), is the work of a much later remarkable polymath (more than forty works are ascribed to him), not characteristically written in the spirit of a particular sectarian tradition but very true to the Tantric spirit of the YH. It is clear and useful.[17] There are other commentaries of lesser interest.

It may be useful here to draw the reader's attention to the fact that Indian religious or philosophical texts, often obscure or arcane or cast in brief elliptical statements,[18] were meant to be made explicit by commentaries given orally through the teaching of masters or in written exegetical works. This is how Indian traditions appeared and developed, permitting "change in continuity." Truth being deemed to have been proclaimed in the origins of time—or out of time—in the Veda, or by deities, nothing could be added to it except by way of commentaries and explanations.

A problem that arises concerning the text of the YH is its relationship to the VM/NṢA. The three chapters of the YH have often been considered to be the latter part of a work in eight chapters, the first five of which constitute the VM/NṢA. The YH begins with the Goddess asking Bhairava to explain to her "the many unknown elements that are in this Vāmakeśvaratantra" (*vāmakeśvaratantre 'sminn ajñātārthas anekaśaå*). The YH would thus appear to be an esoteric complement to the more exoteric VM, which is a work of erotic magic and ritual, whereas the YH is mainly metaphysical and devotional, even in its third chapter on the *śrīcakrapūjā*. To this can be added that Amṛtānanda sometimes refers to the VM in his Dī, notably when explaining why a particular point is or is not mentioned in the YH or in his own commentary, and that Bhāskararāya later wrote his commentary, *Setubandha*, on all eight chapters of the two texts as if they constituted a single work, and he states explicitly that the YH is the latter half of the Tantra: *tantrottarārdham*.

There are, however, convincing reasons to believe that these two works are related but distinct texts, probably of different periods. For instance, Śivānanda and Vidyānanda never refer to the YH in their commentaries on the NṢA. Jayaratha, when commenting on the VM, mentions several earlier commentators on the same, while Amṛtānanda, in his DĪ, says that he is the first to comment on the YH. Not only is the spirit of the two works very different, but the YH also gives the *śrīvidyā* in the so-called *hādi* form, whereas the NŚA/VM gives it in the *kādi* form.[19] For these reasons and several others, we believe that the VM and the YH are two different works, the VM being the earlier one and the YH being composed to complement it philosophically, which is why these two texts came, at some later period, to be considered as two sections of one work.

THE ŚRĪVIDYĀ or Tripurā tradition constitutes one of the "transmissions"—the *dakṣināmnāya*—of the Kula, and the YH, which is one of its basic texts, is a Tantric work. It is Tantric both in its spirit, its theology, and its metaphysics and in its ritual practices and forms of worship.

It is Tantric in its conception of the supreme deity as inseparably male and female, Bhairava and Tripurasundarī, the latter being, theologically, the supreme goddess but metaphysically subordinated to Bhairava, who is Śiva. The Goddess is also Śakti, the divine universal power that creates and animates the cosmos in all its aspects, human, material, mundane, or supramundane, her power spreading out as a hierarchy of feminine deities or energies radiating concentrically from her; this characteristically Tantric "mandalic" aspect of the pantheon is found in the whole of South Asia. It is illustrated here by the *śrīcakra* with the deities who abide in it.

Also Tantric is the notion of the *kuṇḍalinī*, the divine cosmic power present in the human body. The Tantric adept lives with the image of this both human and divine power present in the image of his body, this structure of centers (*cakras*, etc.) or nodal points (*granthis*) connected by subtle tubes or channels, the *nāḍis*, where the life breath, the *prāṇa* (*prāṇas*, rather, for they are numerous) circulates along with the mantras.

This structure, imagined, visualized, even sometimes "felt" as present ("intraposed") within his physical body by the yogin, is usually called "subtle body" in English. We do not use this expression because it is a misnomer. In *all* Sanskrit texts, the term *sūkṣmaśarīra* (or *sūkṣmadeha*), which means "subtle body," designates not this structure but the transmigrating element in the human being, which is made up of different *tattvas* and therefore has no shape, no visible aspect. It cannot be visualized as is the inner structure of *cakras* and *nāḍis*. We call it yogic body or imaginal yogic body, not subtle body.

The presence and the meditative and ritual use of this purely mental (but existentially perceived) image of the body is fundamentally Tantric, even though it is used by most non-Tantric practitioners of yoga. Also Tantric, of course, is the worship beginning with an inner (*āntara*), entirely mental *pūjā*, followed by the outer (*bāhya*) worship organized following the traditional Tantric pattern, which includes not only visualisations (*dhyāna*) but also yogic phases during which the officiating adept is to awaken his *kuṇḍalinī*. The *pūjā* ends with a *japa* of the *śrīvidyā*, which is, in fact, a practice of *kuṇḍalinī* yoga. The offerings made during the worship, being Tantric, include meat and alcohol. But there are no sexual rites.

We will comment further on these Tantric aspects, and mention other ones, as they occur in the three chapters of the YH. Here we underline only a few particular points.

Yoginī

The Yoginī of the title is the goddess Tripurasundarī. Amṛtānanda, in his DĪ, explains that she is so called because she manifests the coming together (*yoga*) of all the constitutive elements of the universe. She bears this name, he says, because she is eternally in union, *yoga*, with Śiva. These explanations are of some value insofar as they underscore the at once transcendent and immanent nature of the Goddess Śakti and her indissoluble union with Śiva.

The name Yoginī is also interesting as a reminder of the links between the Tripurā tradition, as an *āmnāya* of the Kula, with the ancient (but still surviving) Yoginī cults. This tradition having as its main deity a goddess who is the supreme power, Śakti, surrounded by a retinue of feminine secondary deities/powers—*ṣaktis*, which are also Yoginīs—could be called Śākta. But the so-called Śākta systems developed in a Śaiva context and are in effect Śaiva. Metaphysically, Tripurasundarī is subordinated to Paramaśiva, the supreme level of the godhead. The YH is expounded by Bhairava, the fearsome form of Śiva, in answer to a question of the Goddess. True, he does so because she orders him ("I am ordered by You," *tvayāham ājñaptaḥ*), but this order is a form of his own will (*madicchārūpayā*, 3.202). As the DĪ explains, the universe is the "play" (*līlā*, *kṛḍ*) of Śakti, but Śiva is her master. Theologically, in the devotion and worship of her devotees, the Goddess is supreme; but if Śiva and Ṣakti are inseparable, Śiva, the masculine aspect of the total supreme godhead, is higher: Ṣakti is Śiva's energy. Tripurā's tradition is therefore Śaiva.[20]

Surrounded by the Yoginīs abiding in the *śrīcakra*—in the cosmos, that is—Tripurasundarī is the first of them, infusing them with her power and presiding over their activity. They emanate from her in a hierarchical order, embodying and spreading her power on all planes of the cosmos and fulfilling the functions allotted to them. As Bhairava says in YH 3.194: "You alone it is, Enchantress of the worlds, who are playing under the guise of these [deities]." They are aspects (*rūpa*) she takes on in her cosmic play.

In the Tantras and the Purāṇas, the Yoginīs are usually said to be sixty-four in number, which is eight times eight, that is, eight times the Eight Mothers (*aṣṭamātaraḥ*, *aṣṭamātṛkā*).[21] In the third chapter (3.193), the YH multiplies this number by ten million, mentioning sixty-four crores[22] of Yoginīs, to be worshipped in an eightfold ritual. In the *śrīcakra*, however, although they are in eight groups (plus the Goddess), corresponding to the structure of the diagram, they number seventy-eight. Their names also are not those usually found in the Purāṇas.

Hṛdaya

The great secret (*mahāguhya*) disclosed to initiates by the YH is the *Yoginīhṛdaya*, the "Heart of the Yoginī," by which is meant the supreme reality, the supreme divine plane where the Goddess, consciousness (of) itself, manifests her power and her glory. She does this by means of the *śrīcakra* and the *śrīvidyā*, which are not a mere ritual diagram and a mere mantra but her visual, or diagrammatic, and her phonic form, two aspects of her cosmic creative (and destructive) power.

The heart as the supreme reality, as the spiritual plane, and as the center in the human body (or, more exactly, in the image of the body) where this reality is revealed and experienced is an ancient Indian notion. It was taken over and developed in nondualist shaivism by such authors as Utpaladeva, Abhinavagupta, and Kṣemarāja, who described it in his commentary on the Śivasūtras as being "the light of consciousness since it is the place where everything abides" (*viśvapratiṣṭhasthānatvāt citprakāśo hṛdayam*). He also describes it as throbbing and flashing consciousness (*sphurantīṃ saṃvidam*) or as both made of the world and transcending it (*viśvātmakaṃ taduttīrṇam*). It is therefore the total plenitude of the godhead as mystically experienced in one's heart.[23] (We must not forget that in traditional India, the center of consciousness is in the heart, not in the brain.)

Mudrā

Mudrās do not play a fundamental role in the YH. Their case, however, needs to be mentioned here because of the particular conception of *mudrās* in Tantric texts. They are not mere symbolical gestures evoking a deity or some person or entity, object, or feeling, as is true of the *mudrās* (or *hastas*) of dance or theater. They are both evocative/invocative gestures and—in the case of deities or powers—the supernatural entity they evoke or symbolize. They are both bodily gestures or attitudes by which the performer invokes and makes present (and, up to a point, identifies with) the entities they symbolize *and* these very entities. The nine *mudrās* described in *śl.* 59–61 of the first chapter of the YH are nine deities, ancillary goddesses of Tripurasundarī made present by a gesture whose performance (together with the mental visualization) identifies the adept with that deity. (Such deities are to be worshipped during the *śrīcakra pūjā*, as we shall see in the third chapter.)

Gestures are an important element in human communication. They play a role in support of language. They also supplement it. In ritual, they have meaning and power, and they act, usually by accompanying a mantra but also sometimes by their own visual/bodily power; this appears clearly here in chapter 1.

For many texts, *mudrās* are more than gesture; they are mystical attitudes, and in practicing them, the yogin identifies with a deity or even with the absolute. Such is the case, for instance, with the *mudrās* described in the *Vijñānabhairava* or those described in chapter 32 of Abhinavagupta's *Tantrāloka*, where he explains that the *mudrā*, together with the mental concentration of the adept, brings about the presence of the deity invoked and identifies the adept with it.

Metaphysics

The philosophical conceptions of the YH can be said to be those of the nondualist Kashmirian shaivism, and especially those of the *pratyabhijñā*-based

Trika as expounded notably by Abhinavagupta. This is one more reason for believing the YH to have been elaborated, if not in Kashmir, then at least, and certainly, in circles where the Kashmirian Śaiva tradition was active.

The supreme reality (*paramaṃ mahat*, *mahātattva*, or *mahāsattā*, the "Great Being") is described as transcendent, undivided (*niṣkala*, 1.27), transcending space and time, pure light (*prakāśa*, 1.11),[24] and consciousness (*saṃvit*, 1.10). It is also the phoneme *A*, the "unsurpassed" or "peerless one" (*anuttara*). This absolute flashes forth, vibrates luminously (*sphurattā*, *ullāsa*). It expands as a luminous wave (*sphuradūrmi*, 1.10) by its own free will (*svecchayā*, 1.9) and manifests thus the whole cosmos made up of the thirty-six *tattvas*, from Śiva to the earth (*pṛthivī*, 2.32–33). This universe, manifested[25] as if by play (*līlā*), is pervaded by the divine power or energy; everything, from the gods to this earthly world, is in fact the Goddess herself, supreme splendor (*paraṃ tejas*, 1.72), "surrounded by the sparkling waves of her multitudinous energies" (1.55). Of this manifestation, the Goddess is luminously conscious (*prakāṣāmarśana*) as it unfolds "on the screen of her own self" (*ātmabhittau*, 1.56). She vibrates (*spandarūpiṇī*), being immersed in bliss (*ānanda*). Although transcendent (*viśvottīrṇa*), the Goddess as supreme power (*paramaśakti*) is also immanent, "made of the world" (*viśvamaya*), that is, embodied in everything that exists. The cosmos is her manifested form, but although she is shining, "Flame of the essence of divine play" (*divyakrīd rasojjvala*, 2.76) as the absolute, she is ever pure, undivided light and bliss. All these notions and the terms used are typical of nondualist shaivism.

The YH, however, is not a philosophical treatise aiming at expounding particular metaphysical tenets. Neither was that the aim of the Dī, in spite of the fact that its interpretation of the sutras always develops their metaphysical import. The aim of this text (and of practically all Indian metaphysical systems)[26] was, while conveying an esoteric teaching, to show a way toward liberation—more precisely to a Tantric form of liberation in this life, *jīvanmukti*, which is both liberation from the fetters of this world and domination over it. This is the raison d'être of the three chapters of the YH.

Chapter 1: Cakrasaṃketa (86 ślokas)

The YH does not say here how to draw the *śrīcakra* (nor does Amṛtānanda in the Dī). It describes how it appears as an outward manifestation of the power of the Goddess, who is deemed to have agreed with her consort,

Śiva, to be present with him in the *śrīcakra*, hence the title of the chapter, *Cakrasaṃketa*. What is described is a cosmic process bringing about the existence of the *cakra* that embodies this process and mediates it to the *sādhaka* who is to visualize mentally its aspect and its dynamism through an intense identifying form of meditation called *bhāvanā*.[27]

After presenting the dialogue, in the Absolute, between the Goddess and Bhairava, which makes up the text of the YH, the chapter first describes the cosmic unfolding of the *śrīcakra* from the central *bindu* to the outer square (*śl.* 10–21). Then the adept, following a reverse movement, since he is a human being, is to visualize and perceive within himself the three main constituent parts of the *cakra*, going from the outer square to the center. Now, once the meditation of the *sādhaka* has reached the central *bindu*, he is to evoke and follow mentally the ascending levels of phonic energy (the *kalās*, "parts"), from *ardhacandra* to *unmanā*, of the utterance (*uccāra*)[28] of the *bīja HRĪṂ*, the basic mantra of the Goddess.

The mental process goes thus from the spatial, visual domain of the diagram to the oral one, as if sound were felt as a subtle extension of space. The adept is to meditate there on three planes of the Word, *vāc*, from the supreme, *parā*, to the intermediate, *madhyamā*,[29] and to evoke the fifty phonemes of the Sanskrit alphabet while also meditating such entities as *pīṭhas* or *liṅgas* (*śl.* 37–49). He is to conceive the *śrīcakra* as being the universe produced by the will (*icchā*) of the deity, a will that is eventually to become action (*kriyā*) and which is then *mudrā* "because it rejoices [*mud*] the universe and makes it flow [*rā*]."[30] Stanzas 57–71 then describe ten *mudrās* that are both ritual hand gestures and aspects of the Goddess, corresponding also to the nine parts of the *śrīcakra* (and to its entirety). The *mudrās* symbolize or, more accurately, are actually stages in the progression of the *sādhaka* from the outer world where he lives to the godhead.

Other meditations on the *śrīcakra* are then prescribed, all meant to help the adept to realize the metaphysical import of the diagram as the form the Goddess takes on in her cosmic creative (and destructive) play; added to the preceding ones, this *bhāvanā* will lead him to liberation.

Chapter 2: Mantrasaṃketa (85 ślokas)

Although this chapter is entirely based on the phonetic pattern of the *śrīvidyā* (in which the Goddess and Śiva have agreed to meet; this is the *saṃketa* of the chapter's name), its syllabic composition—its "extraction," *uddhāra*,[31] as it is usually called—is not given. In this, the YH differs from its parent text, the NṢA, which does give it. It appears, however, that the *śrīvidyā* is considered to be made up of fifteen syllables grouped in three clusters, as follows: *HA SA KA LA HRĪṂ* • *HA SA HA KA LA HRĪṂ* • *SA KA LA HRĪṂ*. This is, as we have said, the *śrīvidyā* in the so-called *hādi* form, because it begins with *HA*. There is also another form, called *kādi* (because the first cluster begins with *KA*): *KA E I LA HRĪṂ*. These two forms are used in two Tripurā traditions called, respectively, *hādimata* and *kādimata*, which seem to have existed from comparatively ancient times since they are mentioned by such authors as Śivānanda (13th c.).[32] The three clusters of the *śrīvidyā* are called *kūṭa*, which means "summit" or "group"; they are also called *bīja* or *piṇḍa*.

The *mantrasaṃketa*'s purpose is to give six different "meanings" (*artha*) by means of allegorical symbolical interpretations of its syllables—that is, to expound six different ways to understand, perceive, and experiment by *bhāvanā* its inner nature and hidden meaning, a practice that will lead the *sādhaka* toward liberation. These interpretations are abstruse and often far-fetched, and we have not always understood them in spite of help received from Professor V. V. Dvivedi of Varanasi.

The chapter begins by enumerating the *vidyās* (i.e., mantras) of the nine *cakreśvarīs*, the regent deities of the nine parts of the *śrīcakra*, which the adept must place by *nyāsa* on nine parts of his yogic body and worship there as present in the nine constitutive *cakras* of the *śrīcakra*. Then is expounded the first *artha*, the *bhāvārtha* (*śl.* 16–25). It is based on symbolical values given to the syllables of the *vidyā*, the three parts of which are described as resulting from the union of Śiva and Śakti, from whose interactive union (*saṃghaṭṭa*)[33] the "flow," the creative play of the mantra, is deemed to issue. This very flow expressed by the phonetic constituents of the *śrīvidyā*, manifests, sustains, animates, and ultimately reabsorbs the cosmos, a process the adept must experience spiritually through a *bhāvanā* in which the three parts of the mantra are experienced as fused with his *kuṇḍalinī*. The power of the *vidyā* also takes on here the form of the *kāmakalā* (*śl.* 21–25), a diagram whose symbolism, based on the sexual union of Śiva and Śakti, is both visual and phonic.[34]

The *saṃpradāya artha*, the "traditional meaning" (*śl.* 26–48) shows how the cosmic process is pervaded by the *śrīvidyā*, that is, by the united Śiva and Śakti. To this effect, the YH explains how the constitutive elements of the universe—*tattvas, guṇas, prāṇas,* and so forth, even the gods—come to be manifested. All of this is grasped and experienced by *bhāvanā.*

The *nigarbha artha,* the "inner meaning," very briefly considered, (*śl.* 48–51), is the essential oneness of Śiva, the guru, and the self of the *sādhaka,* who is to realize it by *bhāvanā,* thanks also to his devotion and to the power of the guru's gaze (*nirīkṣaṇa*).[35]

The *kaulikārtha,* the Kula meaning of the *vidyā* (*śl.* 51–68), is meant to bring about a realization by the adept of the essential oneness of the *cakra,* the godhead, the *vidyā,* the guru, and his own self. The *śrīcakra* is shown as being born from the phonemes of the *vidyā;* as being the cosmic, essential body (*vapus*) of the Goddess; and as having the *vidyā* as its essential nature. The Goddess is described as present in the cosmos as five different groups of divine aspects or entities, Yoginīs and so on. The adept is to realize and experience by *bhāvanā* that all of this is present in the *cakra* and in the *vidyā* and in his own body and that of the guru. To realize this is to gain liberation.

The *sarvarahasya,* the "most secret of all" *arthas* (*śl.* 69–72), is secret because it is a most direct way to fusion with the godhead. It is a *kuṇḍalinī* yoga practice where the parts of the *śrīvidyā,* the fifty Sanskrit phonemes, and the thirty-eight cosmic *kalās* are interiorized by the adept and made to ascend with his *kuṇḍalinī.* He thus experiences a cosmic pervasion leading to liberation.

Finally, the *mahātattva artha,* the one concerning the highest reality (*śl.* 73–80), is the nondual realization of the Absolute "in the flashing forth of the essence of the divine play." This *artha* is meant for the "heroes" (*vīra*), followers of the *kaulācāra,* the practice of Kula, who participate in the ritual meetings of the Yoginīs (*yoginīmelana*). The practice described here seems to be mainly meditative, not actually sexual. It shows, however, the surviving links of the Tripurā tradition with the earlier *kāpālika* Kula practices, an aspect that the adepts of the South Indian Śrīvidyā later tried to blot out.

Chapter 3: Pūjāsaṃketa (204 ślokas)

This chapter is the longest of the YH. It accounts for more than half of the work. Although the Goddess is to be visualized during the worship, which is performed on the *śrīcakra* without any material icon, she is not described here as she is, for instance, in *śl.* 130–146 of the first chapter of the NṢA. Only her theological and metaphysical traits as the supreme deity are given. Tripurasundarī, in NṢA, is described as a beautiful young woman, luminous like the rising sun, having three eyes, a half-moon on her forehead, and a crown of jewels on her hair. She wears gold bracelets, is clad in a red garment, and is seated on a lotus. She holds in her two upper hands a noose (*pāśa*) and an elephant-goad (*aṅkuśa*) and in her two lower hands a bow (*dhanus*) and arrows (*bāṇa*). These four attributes are quoted in YH 1.53 as those of Kāmeśvara and Kāmeśvarī, who, taken together, are forms of Tripurasundarī.

The first *pūjā* described is the *nityāpūjā*, the worship all Hindus must perform daily. Some are occasional (*naimittika*) rites, and a few are optional (*kāmya*).[36] It is not described in full detail, except for the *nyāsa* and the *japa*, two rites meant to identify the officiating adept with the deity. Some rites are hardly dealt with. The YH underscores the parts of the ritual that aim more specifically at helping the *sādhaka* to identify with the godhead, which is the raison d'être of the YH but which is an essential aspect of Tantric worship. Its performance is a means, if not to gain, at least to progress toward liberation. In fact, no Tantric worship may be performed if one is not already divinized by a preliminary ritual. It is said, *nādevo devam arcayet* ("One who is not God must not worship God"). But although he is thus already ritually divinized, the officiant must still perform during the worship several rites that will advance him toward the goal of identification with the deity he worships.[37] In such a view, the ritual is seen more as a spiritual exercise than as a mere worship of the deity.

This explains why the chapter begins by saying that there are three sorts of *pūjā*, the lowest of which is the ritually performed one. The highest one (*śl.* 3a, 4b–7), the "supreme worship," is purely spiritual. It is a *bhāvanā* associated with an ascent of the *kuṇḍalinī*, by which the adept experiences mystically his unity with the supreme Śiva. It is the total plenitude of the absolute I (*pūrṇāhaṃbhava*), an experience of the nature of the Goddess as the flashing forth of consciousness. The second sort is "nonsupreme" (*apara*). It is the *cakrapūja* as described in this chapter. Bhairava says here (*śl.* 3b) that he performs it ceaselessly; it is a divine, not a human, activity. Then there is (*śl.* 4a) the "supreme-nonsupreme worship" (*parāparāpūjā*). It consists in "seeing all that appears of itself" and especially, it seems, all rites as being in truth of a purely spiritual nature.

The description of the nonsupreme (*aparapūjā*), ritually performed worship begins next. It fills *śl.* 8–199. It conforms to the usual pattern of the Tantric worship, whose dual (if somewhat contradictory) aim is to identify the performer with the deity while worshipping her. It includes the following items:

Four succeeding series of ritual placings (*nyāsa*) of mantras, of deities, and of the *śrīcakra* on the body of the officiating adept (*śl.* 8–89).

The construction of the throne (*āsana*) of the Goddess and the offering of a propitiatory oblation (a *bali*) to the Yoginīs (*śl.* 90). This is where an "inner sacrifice" (*antaryāga*), or "worship of the self (*ātmapūjā*), should normally take place, but the YH does not mention it.

Removal of obstacles (*vighnabheda*) (*śl.* 92–93).

Worship of the sun (*sūryapūjā*). This is a preliminary rite of all Śaiva cults, with the sun being worshipped as an aspect of Śiva (*śl.* 94–95).

Drawing of the *śrīcakra* on which the ritual worship is to be performed (*śl.* 95–97).

Offering of the "common *arghya*"—consecrated water and so on—on a special diagram; worship of the *āsana* and *pīṭha* and of the *kalās* of fire, sun, and moon (*śl.* 98–100).

Preparation of the "special *arghya*" (*viṣeśārghya*), which, as appears later on, includes wine, and offering it to Bhairava and to the succession of masters (*gurupaṅkti*) (*śl.* 103–104).

Inner oblation (*homa*) in the "fire of desire" (*kāmāgni*). This is normally performed materially at the end of the ritual. Here it is an interiorized, mystical oblation (*śl.* 105–108).

Śrīcakrapūjā, worship of the Goddess and of her retinue of deities (*āvaraṇadevatā*) with sixteen offerings or services (*upacāra*), on each of the different parts of the *śrīcakra*, from the outer square to the center (*śl.* 109–161). This is the main part of the *pūjā*. It ends with the offering of the "lamp of Kula" (*kūladīpa*), together with wine and pieces of meat (*śl.* 165–168).

Japa of the *śrīvidyā* (*śl.* 169–188).

"Satisfaction" (*tarpana*) of the deities of the *cakra* with offerings of wine, meat, and fish (*śl.* 190).

Occasional (*naimittika*) rituals to be performed on certain days to the Yoginīs of the *śrīcakra* (*ṣ̊l.* 191–197).

Taking in by the officiant of the leftovers of the offerings to the deity and final *bali* to Baṭuka and Kṣetrapāla.

The last stanzas (199–204) deal with the fruits, worldly or otherworldly, resulting from the performance of the *pūjā*.

All of these rites will be explained and discussed later, with the translation of chapter 3. The following, however, may be said now about some of them.

Nyāsa

Eighty-one stanzas, nearly one-fifth of the chapter, are taken up by the prescription of this long and complex ritual, which is indeed important since it infuses the body of the officiating adept with the powers of the Goddess, identifying him with her. First, six different "forms" (*rūpa*)—we could say epiphanies, divine and cosmic—of the Goddess are placed. This ritual placing (or imposition) being sixfold, it is called *ṣoḍhānyāsa*. It is considered particularly important and efficacious. It is prescribed and extolled in many of the texts, ancient or modern, of the Tripurā/Śrīvidyā tradition. It is also mentioned in other Śaiva traditions.[38] Next (*śl.* 41–68) comes the *nyāsa* of the *śrīcakra*, first of its nine concentric parts, then of the deities abiding in those parts, going from the outer square, imposed on the extremities of the body, to the Goddess, imposed on the heart. This is followed by another placing (the third series of *nyāsas*) of these deities, starting with the Goddess and ending with the Siddhis of the outer square. These two rites will increase the feeling of identification of the officiant with the Goddess by an interiorization of her diagrammatic cosmic form. The YH says (*śl.* 81) that he is now to consider himself as inseparable from her (*svābhedena cintayet*). Then, as a fourth series of *nyāsas* (*śl.* 81–86), come eight different placings of various entities on the hands and on other parts of the body. The *nyāsas* end with a libation (*saṃtarpana*) to the Goddess, which is, in fact, a meditative practice with an ascent of *kuṇḍalinī*; this somehow confirms the ritual identification of the adept with the deity he worships.

Śrīcakrapūjā

This is not a worship of the *śrīcakra* but a worship, performed on the *cakra*, of Tripurasundarī, who resides in its center while also pervading it, and of all the deities of her retinue placed in concentric tiers around her in the different parts of the diagram. They are worshipped going from the outer square to the inner triangle, the Goddess herself being worshipped in the whole *śrīcakra* since it is her diagrammatic cosmic form.

We have already enumerated the different parts of this *pūjā*. We note here, however, that in each of the constituent parts of the *śrīcakra*, a Siddhi is worshipped, which is both a deity and a supernatural, magical power. Thus, the worship in each of the *cakras* confers on the *sādhaka* one of the eight main magical powers, the *mahāsiddhis*, *aṇimā*, and so on.[39] The ritual worship, therefore, is not only a means to approach the Goddess and identify with her but also a means to acquire supernatural powers, as is expressly stated in *śl.* 189 and 203 of the chapter. This is in conformity with the Tantric conception of liberation in this life, which confers worldly powers along with liberation.

The *pūjā* is made up of a number of sometimes complex rites organized as a dynamic, coherent ritual process, with two intermediate meditative periods, carrying the worshipper from the outer, ordinary world to the realm of the gods, a process during which he acts out symbolically an inner transformation from his condition of a mere mortal being to that of *jīvanmukti* by identification with the godhead. Progressing along this structured ritual and spiritual path, the officiating adept, after "entering" the diagram by paying homage to the lower and most external deities abiding in the outer square, the *bhūgṛha*; purifies his hands and his *prāṇa* (in the two lotuses); then causes his *kuṇḍalinī* to ascend and feels thus absorbed into the cosmic energy (the *kulaśakti*), which is also present in his body, this in the *cakra* of fourteen triangles. As he concentrates on an inner subtle phonic resonance (*nāda*), he raises his *kuṇḍalinī* again from the *mūlādhāra* to the *ājñācakra* (in the first *cakra* of ten angles), and then, along with the *kuṇḍalinī* (in the second ten-angles *cakra*), he becomes absorbed in his own essence. After that, as his *prāṇa* is concentrated in his heart (*cakra* of eight triangles), he realizes the pure essence of consciousness, and (having attained the central triangle) he worships the higher deities destructive of the cosmos surrounding the Goddess, which means that he rises to the source of the universe. The worship having now reached the central *bindu* "whose nature is that of the supreme *brahman*," the adept worships Tripurasundarī in the whole *śrīcakra* since she pervades it. This he does "in total freedom," that is, with the absolute liberty of one who has outsoared (ritually, of course) all limitations.

Perceived in this way, as a movement from this world to the supreme deity, the *pūjā* is for the adept not a random succession of discrete ritual actions but a total and fulfilling existential experience of participation in the divine, a coherent progress toward the Absolute realized by an identification with the cosmic play of the Goddess.

Japa

Finally comes the *japa*, the recitation of the *śrīvidyā*, the *mūlamantra* of the Goddess, a rite performed in the last part of all ritual Hindu worships. The *japa* prescribed here is, however, not really a recitation. It is a complex spiritual and yogic exercise associating the enunciation (*uccāra*) of the *vidyā* with visualizations and with the ascent of *kuṇḍalinī*. The *uccāra* is, in fact, an upward movement of the phonic resonance of the *śrīvidyā* along the *suṣumnā*, going from the *mūlādhāra* up to the *dvādaśānta*,[40] inseparable from the ascent of the *kuṇḍalinī*. It is therefore a practice of Tantric mantrayoga where the *śrīvidyā* is used as a means to facilitate the fusion of the adept with the cosmic divine power of the Goddess.

The *japa* is made up of four meditative-yogic practices:

Japa of the three parts of the *śrīvidyā* (*śl.* 169–173). This consists in visualizing the three parts and the nine constituent *cakras* of the *śrīcakra* as tiered along the *suṣumnā*, then to perceive the *kalās* of the subtle vibration of the *bīja HRĪṂ*, which ends these three parts (*kūṭa*) of the mantra as ascending from the *mūlādhāra* to the heart, then from the heart to the *ājñācakra* and thence up to the *dvādaśānta*, where the threefold phonic vibration reaches the plane of *unmanā*, the "transmental," and dissolves into the silence of the Absolute, with which the adept also fuses. Table 3.1 in chapter 3 shows the pattern of this *japa*.

Japa of the sixfold void, *śūnyaṣaṭkam* (*śl.* 174–175). This practice involves only the *uccāra* of the three *HRĪṂ* and their *kalās*, the *uccāra* being organized along six "voids," or points of the yogic body. It does not seem to include visualizations. Like the first one, it leads to a fusion with the Absolute "in the central void of the divine undivided Consciousness," says the DĪ.

Japa of the five states of consciousness, the *avasthās: jāgrat*, waking; *svapna*, dream; *suṣupti*, dreamless sleep; *turya*, the "fourth" state; and *turyātīta*, "above the fourth" (*śl.* 176–180). It is also an *uccāra* of the *śrīvidyā* with which the adept experiences these states, from the ordinary waking state up to the highest, "above the fourth," which is identical with the absolute divine Consciousness.

Japa of seven "equalizations," *viṣuvas* (*śl.* 181–193). This is the longest practice, since it includes seven *japas*. It is also the most difficult to understand, since the nature of these *viṣuvas*—apparently states of equilibrium of the *prāṇas*—does not appear clearly. It is also a meditative practice whose aim, as with the preceding ones, is to bring about a fusion of the adept with the Absolute. It is a somatopsychic—bodily, mental, and spiritual—practice; in the Tantric domain, whatever is experienced spiritually is also "lived" in the body.

Finally, the third chapter describes the last offerings of the *pūjā*. It ends, too (*śl.* 188–189), by promising the adept who has performed all of these deifying rites or practices (and who is, we may believe, on the way to liberation) not liberation, *jīvanmukti*, but that he will rapidly be in possession of all possible supernatural powers. This may strike us as something of an anticlimax. But on the one hand, is this ritual worship meant to lead progressively, by its daily practice, toward liberation, or is it not rather an acting out of such liberating experiences? Be that as it may, the fact is that the *śrīcakrapūjā*, being performed repeatedly every day, cannot but create mental impregnations (*vāsanas*) which can eventually bring the performer, if not to liberation, at least to its threshold. This salvific efficacy can act progressively with the repeated performance of the *pūjā*, whereas the magical powers are "rapidly" obtained; both can therefore be given by the same ritual. On the other hand, in the Tantric perspective, liberation and powers are inseparably linked: a *jīvanmukta* may despise supernatural powers, consider them as fetters, but he is necessarily endowed with them. We may recall here the Śivasūtras, or Abhinavagupta stating that whatever the *jīvanmukta* says is mantra and that all of his actions are *mudrās*; these are supernatural actions resulting from the condition of liberation in life. The Tantric perfection is metaphysically not of this world, but it takes place in it. It is not disincarnate. It is total plenitude (*pūrṇa*). It is experienced, "lived," on all planes of being. The liberated person is free from the fetters and illusions of this world: he or she outsoars it but also dominates it. The quest of a magical domination of the world is, as much as the hope for liberation, an Indian dream.

THE EDITION USED for this translation is the one prepared, on the basis of several manuscripts, by Pdt. Vrajvallabh Dvivedi, former head of the Yoga-Tantra Department of the Varanasi Sanskrit University, which was published by Motilal Banarsidass in Delhi in 1988, together with

Amṛtānanda's commentary, the *Dīpikā*. It is a good edition both of the YH and of the commentary. Professor Dvivedi kindly let me use it before it was published for the French translation I made of this work.[41] For this, and for the help he otherwise extended me, I wish to thank him once more very sincerely. The YH—of which a large number of manuscripts exist in India and Nepal—was first edited in 1923, together with the commentaries of Amṛtānanda and of Bhāskararāya, by Gopinath Kaviraj; this edition is still available, but it is not very reliable. The YH was also published together with the *Nityāṣoḍaśikārṇava* and with the *Setubandha* of Bhāskararāya as vol. 53 of the Ānandāśram Sanskrit Series.

I

Encounter in the Cakra

CAKRASAṂKETA

THE *YOGINĪHṚDAYA* BEGINS with the Goddess asking her consort, Bhairava, to enlighten her on the secret teachings of the Vāmakeśvaratantra—by which is meant either the text of this name or a larger textual ensemble of the Tripurā/Śrīvidyā tradition (see introduction, above). This dialogue being carried out between two deities is viewed as taking place out of time, in the Absolute.

On the complex meaning of the term *saṃketa*, which cannot be satisfactorily translated by one word and which we try to render here both by encounter (or co-presence) and by agreement, see the introduction, above. It is this commonly agreed presence of Śiva/Bhairava and the Goddess in the *śrīcakra* that transforms it in the (visible) embodiment of the different aspects of the cosmic creative and reabsorbing power of the Goddess united with Bhairava. It gives its powers and efficacy to the *śrīvidyā* and ensures the soteriological efficacy of the *pūjā*.

The Goddess said:
śrīdevyuvāca

O God of gods, great God, expanding in total fullness, there are in this Vāmakeśvatatantra many unknown elements //1// please reveal them entirely, O Bhairava!

devadeva mahādeva paripūrṇaprathāmaya /

vāmakeśvaratantre'sminnajñātārthas tvanekaśaḥ //1//

tāṃstān arthān aśeṣeṇa vaktum arhasi bhairava /

Bhairava said:
śrībhairava uvāca

Hear, O Goddess, the great secret, the Heart of the Yoginī, supreme. //2// What I tell you now out of love for you is to be kept carefully hidden. On earth, it has [always] been taught and received by word of mouth. //3// It must not be given to the disciples of other [masters], nor to unbelievers, O Goddess! nor to those who do not wish intensely to hear it, or who do not give over riches. //4//

śṛṇu devi mahāguhyaṃ yoginīhṛdayaṃ param //2//
tvatprītyā kathayāmy adya gopitavyaṃ viśeṣataḥ /
karṇāt karṇopadeśena samprāptam avanītalam //3//
na deyaṃ paraśiṣyebhyo ṇāstikebhyo na ceśvari /
na śuśrūṣālasānāṃ ca naivānarthapradāyinām //4//

It can be given to [someone] who has been examined and tested during half a year. As soon as one knows it, O Woman with beautiful hips! one attains the state of *khecara.* //5//

parīkṣitāya dātavyaṃ vatsarārdhoṣitāya ca /
etajjñātvā varārohe sadyaḥ khecaratāṃ vrajet //5//

Secrecy is always insisted upon in Tantric traditions, which are initiatory. The teaching is therefore transmitted secretly by the master, the guru, to a carefully chosen disciple, intent on acquiring the esoteric knowledge of the tradition, fully devoted to his master and careful not to divulge the doctrine to unbelievers. The mention of those who give over riches may well surprise us, but it was traditionally considered one of the ways to gain knowledge—or at least a means to approach a master.[1] More generally, as is often said in ritual texts, to spend lavishly on costly rituals is meritorious or even a religious duty: one must never be stingy in one's relationship with the deity. We must not forget that in India, poverty is not meritorious; it is an imperfection, a stigma, the result of the play of karma, therefore not unmerited.

As for *khecaratā,* it is a supernatural power (a *siddhi*) consisting in being able to move (*caratā*) freely in space (*khe*) but, more specifically, to move—that is, to fuse spiritually—in the inner space or sky, the heart, the central void (*kha*) of consciousness. The Sanskrit term *kha* means a hole, an opening, and, more technically, the void for the axle in the hub of a wheel, a notion metaphysically transposed to mean the "void" (*śūnya*), which is the "central" inner essence of the deity: one who moves (*cara*) in that void is identified with Śiva. The state of *khecaratā* is thus the highest spiritual attainment: liberation.

The teaching as expounded by Bhairava now begins:

> O Supreme Goddess! Threefold is the agreed co-presence of the goddess Tripurā: the agreement[2] concerning the *cakra*, and those concerning the mantra and the worship. //6//
>
> *cakrasaṃketako mantrapūjāsaṃketakau tathā* /
>
> *trividhas tripuradevyāḥ saṃketaḥ parameśvari* //6//

As stated in the introduction above, the adept must realize and experience ritually and mystically the divine co-presence of the two aspects, male and female, of the supreme deity during the practices and observances prescribed in the three chapters of the YH, their spiritual efficacy resulting from this active, dynamic co-presence.

The first chapter will now describe this divine presence and power as found and understood in the *śrīcakra*:

> As long as one does not know this threefold agreement, one will not be recipient of the supreme authority [inherent] in the *cakra* of Tripurā. //7//
>
> *yāvad etan na jānāti saṃketatrayam uttamam* /
>
> *na tāvat tripurācakre paramājñādharo bhavet* //7//

The YH now describes the agreement concerning the *cakra*, that is to say, both the diagrammatic structure of the *cakra* with the deities who reside there and the understanding the disciple must have of this *cakra* as embodying the cosmic manifestation of the power of the Goddess united with Śiva.

> This [*cakra* includes] five energies directed toward emanation (*sṛṣṭyā*), and four fires turned toward resorption (*layena*). The *cakra* is [therefore] produced by the conjunction of five energies and four fires. //8//
>
> *tacchaktipañcakaṃ sṛṣṭyā layenāgnicatuṣṭayam* /
>
> *pañcaśakticaturvahnisaṃyogāc cakrasambhavaḥ* //8//

The concentric series of triangles that make up the *śrīcakra* result from the intersections of five triangles apex downward:[3] the energies or powers (*śakti*), the female aspect of the godhead, and four triangles apex upward: the so-called fires, the male aspect. The energies (*śakti*) are creative. The cosmos appears through their play. Fire, on the contrary, evokes destruction, resorption. The total cosmic play of the Goddess, who creates and dissolves the universe, is thus implicitly present in the very pattern of the *śrīcakra*.

> I will tell you, O Perfect One, the descent [on earth] of your *cakra*.
>
> *etac cakrāvatāraṃ tu kathayāmi tavānaghe* /

The *śrīcakra* being the diagrammatic form of the Goddess is a divine, transcendent reality. It therefore comes down to earth (a process known as *avatāra*) so as to be perceived and worshipped by the adepts or devotees. This happens because the Goddess wills it:

> When She, the Supreme Power, [becoming] out of her own free will embodied as all that exists (*viśvarūpiṇī*), perceives herself as flashing forth, the *cakra* then appears. //9//
>
> *yadā sā paramā śaktiḥ svecchayā viśvarūpiṇī* //9//
>
> *sphurattām ātmanaḥ paśyet tadā cakrasya saṃbhavaḥ* /

The *śrīcakra* being the cosmic form of the Goddess results from the same act of consciousness or awareness (*vimarśa*) of the deity as the cosmos. As Amṛtānanda says in the Dī, "The intensely luminous flashing forth of the Supreme Power is nothing else than the emission of the cosmos." The apparition of the *śrīcakra* is therefore described in *ślokas* 10–17 in terms of a cosmic process that simultaneously manifests the geometric pattern of the *śrīcakra* and brings about the apparition of the deities that abide in the *cakra* and animate, nay manifest it, by their power. This is why the process is described starting from the center, that is, from the Goddess.

Note that each of the nine constituting parts of the *śrīcakra* is called *cakra*. (See figures 1.1 and 1.2.)

> From the void letter *A* and from that which ends by emission, [that is] from the *bindu*, vibrating consciousness whose supreme nature is light and which is united with the flashing flow [of divine power, appears] the throne of the *bindu* (*baindavāsana*) which is the [birth] place of the flow made up of the three *mātṛkās*. It then assumes a threefold aspect. // 10cd–12a //
>
> *śūnyākārād visargāntād bindoḥ praspandasaṃvidaḥ* //10//

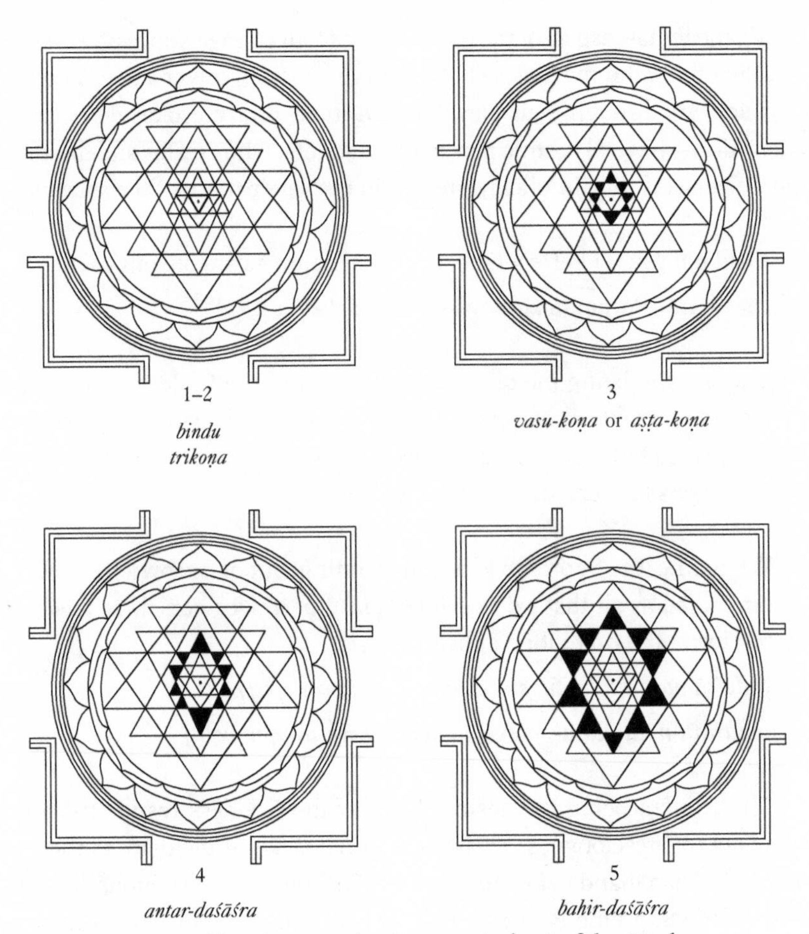

FIGURES I.1 AND I.2 The nine constitutive parts (*cakras*) of the *śrīcakra*.

prakāśaparamārthatvāt sphurttālaharīyutāt /
prasṛtaṃ viśvalaharīsthānaṃ mātṛtrayātmakam //11//
baindavaṃ cakram etasya trirūpatvaṃ punar bhavet /

"The void letter *A*" (*śūnyākāra*) is to be understood as the supreme Śiva, and since Śiva precedes creation, it is considered as void. *A*, the first letter of the Sanskrit alphabet, is traditionally considered the origin and substrate of the whole alphabet, which, in the Śaiva system of phonetic emanation, is the source and essence of the cosmos. Hence the identification of *A* with the supreme deity.

FIGURES 1.1 AND 1.2 (Continued)

The *bindu*, the *anusvāra*, the nasal addition to the preceding vowel (*A*, in this case), written as a dot over the letter it prolongs, is conceived of as the fusion of Śiva and Śakti into one point of concentrated energy: the notion is both visual (a dot) and metaphysical. *Bindu* is thus metaphysically both the totality of the Absolute and the power that will manifest the universe. Being a concentrate of creative power, *bindu* is always described as luminous and vibrating, throbbing.

The "flow of the three *mātṛkās*" issuing from it are (says the DĪ) the three levels of the Word: *paśyantī, madhyamā,* and *vaikharī*,[4] which is another way of saying that the central *bindu* is the birthplace of the whole cosmos, while underlining the fact that the levels of the cosmos appear together with those of the Word and with the letters of the Sanskrit alphabet, which, as we shall see, are in effect associated with the different parts of the *śrīcakra*.

The triangle surrounding the *bindu* is said to have a threefold aspect insofar as the two triangles (one of energy, one of fire, therefore one female, one male) are added to the central one, which makes three times three. This is why the triangular *cakra* surounding the *bindu* is called *navayoni*, ninefold womb. This *navayonicakra* is associated with, or rather brings about the apparition of, nine elements, as follows:

> [Thus appear] *dharma* and *adharma*, then the [four] *ātman*,[5] the knower, what is to be known and knowledge: the *cakra* is thus a ninefold womb. It is immense, a compact mass of consciousness and bliss. A division of mantras in nine [corresponds to] this ninefold *cakra*. //12–13//
>
> *dharmādharmau tathātmanau mātṛmeyau tathā pramā* //12//
>
> *navayonyātmakam idaṃ cidānandaghanaṃ mahat* /
>
> *cakraṃ navātmakam idaṃ navadhā bhinnamantrakam* //13//

Dharma[6] is the socioreligious Hindu law, *adharma* its opposite, for there is no rule without its contrary. The four *ātmans*—a notion developed notably in Vedānta—correspond to four levels of the Self as consciousness, from the Absolute to the living being. Together with the knowing subject, objectivity, and knowledge, they make up the whole cosmic manifestation. This is why this *cakra* is considered the womb—the ninefold womb (*navayoni*)—of the universe. This *cakra* is said to include nine mantras, those of the of the regent-goddesses (*cakreśvarī*)[7] of the nine parts (*cakras*) of the *śrīcakra*.

The three categories—knower (*pramātṛ*), object of knowledge (*prameya*), and means of knowledge (*pramā* or *pramāṇa*)[8]—are deemed to recapitulate the totality of the world as experienced by the subject who "knows," perceives what is to be known: the objectivity and who does this using means or criteria of knowledge. It is a very common philosophical notion, which we will meet several times here.

> [This ninefold *cakra*] is present in the [next *cakra*], of eight triangles, in the form of Ambikā, surrounded by vowels, it is the dynamism of consciousness,[9] the fire of resorption rising from the throne of the *bindu*. //14//

baindavāsanasaṃrūḍhasaṃvartānalacitkalam /

ambikārūpam evedaṃ aṣṭārasthaṃ svarāvṛtam //14//

The *cakra* of eight triangles results from the expansion of the *navayoni*, says the DĪ. This is why the *navayoni* is said to be present in it as Ambikā, the Mother, the Goddess, who dominates and brings together the three first energy-goddesses, Vāmā, Jyeṣṭhā, and Raudrī, and who is to be imagined as encircled by the fifteen "vowels," from *A* to *bindu*, the sixteenth one, *visarga*, remaining inside.

The two next *cakras* are made up of ten triangles:

> The [first of the two *cakra*] of ten triangles is a shining form born from the flashing forth of the nine triangles. It causes the luminosity of the ten phonemes, from the one preceding *śakti*[10] to the last of the nine [following ones]. //15// It is the support of the light of the ten subtle and gross elements. The flashing form of the second ten-pointed [*cakra* is associated with the ten] phonemes beginning with *krodhīśa*. //15–16//
>
> *navatrikoṇasphuritaprabhārūpadaśārakam /*
>
> *śaktyādinavaparyantadaśārṇasphūrtikārakam //15//*
>
> *bhūtatanmātradaśakaprakāśālambanatvataḥ /*
>
> *dvidaśarasphuradrūpaṃ krodhīśādidaśārṇakam //16//*

The nine triangles are the eight of the *navayoni* together with the so-called *baindavāsana*, the throne of (or the throne that is) the *bindu*. In each of the ten triangles of this *cakra* is a phoneme, beginning with *YA* (which, in the Sanskrit alphabet, precedes *RA*) and going up to the last phoneme, *KṢA*.[11] The light (*prakāśa*)—the essence, that is—of the ten gross and subtle elements (*bhūta* and *tanmātra*) abides also in these ten triangles. The ten phonemes "beginning with *krodhīśa*" are the five guttural and the five palatal phonemes, from *KA* to *ÑA* (*krodhīśa*[12] being a name for *KA*); they are associated with the objects of the senses and the organs of action (speech, etc.).

> The transformation of the luminescence of the [first] four *cakras* conjoined [with the *cakra* of ten angles] results in the fourteen-angled one whose nature is that of sense perception and of the sense organs. [The next *cakra*] is made up of the expansion, in the highest sense, of the

phonemes from *khecarī* to *jayā*, its nature being therefore that of the luminescence of Raudrī flashing forth as fire and energy. //17–18//

catuścakraprabhārūpasaṃyuktapariṇāmataḥ /

caturdaśārarūpeṇa saṃvittikaraṇātmanā //17//

khecaryādijāyantārṇaparamarthaprathāmayam /

evaṃ śaktyanalākārasphuradraudrīprabhāmayam //18//

The *cakra* of fourteen triangles is associated with sense perception (*saṃvitti*) and the five senses of apperception and the five of action, to which are added mind (*manas*), "egoity" (*ahaṃkāra*), and intellect (*buddhi*)[13], to these—so as to have a total of fourteen—is added a fourth element, which, according to the Dī, is *citta*, the limited empirical consciousness.

[Then appear] the square, a form of Jyeṣṭhā, and the threefold circle, a form of Vāmā. //19a//

jyeṣṭhārūpacatuṣkoṇaṃ vāmārūpabhramitrayam /

The square is the outer quadrangular part of the *śrīcakra*, sometimes called *bhugṛha*, the house of the earth, since it is the part of the diagram deemed to be metaphysically on the level of the earth. The "threefold circle" refers to the two eight- and sixteen-petal lotuses with the three circular lines that enfold them.

Another vision of the nature of the *śrīcakra*, as associated with the fivefold cosmic division of the *kalās*, is now propounded:

The inner triangle participates in consciousness (*cit*). The eight triangles, of *śāntyātīta*[*kalā*]. //19// The two ten-pointed [*cakras*] as well as the fourteen-pointed one are part of *śānti*[*kalā*]. [The one that] is surrounded by eight petals is made up of the effulgence of the *vidyākalā*. //20// The sixteen-petaled lotus shining clearly is in the body of the *pratiṣṭhā*[*kalā*]. When the aspect of the *nivṛtti*[*kalā*] shines forth, the square shines. //21//

cidaṃśāntas trikoṇam ca śāntyatītāṣṭakoṇakam //19//

śāntyaṃśadvidaśāraṃ ca tathaiva bhuvanārakam

vidyākalāprabhārūpadalāṣṭakasamāvṛtam //20//

pratiṣṭhāvapuṣā spaṣṭasphuraddvyaṣṭadalāmbujam /

nivṛttyākāravilasaccatuṣkoṇavirājitam //21//

One of the divisions of the cosmos of the Tantric traditions is that of the *kalās*. It is part of an all-embracing cosmic and soteriological conception that divides the ways of apparition and maintenance of the cosmos (and the ways toward liberation) into "six paths" (or ways, *adhvans*): the *ṣaḍadhvan*. It is a sixfold division into two groups of three notions or entities, all spreading from the deity to our world, to create and animate the cosmos, and manifest ways also to be followed, going upward, toward liberation.

These *adhvans* are: the way of time (*kālādhvan*), which includes the phonemes, the mantras, and the "words," entities that exist in time, not materially; and the way of space (*deśādhvan*), which includes the *kalās*, the *tattvas*, and the *bhuvanas*, which are more concrete elements, existing in space. The *bhuvanas* are the infernal, terrestrial, and divine "worlds," numbering usually 224. The *tattvas* are the thirty-six entities or cosmic levels, from Śiva to the earth. The *kalās*, "portions," are divisions too complex to be described here. They include *tattvas* and *bhuvanas* in addition to phonemes, mantras, and "words" (*padas*). The highest *kalā* is *śāntyātīta*, "transcending *śānti*," made up of Śiva and Śakti; then comes *śānti*, made up of the next three *tattvas*; then *vidyā*, made up of the *tattvas* from *puruṣa* to *māyā*; then *pratiṣṭhā*, from *prakṛti* to water; and finally, *nivṛtti*, earth.

The correspondences between the parts of the *śrīcakra* and the five *kalās* are logical since they both give expression to the same cosmic hierarchy, going from the deity to our world: the creative and animating process of emanation, embodied diagrammatically by the pattern of the *śrīcakra*, which *is* the Goddess, as creating and embodying the cosmos.

An opposite movement is shown in *ślokas* 22–24, the parts of the *śrīcakra*, with their attending deities, being enumerated in the reverse order, from the outer square to the center, according, that is, to the process of resorption (*saṃhārakrameṇa*), a process that goes metaphysically from the level of this world to the plane of the supreme deity and is also symbolically present in the *śrīcakra*. The nine parts are quoted not by their names but by the divine entities or deities abiding in them. These are divided in three groups:

> In the nine *cakras*, Trailokyamohana and so forth, O Sureśvarī! are found *nāda*, *bindu*, *kalā*, Jyeṣṭhā, Raudrī then Vāmā, //22// as well

as Viṣagnī, Dūtarī, and Sarvānandā, in this order. *Nāda* and *bindu* are undivided, Kālī has the nature of will, //23// Jyeṣṭhā is knowledge, the remaining ones being activity. The *cakra* is thus threefold. It is a form of *kāmakalā*; its essential nature is expansion. //24//

trailokyamohanādye tu navacakre sureśvari /

nādo binduḥ kalā jyeṣṭhā raudrī vāmā tathaḥ punaḥ //22//

viṣagni dūtarī caiva sarvānandā kramāt sthitāḥ /

niraṃśau nādabindū ca kalā cecchāsvarūpakam //23//

jyeṣṭhā jñānaṃ kriyā śeṣam ity evaṃ tritayātmakam /

cakraṃ kāmakalārūpaṃ prasāraparamārthataḥ //24//

The Dī explains the triplicity of the *śrīcakra* mentioned in these three stanzas as linked to three forms of energy-goddesses, each being present in a group of three *cakras*. Thus, the peaceful, *śāntā*, which is consciousness (*cit*), is indivisibly present in the outer square and in the sixteen-petal lotus, with *nāda* and *bindu*. The eight-petal lotus is made of the energy of will (*icchā*). Jyeṣṭhā is the energy of knowledge (*jñāna*) and is present in the fourteen-triangle *cakra*. The remaining five *cakras* (the two ten triangles, *navayoni*, central triangle, and *bindu*), in which are located the goddesses Raudrī, Vāmā, Viṣagnī, Dūtarī, and Sarvānandā, are pervaded by the energy of activity (*kriyā*). The *śrīcakra* is thus pervaded by the three basic energies of Śiva, their places in it being inverted, since the highest, *śāntā*, is in the outer square and the lowest in the center, an inversion that expresses the omnipresence of the whole energy of Śiva in the whole diagram.

To say that the *śrīcakra* is a form of *kāmakalā* is to say that it is a form of the (sexual) union—and therefore both embodying and causing the expansion/emanation of the cosmos—of Śiva and Śakti expressed by the *kāmakalā*.[14]

Yet another manner of conceiving and making a yogic and meditative use of the *śrīcakra* is expounded in the following eleven *ślokas* (25–35):

In *akula*, in what is called *viṣu*, in energy and in fire, then in [the *cakra* of] the navel, in the *anāhata*, the [*vi*]*ṣuddha*, the uvula, the forehead, //25// in the moon and the half [moon], in *rodhinī*, *nāda*, *nādānta*, and *śakti*, then in *vyāpikā* and in the domain of *samanā* and *unmanā*, //26// then in the *mahābindu*, one must meditate in this way the [*śri*]*cakra* in a threefold manner.

Up to the *ājñā* [*cakra*, the meditation] is said to be with parts (*sakala*), then up to *unmanā* it is with and without parts (*sakalaniṣkala*). On the supreme level, it is without parts (*niṣkala*). It is [therefore] threefold.

On the forehead [the *kalā*] is round, like a lamp; [the enunciation, there, lasts] a half a mora.[15] //28// *Ardhacandra* [located above it] has the same aspect and lasts one fourth of a mora. *Rodhinī*, appearing like moonlight is triangular in shape; it lasts an eighth of a mora. //29// [*Nāda*, to be visualized as] a line between two dots, is shaped like a penis, scintillating like a jewel, lasts a sixteenth of a mora. //30// Lasting half as long is *nādānta* flashing like lightning, in the shape of a plow, with a *bindu* on its right. Then *śakti* like an upright line above and to the left of two *bindus*. //31// *Vyāpikā* appears when *bindu*, by its play, becomes triangular. *Samāna*, then, is a straight line between two *bindus*. *Unmanā* [appears] when the play of *bindu* produces a straight line.[16]

The essential body[17] of *śakti*, etc., shines like twelve blazing suns. //33// The fractions of mora of the [enunciation] from *śakti* onward are $^1/_{64}$ of a *mora*, then two times less, then again half as much for *manonmanī*. Then [comes] *unmanī*. //34//

Higher still, [there is] the Supremely Great, transcending the limitations of time or space, of innate beauty, overflowing with supreme bliss. //35//

akule viṣusaṃjñe ca śākte vahnau tathā punaḥ /

nābhāv anāhate śuddhe lambikāgre bhruvo 'ntare //25//

indau tadardhe rodhinyāṃ nāde nādānta eva ca /

śaktau punar vyāpikāyāṃ samanonmanigocare //26//

mahābindau punaścaivaṃ tridhā cakraṃ tu bhāvayet /

ājñāntaṃ sakalaṃ proktaṃ tataḥ sakalaniṣkalam //27//

unmanyantaṃ pare sthāne niṣkalaṃ ca tridhā sthitam /

dīpākāro 'rdhamātraś ca lalāte vṛtta iṣyate //28//

ardhacandras tathākāraḥ pādamātras tadūrdhvake /

jyotsnākārā tadaṣṭāṃśā rodhinī tryaśravigrahā //29//

bindudvayāntare daṇḍaḥ śevarūpo maṇiprabhaḥ /

kalāṃśo dviguṇāṃśaś ca nādānto vidyujjvalaḥ //30//

halākāras tu savyasthabinduyukto virājate /
śaktir vāmasthabindūdyatsthirākārā tathā punaḥ //31//
vyāpikā binduvilasattrikoṇākāratāṃ gatā /
bindudvayāntarālasthā ṛjurekhāmayī punaḥ //32//
samanā binduvilasad ṛjurekhā tathonmanā /
ṣaktyādīnāṃ vapuḥ sphurjaddvadaśādityasaṃnibham //33//
catuṣṣaṣṭis tadūrdhvakaṃ tu dviguṇaṃ dviguṇaṃ tataḥ /
ṣaktyādīnāṃ tu mātrāṃśo manonmanyas tathonmanī //34//
deśakālānavacchinnaṃ tadūrdhve paramaṃ mahat /
nisargasundaraṃ tat tu parānandavighurṇitam //35//

The YH prescribes here to meditate, that is, to visualize each of the nine constituent parts of the *ṣrīcakra* in each of nine bodily *cakras* (also called *padma*, lotus) tiered along the *suṣumnā*, from its lowest part to the *mahābindu*, a system of *cakras* proper to this text (see figure 1.3).

As the Dī explains, these *cakras* are the following: at the base, at the root of the *suṣumnā*, is the *akulapadma*, a red thousand-petal lotus, turned upward, above which is another, eight-petal lotus supporting a third, six-petal lotus. These three elements form what is called *viṣu*, a word that means poison but is taken to come from the Sanskrit root *VIŚ*, to enter or be present, this lotus being deemed to pervade in essence all thirty lotuses tiered along the *suṣumnā*. What these thirty lotuses are is not explained by the Dī, but the YH probably refers to secondary subtle centers (*ādhāra*, *sthāna*, etc.), which we will meet later. Above these lotuses are the usual seven *cakras*: *mūlādhāra* ("fire"); *svādhisthāna*, considered as the place of *śakti*; *maṇipūra*; *anāhata*; *viṣuddha*; *lambika* (on the uvula); *ājñā* (or *bhrūmadhya*), above which the yogin is to meditate on the *bindu*. On the top of the head is another thousand-petal lotus, on the *brahmarandhra*. All this is usual.

But now the *bhāvanā* takes on a different aspect, since the adept is to "meditate" the *kalās*, the subtle phonic "parts" of the *bīja HRĪṂ* starting with the *bindu* (the *anusvāra Ṃ*, that is, which prolongs the *M* of *HRĪṂ*) and ending with *unmanā*. He is to cause to appear in his mind (*bhāvayet*) all these *kalās*, seeing them mentally as described in *ślokas* 27–34. The Dī explains that in this meditation, the conventional shapes and colors of the *kalās*, along with the aspect of the deities abiding in the nine bodily centers, are to be visualized.

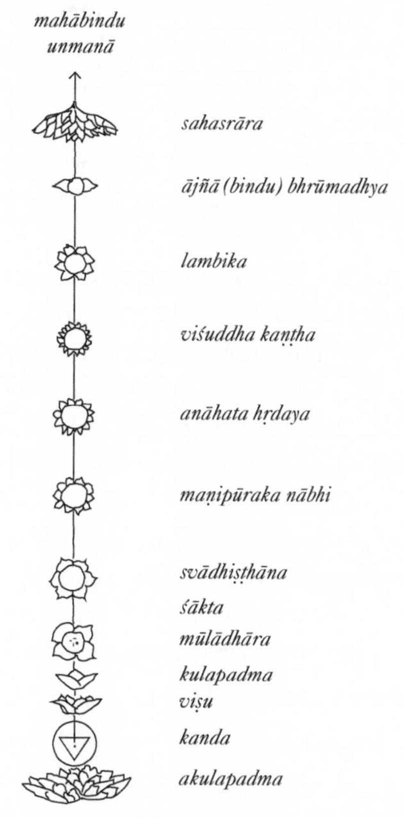

FIGURES 1.3. The *cakras* tiered between the two one-thousand-petaled lotuses.

The adept should do this while giving to each of these mental images the prescribed length of time. These, however, are so infinitesimal as to be entirely theoretical. We may therefore surmise that they are meant merely to express the extreme subtlety and transcendence of these phonic elements.

When this supreme *kalā* sees the flashing forth of the Self, assuming the aspect of Ambikā, the supreme Word is being uttered. //36//

ātmanaḥ sphuraṇaṃ paśyed yadā sā paramā kalā /

ambikārūpam apannā parā vāk samudīritā //36//

When the supreme Goddess perceives herself as identical with the supreme Śiva—that is, when the supreme godhead, in total plenitude, at once male and female, becomes conscious of this state—she becomes

Ambikā, the Mother, the origin, in other words, of all that is. She is then also the supreme Word (*parā vāk*), which is the basic ground and substrate of the universe, and the absolutely peaceful, Śāntā, energy deity.

This metaphysical level is to be imagined diagrammatically as in the center of the *śrīcakra*.

The creative function of the levels of the Word is then shown as visibly embodied in the geometrical structure of the inner triangle of the *śrīcakra*:

> When she turns toward [creation] so as to manifest the universe which is held [within her] as a seed, taking on the form of a hook,[18] [she becomes] Vāmā because she vomits the universe. //37// Then, being the energy of will, this very [goddess] embodies herself as the visionary [word]. Then, as energy of knowledge, she is Jyeṣṭhā, and the intermediate word is being enunciated. //38// With the conservation of the universe, her form spreads out as a straight line. Then, on the level of resorption, she takes on the form of *bindu*. //39// When the reverse process takes place, she flashes forth in a body [shaped like] a *śṛṇgāṭa*. She is then energy of action. She is Raudrī, the corporeal [word], appearing as the universe. //40//
>
> *bījabhāvasthitaṃ viṣvaṃ sphuṭīkartuṃ yadonmukhī* /
>
> *vāmā viśvasya vamanād aṅkuśākāratām gatā* //37//
>
> *icchāśaktis tadā seyaṃ paśyantīvapuṣā sthitā* /
>
> *jñānaśaktis thatā jyeṣṭhā madhyamā vāg udīritā* //38//
>
> *ṛjurekhāmayī viśvasthitau prathitavigrahā* /
>
> *tatsaṃhṛtidaśāyāṃ tu baindavaṃ rūpam āsthitā* //39//
>
> *pratyāvṛttikrameṇaivaṃ śṛṅgāṭavapur ujjvalā* /
>
> *kriyāśaktis tu raudrīyaṃ vaikharī viśvavigrahā* //40//

These four *ślokas* describe the process whereby the Goddess, having perceived herself as the supreme (divine) limiting creative power (*paramakalā*), manifests the universe through the three stages or levels of the Word (*vāk*), starting out from *paravāk*, the supreme Word, which is the eternal, omnipresent, pervasive ground of the whole process. This process, in the metaphysics of nondualist shaivism, brings about the cosmic manifestation as resulting from the Word: the world exists because it has been and is eternally being enunciated, expressed by the supreme deity, which is essentially Word.

There are, based on *parā*, three stages or levels in this process. First is the visionary (*paśyantī*) word, in which there appears in the divine consciousness a vision of what will be manifested—the word and the vision being inextricably mixed. Then comes the plane of *madhyamā*, the intermediate word, in which there appears a differentiation between elements of word or speech and in which the lineaments of the objective world appear but still ideally.

There is a third and lower plane of the word, that of *vaikharī*, the "corporeal,"[19] in which words and objects appear manifested and separately.[20] But in the present case, what appears after the intermediate word is not the next stage of manifestation but the opposite movement: toward resorption, with the *bindu*, the dot in the center of the central triangle. This is because the whole process takes place within the deity and because creation and destruction are always present together in the supreme godhead.

This process, which unfolds on the highest divine plane, is thus described as resulting from the Goddess assuming the aspect of four goddesses and of four energies. First is Ambikā, the Mother of creation, together with the highest peaceful (*śāntā*) goddess form of energy, on the plane of *parā vāk*. Then comes *vāmā*, "because she vomits the universe" (*viśvasya vāmanāt*), projects it outside, that is, together with the energy of will (*icchā*). She also visualizes ideally the universe in herself, the level of the word being *paśyantī*. After this comes the goddess Jyeṣṭhā, together with the power of knowledge (*jñānaśakti*), since she takes cognizance of her creation on this plane. It is the level of *madhyamā vāk*.

Since the creative movement stops here and a reverse, resorption movement appears, the Goddess takes on now the form of the fearsome Raudrī, deemed to arise together with the divine power of action (*kriyāśakti*), described as abiding in the central *bindu* wherein all powers are united and concentrated. The central triangle is thus complete, its three sides being made by the forms taken on by Ambikā, Vāmā, and Jyeṣṭhā, with Raudrī on *bindu* in the center.

What the adept is to realize here is the first creative movement of the supreme Goddess manifesting the inner triangle of the *śrīcakra* together with the four basic forms of energy and four forms of herself as four energy-goddesses, while retaining all this within herself: hence the fourth goddess, Raudrī, and the return to the *bindu*.

In or around this central triangle, other entities are now to appear:

> While manifesting[21] everything that exists in essence then externally, these four energies [produce] KA PŪ JĀ O, in that order. //41//

These *pīṭhās* are located respectively in the bulb, the word, the form, and beyond all form. Their forms are respectively those of a square, a circle with six *bindus*, a half-moon, and a triangle. They are known as being yellow, smoke-gray, white, and red. //42–43//

bhāsanād viśvarūpasya svarūpe bāhyato 'pi ca /

etāś catasraḥ śaktyas tu kā pū jā o iti kramāt //41//

pīṭhāḥ kande pade rūpe rūpātīte kramāt sthitāḥ /

caturasraṃ tathā binduṣaṭkayuktaṃ ca vṛttakam //42//

ardhacandraṃ trikoṇaṃ ca rūpāṇy eṣāṃ kramena tu /

pīto dhumras tathā śveto rakto rūpam ca kīrtitam //43//

The four basic energies, from *śāntā* to *kriyā*, present in the central triangle around the Goddess are now said to bring about the apparition of more concrete cosmic elements, the *pīṭhas*, which are the four main seats or centers of presence and power of the Goddess. They are quoted by the initials of their names, which are Kāmarūpa, Pūrṇagiri, Jālandhara, and Oḍḍiyāna, four places ensuring "geographically" the concrete presence of the Goddess in the Indian subcontinent.[22] A characteristic of Tantric sacred geography is that it is mentally and bodily interiorized, so the *pīṭhas* are also to be visualized by the adept on four points of his yogic imaginary body. The bulb (*kanda* in Sanskrit) is a bulge in the lower part of the *suṣumnā* usually considered as the center from which issue and radiate in the body the 72,000 *nāḍīs*, the channels in which the *prāṇa* circulates. It is also assimilated to the lower yogic center, the *mūlādhāra*.

The three terms "word" (*pada*), "form" (*rūpa*), and "beyond the form" (*rūpātīta*)—together, usually, with *piṇḍa* rather than *kaṇḍa*—are the names of four centers of the yogic body. According to the DĪ, "word" refers to the *haṃsa*, which we may understand here as the inner breath in the heart. The "form" (*rūpa*) would be the *bindu*, on the forehead, on the so-called *ājñā* center. "Beyond the form" (*rūpātīta*) refers to the *brahmarandhra*. The *pīṭhas* appear thus as tiered along the *kuṇḍalinī*, where they are to be visualized as colored geometrical shapes, which are, in fact, those of the *maṇḍalas* of four elements, the *tattvas* of earth, water, fire, and air. Their being associated with *cakras* of the yogic body, from the base to the summit of the *kuṇḍalinī*, correlates cosmic and human levels. This practice (since the *pīṭhas* are to be visualized and "interiorized") is thus at once mental-spiritual, diagrammatic-visual, bodily (in the yogic sense), and cosmic, the description of this part of the *śrīcakra* being at the same time the prescription of a yogic practice. This is one more instance of the tantric association of ritual and yoga.

Now *liṅgas* are described as present in the same places:

> The self-existing *liṅga*, the *bāṇaliṅga* and the *itara*, then the supreme [one], O Dear One, are present in the *pīṭhas*. //44//
>
> They shine like gold, [like] the bandhūka flower, the autumn moon. The great *svayambhuliṅga* is surrounded by the vowels and is three-pronged. //45// The *bāṇaliṅga*, triangular, is encircled by the phonemes from *KA* to *TA*. [The *itara*] is shaped like the round flower of the Kadamba and is encircled by the letters from *THA* to *SA*. //46// The supreme *liṅga* is subtle; it is enclosed by all the phonemes. It is the *bindu*, root of supreme bliss, arising from the eternal plane. //47//
>
> *svayambhūr bāṇaliṅgaṃ ca itaraṃ ca paraṃ punaḥ* /
> *pīṭheṣvetāni liṅgāni saṃsthitāni varānane* //44//
> *hemabandhūkakusumaśaraccandranibhāni tu* /
> *svarāvṛtaṃ trikūṭaṃ ca mahāliṅgaṃ svayambhuvam* //45//
> *kāditāntākṣaravṛtaṃ bāṇaliṅgaṃ trikoṇakam* /
> *kadambagolakākāraṃ thādisāntākṣarāvṛtam* //46//
> *sūkṣmarūpaṃ samastārṇavṛtaṃ paramaliṅgakam* /
> *bindurūpaṃ parānandakandaṃ nityapadoditam* //47//

The *sādhaka* is to imagine these *liṅgas* as being on the same places as the *pīṭhas*: three on the three angles of the inner triangle, the fourth on the *bindu* in the center. Since *liṅgas* are icons of Śiva, we may assume that to conceive them as placed on the *pīṭhas*, the seats of the Goddess, is to mark symbolically the co-presence (the *saṃketa*), the union, of these two, male and female, aspects of the supreme deity.[23]

A *liṅga* is an icon of Śiva of any aspect, shape, or material, not necessarily the more or less visibly phallic image one usually means when using the term.[24] *Liṅgas* are classified in Tantras or in iconography manuals under different names and categories, notably that of "special" (*śiṣṭa*) *liṅgas*, which is the case of those mentioned here, where their shape and color are specified for the adept to visualize them.

The self-existing (*svayambhu*) *liṅga* is normally any sort of natural object that has been declared to be a visible icon of Śiva. In the present case, it is described as three-pronged (that is, says the DĪ, having three *bindus* on its summit) and golden in color. *Bāṇalingas*, as a rule, consist mostly of quartz and are egg-shaped pebbles. Here it is triangular and red. The *itaralingas*, as their names indicate (*itara* means "other"), are normally all other sorts of *liṅgas*. Here it is said to be round like a ball and white. The *paraliṅga* is colorless, invisible, since it is above the field of the senses. It is, says the DĪ, "the root made of bliss of the liana extending from *A* to *KṢA* whose boughs are the [levels of the Word] *paśyantī*,[25] etc., and whose imperishable root is the supreme (*parā*) word. It 'arises from the eternal plane' because the *mātṛkā* is eternal. This *liṅga* arises as the primordial vibration (*prathamaspanda*)[26] from the eternal plane which is to be reached by all those who wish to be liberated from the fetters of this world."

Here, too, the phonemes of the Sanskrit alphabet are present but in their subtle form, as the *mātṛkā*, the "mother" of the phonemes, not as utterable phonic elements. The vowels are associated with the *svayambhuliṅga* since they are of a higher nature than the consonants, associated with the *bāṇa* and *itara liṅgas*, whereas the whole alphabet, the totality of the power of the Word, is associated with the supreme *liṅga*.

> Such are the *kula* and *kaula* entities expressed by the whole mantra taken as a whole with its three *bījas*. //48//
>
> Such [too] are the states called waking, dream, deep sleep, and fourth, as well as the one beyond, supreme splendor [wherein] appears the consciousness of the Self. //49//
>
> *bījatritayayuktasya sakalasya manoḥ punaḥ /*
>
> *etāni vācyarūpāṇi kulakaulamayāni tu //48//*
>
> *jāgratsvapnasuṣuptākhyaturyarūpāṇy amūni tu /*
>
> *atītaṃ tu paraṃ tejas svasaṃvidudayātmakam //49//*

Having associated the four *liṅgas* with the *mātṛkā* and with the levels of *parā*, *paśyantī*, and so on, that is, with the total power of the Word, the YH now considers these entities to be expressed or predicated (*vācya*), that is, brought to existence by—or to have their essence in—the three parts, here called *bījas*, of the *śrīvidyā* and (for the supreme *liṅga*) by or in the *ṣrīvidyā* taken in its totality. The term *kula* is understood by the DĪ as referring to the three human and cosmic divisions: knower, object of knowledge, and knowledge—or subject, objectivity and cognition; or measurer, measurable, and criteria of measurement—(*pramātṛ-prameya-pramāṇa*, which we have already seen above, *śl.* 12–13), taken separately, *kaula* referring to these three elements taken together.[27]

Then (*śl.* 49) another, human group of four elements is added as present in the center of the *śrīcakra*: the four *avasthas*, which are states or modalities of consciousness going from the ordinary waking consciousness (*jāgrat*) to a fourth (*turya/turīya*) subtle one, these four being subsumed and dominated by a fifth "above the fourth" (*turyātīta*) transcendent state, identical with the supreme uncreated divine Consciousness.[28]

> What comes forth appearing as a self-willed visible layout of everything in the shape of the universe is Consciousness, a form of the Self, beauty of uncreated bliss. //50//
>
> *svecchāviṣmayollekhakhacitaṃ viśvarūpakam /*
>
> *caitanyam ātmano rūpaṃ nisargānandasundaram* //50//

Having shown the goddesses or energies present in or around the central triangle as issuing from the absolute while having it as their essence and substrate, the YH now comes back to the cosmic aspect of the *śrīcakra*: by drawing it out by an act of her own will (*svecchā*) as a visible layout of everything that exists (*viśvamayollekhakhacita*) consisting in the universe (*viśvarūpaka*), the Goddess manifests the universe as the *śrīcakra*, entirely pervaded by her power. The Dī quotes here Kṣemarāja's *Pratyabhijñāhṛdaya*,[29] 2: "By the power of her own will she unfolds the universe on her own screen" (*svabhittau*), that is, on herself as the essence and substrate of all. The Dī also quotes a well-known formula:: "The Lord Śiva gladdens having seen the infinite diversity of the world which he has drawn out with the brush of his own will." Another quote: "the supreme energy inseparable from Śiva has as her body the whole cosmic process."

That the diagrammatic and the cosmic processes are one and the same is again stated, as follows:

> When the measurable, the measurer, and the criteria of measure spread out, the brightness contracts, being will, knowledge, and activity. [Consciousness then] takes on a triangular[30] form. //51//
>
> *meyamātṛpramāṇamānaprasaraiḥ saṃkucatprabham /*
>
> *śṛṅgāṭarūpam āpannam icchājñānakriyātmakam* //51//

What appears now in the supreme Consciousness is the condition of the knower (*pramātṛ*), the empirical subject (the measurer), and what the subject can know (the objects, which are measurable, *meya*), knowledge (*pramā*), and its criteria (*pramāṇa*). This development implies a "contraction" (*saṃkoca*) of Consciousness since it evolves from an absolute fullness and undifferentiation to the differentiated, discursive thought (*vikalpa*) of the empirical, individual subject, an evolution whose dimension here is cosmic: the divine energy takes on the form of the universe without, however, losing her divine, absolute, luminous nature. This is expressed by saying that she acts as the three fundamental divine powers of will, cognition, and activity (*icchā, jñāna,* and *kriyā*). These being three, she becomes threefold, a condition expressed in the YH by saying that she assumes the shape of a water chestnut (*śṛṅgāṭa*).

The YH now says (*śl.* 52–55) how the adept is to conceive meditatively—by *bhāvanā*—and visualize the supreme deity as abiding in the *śrīcakra*:

> [One must see the energy of consciousness as] the resting place of the very nature of Śiva as the sustaining power of the expansion of the forms of the universe, supremely beautiful, resting as on a couch against the hip of Kāmeśvara. //52// Shining, she holds the noose made of the energy of will, the hook which is [energy of] knowledge, the bow and the arrows made of energy of action. //53//
>
> Split into support and supported, divided into eight, bearer of weapons, arising from the *cakra* with eight points, she has the ninefold *cakra* as a throne. //54//
>
> *viśvākāraprathādhāranijarūpaśivāśrayam /*
>
> *kāmeśvarāṅkaparyaṅkaniviṣṭam atisundaram //52//*
>
> *icchāśaktimayaṃ pāśam aṅkuśaṃ jñānarūpiṇam /*
>
> *kriyāśaktimaye bāṇadhanuṣī dadhadujjvalam //53//*
>
> *āśrayāśrayibhedena aṣṭadhā binnahetimat /*
>
> *aṣṭāracakrasaṃrūḍhaṃ navacakrāsanasthitam //54//*

The supreme energy of the godhead, supreme consciousness, is now to be conceived as the metaphysical resting place of Śiva, who supports the expansion of the cosmos. She is also to be visualized as the goddess Kāmeśvarī resting on the lap of the god Kāmeśvara:[31] a division in two of the absolute oneness of the supreme which will bring about the multiplicity of the expansion (through the thirty-six *tattvas*) of the cosmos. This divine pair is described as each bearing the four symbolical "weapons" (*āyudha*, here called *heti*) of Tripurasundarī, each identified with one of the four[32] basic energies of Śiva, and is therefore said to be divided into eight.

Although arising from the *bindu*, in the center of the inner triangle, this pair, which is somehow the Goddess herself, stretches out in the whole *śrīcakra*, which is ninefold, and is thus her throne.

> This is the form in which the supreme splendor abides embodied[33] as the *śrīcakra*, surrounded by the sparkling waves of her multitudinous energies. //55//
>
> *evaṃrūpaṃ paraṃ tejaḥ śrīcakravapuṣā sthitam /*
>
> *tadīyaśaktinikarasphuradūrmisamāvṛtam* //55//

The supreme splendor is the supreme godhead, Tripurasundarī, in her cosmic aspect as the *śrīcakra*, with all the deities that animate it surrounding her. The image is that of a central throbbing core of light and power surrounded, as by the waves of the sea, by the energies emanating from this center.

More technically, but interestingly, the Dī explains as follows this flow of the divine energies as linked to, or embodied as, the *śrīcakra:* "When Kāmeśvara and Kāmeśvarī, who are pure light and reflective awareness [*prakāśavimarśamaya*][34] assume by their own free will the forms of the constitutive parts of the *śrīcakra*, then the energies which constitute these parts surround them in the form of the *āvaraṇadevatās* Kāmeśvarī, Vajreśvarī, Bhagamālinī (etc.)."

As for the word "wave" (*ūrmi*), it is explained as follows: "the supreme Lord, who is light [*prakāśa*] is the sea, Kāmeśvari, which is awareness [*vimarśa*] is the water, the waves being the numberless energies into which they divide themselves. As the waves appear and subside in the sea, so the *cakra* made of the thirty-six *tattvas*, with its energies, appears and disappears there."

Having visualized in this way the *śrīcakra* in its dynamic cosmic aspect, the adept is now to visualize and experience bodily and mentally, while displaying them, nine divinized powers, the *mudrās*, which are deemed to reside in the *cakra* (*śl.* 56–71):

> When Consciousness becomes luminously aware of the universe [appearing] on the screen of her Self, filled with the desire for

action, she [produces it] by her own free will. //56// [She is then] energy of activity, called *mudrā* because she gladdens the universe and makes it flow.

cidātmabhittau viśvasya prakāśāmarśane yadā /

karoti svecchayā pūrṇavicikīrṣāsamanvitā //56//

kriyaśaktis tu viśvasya modanād drāvaṇāt tathā /

mudrākhyā

The awareness that the Goddess, supreme consciousness, has of the universe born from her is said to be luminous since the cosmic manifestation has just been described as an ocean of light. In nondualist Tantric Śaiva traditions, the apparition of the cosmos is viewed as a real transformation of the deity into the universe: she is "made of everything [that exists]" (*viśvamaya*). The world, therefore, is not purely illusory.[35] The creation is also viewed as an image the godhead projects as with a ray of light on herself, as on a screen, which is to say that she is not only the origin but also the substrate of the world. Since the world is being manifested, the energy acting in this case is the energy of activity (*kriyāśakti*).

The interpretation of the term *mudrā* as gladdening (*modana*, from the verbal root *MUD*, therefore *mu*) and causing to flow (*dravayati*, from the root *DRU*, to flow or dissolve, therefore *drā*) is traditional.[36] The term can thus be taken as denoting the blissful flow of the universe, different aspects of which will be shown as appearing in different parts of the *śrīcakra* (which is a cosmic diagram), as a result of the action of such secondary deities as the Mudrās, who embody different aspects or stages of the cosmic activity of the Goddess. They are described in the YH as energy-goddesses, not as hand gestures, the usual meaning of *mudrā*. Only in the Dī (and in Bhāskarāya's commentary) are they shown as gestures (and as deities or energies). These hand gestures are to be displayed by the adept, who will thus not only evoke the *mudrās* as deities but also, through this physical action, experiment in mind and body the cosmic activity of the Goddess as she manifests the cosmos, or, in this case, reabsorbs it, a process parallel to that of the quest for liberation.

When this consciousness, Ambikā, made of three *kalās*, //57// becomes divided into three, she causes the continuous presence [of the Goddess in the *śrīcakra*.]. She is celebrated as pervading the whole *cakra*. //58//

sā yadā saṃvidambikā trikalāmayī //57//

trikhaṇḍārūpam āpannā saṃnidhikāriṇī /
sarvasya cakrarājasya vyāpikā parikīrtitā //58//

Consciousness (*saṃvit*) is said to be made of three *kalās*, since *kalās* are limiting forms of power (see above, *śl.* 21, and n. 10). The term denotes the three energy-goddesses Vāmā, Jyeṣṭhā, and Raudrī, who, taken together, are Ambikā, the Mother of all powers, the Goddess, who, "becoming divided into three," is present as these three goddesses in the whole *śrīcakra* but also as the *mudrās*. As such, she "causes her continuous presence" (*saṃnidhi*) in it, since, in Hindu ritual, a deity is to be actually, continuously, and favorably present in the icon when it is to be worshipped.

Saṃnidhi, or *saṃnidhāna*, is the third of a series of four ritual actions to be performed at the beginning of all worship to ensure this divine presence.[37] The Goddess is, of course, always present in and as the *śrīcakra*. The *saṃnidhi* here is to ensure her presence as *mudrās* who symbolize nine different aspects of her cosmic activity.

> This same [consciousness as Trikhaṇḍā *mudrā*], when [in her, the aspect of] *yoni* increases, [becomes] the universal agitator [Sarvasaṃkṣobhinī] who abides in the *cakra* of the doors and in whom the energy Vāmā dominates. //59//
>
> *yoniprācyuryataḥ saiṣā sarvasaṃkṣobhiṇī punaḥ /*
> *vāmāśaktipradhāneyaṃ dvāracakre sthitā bhavet //59//*

The Mudrās,[38] as divine aspects of the cosmic activity of the Goddess, are now enumerated, going from the outer square section of the *śrīcakra* to its center. The first aspect of this activity to be considered is that of creation, in the outer square (*bhūgṛha*, house of the earth), which corresponds, in the cosmic symbolism of the *śrīcakra*, to the plane of the manifested world. The *mudrā* Sarvasaṃkṣobhinī, the universal agitator, disturbs the cosmos, that is, embodies the action of the Goddess as actively present in this world, not purely quiescent and transcendent.

In Śaiva nondualist systems, the term *kṣobha*, which, like *saṃghaṭṭa*, has sexual connotations, implies creation. As the DĪ says, *sṛṣtir eva kṣobhaḥ*, "agitation is indeed creation" (or "creation is indeed agitation").[39]

The quadrangular external part of the *śrīcakra* is called *cakra* of the doors (*dvāracakra*), because each of its four sides includes a portion

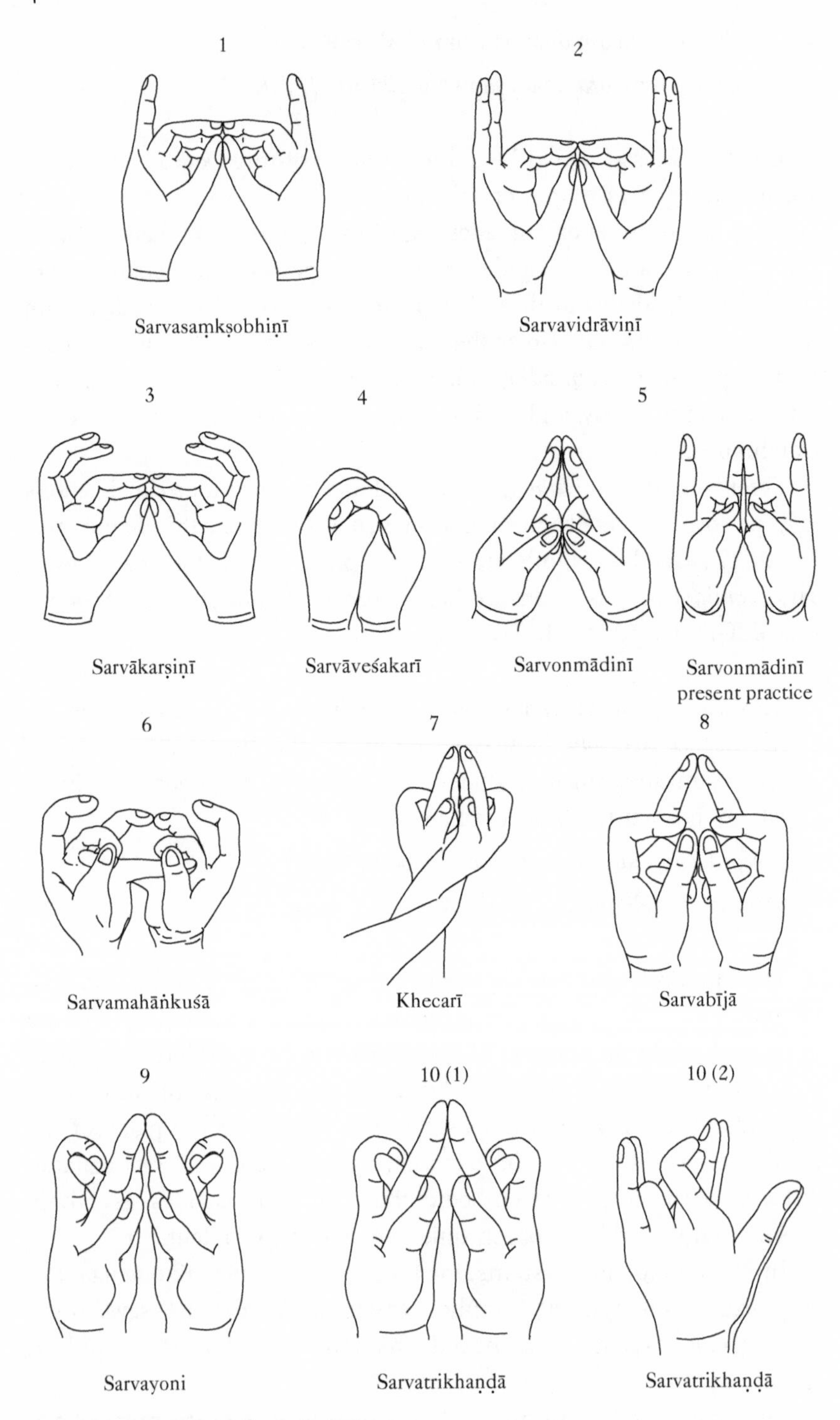

FIGURES I.4 AND I.5 The ten *mudrās.*

technically called a door (*dvāra*), by which the officiating adept can enter or leave[40] the diagram. Being considered on the level of the empirical world, of *māyā*, this *cakra* is fittingly called Trailokyamohana ("delusion of the three worlds"), since the Goddess deludes, enchants, the world by upholding its deceiving nature through her *māyā*.

The goddess Vāmā is so called, it is said, because she "vomits" (*vamati*), that is, brings out, manifests, the world.

The YH mentions only the metaphysical aspect of the *mudrās*, their role as divine energies. They are, however, also hand gestures, to be displayed by the adept. This is explained in the Dī for each of the ten *mudrās*. These explanations are interesting, but translating these passages would take too much space here. Sketches of these hand poses, made by a *paṇḍit* of the French Institute of Indology in Pondicherry, are given in figures 1.4 and 1.5.

> When Jyeṣṭhā predominates, she ensures the conservation of the universe
>
> [which had been] agitated. As the *kalās* of the gross aspect of the phonic subtle vibration, she bestows grace to all. //60// This selfsame Mudrā whose form flashes forth is in the *cakra* called Sarvāśapūraṇa.
>
> *kṣubdhaviṣvasthitikarī jyeṣṭhāprācuryam āśritā /*
>
> *sthūlanādakalārūpā sarvānugrahakāriṇī //60//*
>
> *sarvāśāpūraṇākhye tu saiṣā sphuritavigrahā /*

After the creative agitation caused by Vāmā, the energy-goddess Jyeṣṭhā now causes the preservation (*sthiti*) of the universe. This action is considered to take place (diagrammatically) on the level of the sixteen-petal lotus called Sarvāśapūraṇa ("fulfillment of all wishes"). The *kalās* mentioned here are the sixteen "vowels," from *A* to *visarga*, in their gross, that is, audible, form.[41]

According to the Dī, these *kalās* are also sixteen "attracting" divine energies, Kāmākarṣiṇī and so on, which are to be worshipped in this *cakra* during the *pūjā*.[42]

The Dī gives the name of this Mudrā: Sarvavidrāviṇī ("causing everything to flow") and, naturally, describes the corresponding hand gesture. "Because its nature is conservation," it says, "it consists in raising the joined middle and index fingers and joining the ring and little fingers. Its nature being to attract desires, it causes fullness of divine grace."

> When Jyeṣṭhā and Vāmā are in equilibrium, creation predominates. //61// This Ākarṣiṇī *mudrā* is known as the agitator of the universe.
>
> *jyeṣṭhāvāmāsamatvena ṣṛṣṭeḥ prādhānyam āśritā* //61//
>
> *ākarṣiṇī tu mudreyaṃ sarvasaṃkṣobhiṇī smṛtā* /

The role of this *mudrā* does not seem to differ greatly from that of the preceding one, whose action it seems merely to confirm. Interestingly, the Dī says that if this *mudrā* is attracting (*ākarṣiṇī*), it is "because of the curved position (like a hook) of the two index fingers"; the gesture is given as explaining a metaphysical element. This is one more case of the total interpenetration of the theoretical and the bodily, characteristic of the *mudrās*.

This *mudrā* is localized in the lotus of eight petals called Sarvasaṃkṣobhanacakra, the *cakra* of universal agitation.[43]

> [The *mudrā*] who holds herself in the interval between two *vyomans*, O Maheśvarī! //62// is known as causing the absorption into the deity resulting from the conjunction of Śiva and Śakti. It is an embodiment of the bliss of consciousness, located in the *cakra* of fourteen triangles. //63//
>
> *vyomadvayāntarālasthabindurūpā maheśvari* //62//
>
> *śivāśaktyākhyasaṃśleṣād divyāveśakarī smṛtā* /
>
> *caturdaśāracakrasthā saṃvidānandavigrahā* //63//

The term *vyoman*, which means sky, space, or ether, refers here to secondary centers of the yogic body sometimes also called *śūnya*, void. They are described as numbering five, tiered along the *suṣumnā*, where they are located between the bodily *cakras*, from *mūlādhāra* to *ājñā*. The Dī adds that between these elements there are also five other secondary centers,[44] *bindus*, to be identified with the gross elements (the *mahābhūtas*).

The absorption (*āveśa*) in the union of Śiva and Śakti embodied in this *mudrā*, called Sarvāveśakarī, is displayed in the corresponding hand gesture, which consists in a joining of the hands, the fingers being interlocked. It embodies the bliss of consciousness (*saṃvidānanda*), since the fusion (*saṃśleśa*) of Śiva and Śakti is intensely blissful.

The *cakra* of fourteen triangles where this *mudrā* is to be contemplated is called Sarvasaubhāgyadāyaka ("giver of total happiness").

> When she flashes forth between the *bindus* as a subtle flame, the energy Jyeṣṭhā predominating, she intoxicates all beings. She remains, staying in the [external] *cakra* of ten triangles, O Praised by the heroes! //64–65a//
>
> *bindvantarālavilasatsūkṣmarūpaśikhāmayī /*
>
> *jyeṣṭhāśaktipradhānā tu sarvonmādanakāriṇī //64//*
>
> *daśāracakrāsthāyā saṃsthitā vīravandite /*

This *mudrā*, looking like a flashing flame, extends, according to the Dī, from a *yonibindu* placed in the *mūlādhāra* to a *mahābindu*, on the level of the *brahmarandhra*, therefore along the *suṣumnā*, which means that the experience of the adept is one of *kuṇḍalinīyoga*, not a merely mental, visual one. What with the visual evocation of the *mudrā* in the yogic body as part of a practice of *kuṇḍalinī* yoga, conjoined with the display of the corresponding hand gesture, this practice appears as a particularly complex mental-bodily experience.

The *mudrā*'s name is Sarvonmadinī ("totally intoxicating"). The *cakra* of ten triangles is called Sarvārthasādhaka ("accomplisher of all [human] aims").

> Then the energy Vāmā predominating [again], she becomes the Great Hook. //65// Thus, vomiting the universe, she abides in the second [*cakra*] of ten triangles, being full of joy, remaining in the form of *mudrā*. //66//
>
> *vāmaśaktipradhānā tu mahāṅkuśamayī punaḥ //65//*
>
> *tadvad viśvaṃ vamantī sā dvitīye daśārake /*
>
> *saṃsthitā modanaparā mudrārūpam āsthitā //66//*

The energy-goddess Vāmā is considered to permeate the second *cakra* of ten triangles, named Sarvarakṣākāra ("bringing protection to all"). As we saw previously (*śl.* 37), Vāmā (the word means also left, crooked, oblique) was associated with the left, oblique side of the inner triangle. Now she is similarly associated with the hook *mudrā*, her joy being the bliss of fusion with the supreme godhead. An *aṅkuśa* is a hook or goad of an elephant driver. It is one of the attributes (*āyudha*,[45] "arms") held by Tripurasundarī.

Born from the unifying interaction of *dharma* and *adharma* in the form of intelligence, she destroys the faults of omission in ritual action resulting from differentiated thought. //67// [This *mudrā*,] the supreme *khecarī*, destroyer of the diseases born from differentiated thought, abides, made of consciousness, in the Sarvarogahāra *cakra*. //68//

dharmādharmasya saṃghaṭṭād utthitā vittirūpiṇi /

vikalpotthakriyāloparūpadoṣavighātinī //67//

vikalparūparogaṇāṇāṃ hāriṇī khecarī parā /

sarvarogaharākhye tu cakre saṃvinmayī sthitā //68//

Dharma here means Śiva, and *adharma* is Śakti. That the *khecarī mudrā* should be born from their conjunction, *saṃghaṭṭa* (their total fusion, *sāmarasya*, says the DĪ), is not surprising, since this *mudrā* has a very high position in many *kula* traditions. It is the main *mudrā* described in the *Tantrāloka* (chapter 32), where it is described as a complex bodily-mental attitude deemed to bring about the presence of the deity and unite the adept with it. In the *Parātrīśikā*, a basic Trika work, the highest spiritual state the adept can reach is *khecaratā*, the state of being *khecara*, of moving (*cara*) in the void of consciousness (*khe*[46]), a state described as the state of Śiva (*śivāvasthā*). In such a state, all forms of discursive, differentiated thought evidently disappear.

Then, in the sky [of consciousness], in the flashing forth of the embrace of Śiva and Śakti, making the universe which is there in a subtle form to shine forth perpetually, //69// she holds herself in the Sarvasiddhimaya [*cakra*] as the Great Mudrā whose nature is seed.

Then, in this place where one enjoys the fullness of light, //70// this Yonimudrā which is the power to act, stays in the Sarvānandamaya [*cakra*].

śivaśaktisamāśleṣasphuradvyomāntare punaḥ /

prakāśayantī viśvaṃ sā sūkṣmarūpasthitaṃ sadā //69//

bījarūpā mahāmudrā sarvasiddhimaye sthitā /

saṃpūrṇasya prakāśasya lābhabhūmir iyaṃ punaḥ //70//

yonimudrā kalārūpā sarvānandamaye sthitā /

The luminous state of identification with the union of Śiva and Śakti having been reached while displaying the *khecarīmudrā*, the adept, enjoying the bliss of the full luminousness of the divine consciousness, displays the last *yonimudrā*, which evokes by hand gesture the *yoni* of the Goddess and also the Goddess as *yoni*, source or seed (*bīja*) of the universe. The DĪ says that this *mudrā* embodies the dynamic power of the conscious awareness (*vimarśakalā*) of the supreme deity: the deity, in Tantra, is never static but is dynamic: bliss, absolute total consciousness, but also life, power, as is underlined in the next half-stanza.

The *yoni* being always symbolized by a triangle, this *mudrā* abides therefore in the central triangle of the *śrīcakra*.

The YH concludes:

> This is how the [energy of] activity, whose nature is consciousness, abides in the [*śrī*]*cakra*. //71//
>
> *kriyā caitanyarūpatvād evaṃ cakramayaṃ sthitam* //71//

This half-stanza is commented on as follows by the DĪ: "As has been said before (*śl*. 57), the power of activity is named *mudrā* because she gladdens the universe and makes it flow."

It is therefore only the energy of activity that, dividing herself, beautifies and diversifies herself by the division and the (successive) predominance of the energy-goddesses Vāmā and so on, and assuming the forms of the various *mudrās*, from Saṃkṣobhinī to Yoni, her nature being that of a consciousness (*caitanya*) that becomes the *cakra*, that is to say, that assumes the aspects of the ninefold *cakra*, from Trailokyamohana to Sarvānandamaya. To avoid, however, that one should believe that only the power of activity acts in the *śrīcakra*, the YH adds:

> The awakened must always meditate intensely on the supreme splendor which is will. //72a//
>
> *icchārūpaṃ paraṃ tejaḥ sarvadā bhāvayed budhaḥ* /

The adept must never forget that it is the supreme deity, the united Śiva and Śakti, that acts through the energies of which *kriyāśakti*, that of activity, is the lowest. The YH reminds us, therefore, that the deity acts through her own free will, *svecchayā*. This the devotee must meditate in his heart, perceiving it directly, being however helped by his spiritual master, his guru (who for him is Śiva), and whose compassionate glance falls on him. This is called in Sanskrit *gurukatākṣapāta*, the descent of the glance (bearer of the power of Śiva) of the guru, who thus transmits the divine saving energy of the deity, sometimes called *śaktipāta*.

Two other forms of "encounter" (*saṃketa*) with the *śrīcakra*—different visions and practices of it, that is—are now described:

Now [here] are the threefold and the ninefold encounter of the *cakra*. //72b//

tridhā ca navadhā ca cakrasaṃketakaḥ punaḥ //72//

First the threefold division:

The first [section of the *cakra* is to be imagined as being produced] by one fire and two energies, the [second] one by three fires and the triad of energies, //73// and the [last] as made up of two lotuses and the triple *bhūgṛha*. Five energies, four fires, two lotuses, and the triple earths //74// [constitute thus] the great *cakra* in its complete fullness.

This aspect [of the *cakra*] is explained [thus]: the first [portion] is that of the *navayoni*. To this are added the two [*cakras* of] ten triangles, //75// then the fourteen *yoni* and, immediately after, the third [portion made up of eight and sixteen petals, followed by the triple square.] //76//

[Thus], O Parameśvarī, is described the threefold [aspect of] the *cakra*. The emanation, then, //77// goes from the *navayoni* to the earth and the resorption from the earth to the *navayoni*. Such is the teaching of the treatises.

vahninaikena śaktibhyāṃ dvābhyāṃ caiko 'paraḥ punaḥ /

taiś ca vahnitrayenāpi śaktināṃ tritayeṇa ca //73//

padmadvayena cānyaḥ syād bhūgṛhatritayena ca /

pañcaśakti caturvahnipadmadvayamahītrayam //74//

paripūrṇaṃ mahācakram tatprakāraḥ pradarśyate /

tatrādyaṃ navayoni syāt tena dvidaśasaṃyutam //75//

manuyoni paraṃ vidyāt tṛtīyaṃ tadanantaram /

aṣṭadvyaṣṭadalopetaṃ caturasratrayānvitam //76//

cakrasya triprakāratvaṃ kathitaṃ parameśvari /

sṛṣṭiḥ syān navayonādipṛthivyantaṃ saṃhṛtiḥ punaḥ //77//

pṛthivyādinavayonyantam iti śāstrasya nirṇayaḥ /

The *śrīcakra* is here conceived as made up of three portions. The first one results from the interaction of one triangle apex upward (the "fire") and two triangles apex downward (the "energies"), this constituting the eight-angle figure of the *navayoni*. The next portion is seen as adding to the preceding one two series of three triangles, one male ("fire"), the other female ("energies"), which results in the two ten-triangle *cakras* and the fourteen-triangle one. The third portion is made up of the threefold circle and the square outer portion enclosed by three lines.

The reason the *srīcakra* is to be conceived and meditated upon as made up of three section is—as the Dī explains—that each of these three threefold portions has a particular aspect (*prakāra*). In the central section, resorption (*saṃhāra*) predominates, and in the middle one, conservation (*stithi*) predominates, while manifestation (*sṛṣṭi*) predominates in the outer portion. In addition, in each of these three *cakras*, *saṃhāra*, *sthiti*, and *sṛṣṭi* are respectively considered as predominating. Thus, the dynamism of the *śrīcakra* taken as a whole is that of emanation when going from its center to its outward portion, that of resorption when going from the outer portion to the center.

But since resorption, conservation, and emanation are all present in each of the three sections, the whole *śrīcakra* is, at the same time, entirely permeated by these three aspects of the cosmic activity of the Goddess, who is thus eternally and everywhere at once the creator, the maintainer, and the destroyer of the universe, a fact expressed by this three-times-threefold structure of her *cakra*. As the diagrammatic form of the Goddess, the *śrīcakra* thus symbolizes and expresses her ever living, throbbing, creative, and destructive power. To meditate and realize this mystically, as is here prescribed, is to realize and to fuse with this divine dynamic plenitude. Hence the usefulness of the *śrīcakra*, whose nine sections are now again enumerated and then named:

> [Now], O Parameśvarī, is told in its entirety the *cakra* of Tripurā //78//
>
> through whose knowledge alone one becomes a knower of Tripurā.
>
> The division of the *cakra* into nine, I am telling you, O Dear One! //79//
>
> There must first be the threefold earth,[47] second the sixteen-petal [lotus], then the one with eight petals, then the fourteen triangles; fifth comes the [*cakra* with] ten angles and, sixth, the [other of] ten angles. In seventh position comes the [*cakra* of] eight triangles, then, eighth, the central triangle, the ninth being in the center of [this] triangle. //80–82a//
>
> *etat samaṣṭirūpaṃ tu tripurācakram ucyate //78//*

yasya vijñānamātreṇa tripurājñānavān bhavet /
cakrasya navadhātvaṃ ca kathayāmi tava priye //79//
ādimaṃ bhūtrayeṇa syād dvitīyaṃ ṣoḍaśārakam /
anyad aṣṭadalaṃ proktaṃ manukoṇam anantaram //80//
pañcamaṃ daśakoṇaṃ syāt ṣaṣṭhaṃ cāpi daśārakam /
saptamaṃ vasukoṇaṃ syān madhyatryasramathāṣṭamam //81//
navamaṃ tryasramadhyaṃ syāt

Hear now their names: Trailokyamohana *cakra*, Sarvāśaparipūraka, //82// Sarvasaṃkṣobhaṇa, O Gaurī! Sarvasaubhāgyadāyaka, Sarvārthasādhaka *cakra*, Sarvarakṣākara, supreme, //83// Sarvarogahara, O Goddess! then Sarvasiddhimaya and the ninth, Sarvānandamaya, listen, O Beautiful One! //84//

teṣāṃ nāmāny ataḥ śṛṇu /
trailokyamohanaṃ cakraṃ sarvāśāparipūrakam //82//
sarvasaṃkṣobhanaṃ gauri sarvasaubhāgyadāyakam /
sarvārthasādhakaṃ cakraṃ sarvarakṣākaraṃ param //83//
sarvarogaharaṃ devi sarvasiddhimayaṃ tathā /
sarvānandamayaṃ cāpi navamaṃ sṛṇu sundari //84//

The constituent *cakras* of the *śrīcakra* are enumerated going from its outer portion to its center: from this world, that is, to the supreme Goddess, which is the course of liberation. The Dī explains the names of the *cakras* and the rewards or power the adept is deemed to acquire when worshipping the Goddess and her retinue of ancillary deities and powers abiding in each *cakra*, as we shall see in chapter 3 below, where the different parts of the *pūjā* are described.

Trailokyamohana, "deceiving the three worlds": the three worlds are to be understood as the ensemble formed by the objective world, the apprehension of this duality, and the subject, the "knower" who knows it and who is deceived by duality and discursive thought.

Sarvāśāparipūraka, "satisfying all desires": a satisfaction attained, says the Dī, when complete fusion with the supreme Śiva is attained.

Sarvasaṃkṣobhana, "agitation of the universe": interpreted as alluding to the movement (*saṃkṣobhana*) through which the *tattvas*, from earth to Śiva, are reabsorbed into the supreme godhead.

Sarvasaubhāgyadāyaka, "giver of all happiness": the happiness is that of the union with supreme Śiva.

Sārvārthasādhaka, "accomplisher of all [human] aims": the highest of these aims is liberation (*mokṣa*) by union with the godhead.

Sarvarakṣākāra, "effecting all protection": putting away all obstacles to liberation.

Sarvarogahara, "destroyer of all illnesses": the illnesses are the manifested world, duality, all that is not liberation.

Sarvasiddhimaya, "made of all accomplishments or powers": these are the creation, maintaining, and reabsorption (*sṛṣṭī, sthiti, saṃhāra*) of the cosmos, of which the central triangle is diagrammatically the origin.

Sarvānandamaya, "whose nature is all bliss": this is the nature of the supreme godhead, the eternal union of Śiva and Śakti symbolized by the central *bindu*.

Since the *śrīcakra* is not only the diagrammatic form of the Goddess but also the means to be used to worship her, the YH adds:

> This is where must be worshipped the great Goddess Mahātripurasundarī. Such is, in its perfect fullness, the great *cakra* giver of eternal youth and immortality. //85
>
> *atra pūjyā mahādevī mahātripurasundarī /*
>
> *paripūrṇaṃ mahācakram ajarāmarakārakam //85//*

One could be tempted here to note that the practice of the *śrīcakra* appears to be conferring immortality and not merely liberation, that is, a physical, worldly benefit, not a purely spiritual one. The Dī, however, interprets this by saying that the one who has immortality and liberation is the supreme Śiva. Therefore, what is obtained by the worship of the *śrīcakra* is in effect acquiring the perfect and immortal state of Śiva, a point confirmed by the last *śloka*.

> Thus has been said, O supreme Goddess! the encounter with the great *cakra* of the goddess Tripurā, giver of liberation while still in life. //86//
>
> *evam eṣa mahācakrasaṃketaḥ parameśvari /*
>
> *kathitas tripurādevyā jīvanmukti pravartakaḥ //86//*

2

Encounter in the Mantra

MANTRASAṂKETA

THE PURPOSE OF this chapter is to teach how to understand the inner hidden meaning—and thus the mystical efficacy—of Mahātripurasundarī's mantra, the *śrīvidyā*. As was the case for the *śrīcakra*, this efficacy results from the agreed common presence (*saṃketa*) of Śiva and Śakti in Tripurā's mantra, whose constituent phonemes will be shown to be pervaded by the interactive presence and power of these two, male and female, aspects of the supreme deity and therefore as imbued with saving power. Different aspects assumed by the Goddess, along with cosmic elements, are also shown as expressed by the phonemes of the *vidyā*.

The interpretations given in this chapter of the hidden meanings of the *śrīvidyā* are, however, often extremely far-fetched and sometimes very difficult to understand, even with the help of Amṛtānanda's commentary. Even Professor Dvivedi, whose edition was used to translate the YH and the Dīpikā and with whom I read and discussed this chapter, was in many cases unable to explain the meaning of some stanzas and the corresponding passages of the commentary. We therefore do not expect the reader to find our attempt at deciphering such passages very satisfactory or always fully intelligible.

> I will now tell you the divine presence of [Siva and the Goddess embodied] in the mantra. Whoever knows this becomes, like Tripurā, master of the circle of heroes. //1//
>
> *mantrasaṃketaṃ divyam adhunā kathayāmi te /*
>
> *yad vettā tripurākāro vīracakreśvaro bhavet //1//*

The master of the heroes (*vīra*), that is, of those who have attained the highest knowledge and supernatural powers, is the supreme Śiva. The realization of the inner secret meaning of the *śrīvidyā* leads thus to identification with the supreme godhead.

The *śrīvidyā* being the root mantra (*mūlavidyā*) of the Goddess is considered to be, like the deity, surrounded by secondary (or ancillary) feminine mantras—those of the Cakreśvarīs, the regent-goddesses of the nine parts of the *śrīcakra*, which the *sādhaka* is to assign by *nyāsa* on the nine centers of his yogic body, thus mentally identifying himself with these nine powers. These nine *vidyās* are the following:

> The first is the Karaśuddhikarī, the second one Ātmarakṣikā, the third Ātmāsanagatā; then, after her, //2// [comes] Cakrāsanagatā, then Sarvamantrāsanasthitā. Sādhyasiddhāsana is the sixth one, her nature being that of Māyā and Lakṣmī, supreme. //3// The one called Mūrtividyā is the seventh goddess. The eighth one is the *vidyā* Āvāhinī; the ninth is the supreme Bhairavī, //4// also called Mūlavidyā, subjugating the three worlds.
>
> *karaśuddhikarī tvādyā dvitīyā ātmarakṣikā /*
> *ātmāsanagatā devī tṛtīyā tadanantaram //2//*
> *cakrāsanagatā paścāt sarvamantrāsanasthitā /*
> *sādhyasiddhāsanā ṣaṣṭhī māyālakṣmīmayī parā //3//*
> *mūrtividyā ca sā devī saptamī parikīrtitā /*
> *aṣṭamy āvāhinī vidyā navamī bhairavī parā //4//*
> *mūlavidyā tathā proktā trailokyavaśakāriṇī /*

These nine Vidyās preside over the nine parts of the *śrīcakra*, from the outer square to the central triangle with the *bindu* in its center. To each of them a particular role or function, expressed by her name, is ascribed. The first is Karaśuddhikarī, "purifier of the hands," since the hands of the adept are to be purified before he performs the ritual. He is also to protect himself against all mental or spiritual imperfections and especially against egoism and the illusion of duality, hence the name Ātmarakṣikā, "protector of the Self," of the second Vidyā. The third one, "who stays on the throne of the Self," embodies, according to Amṛtānanda, the consciousness of the unity of the *sādhaka*, the *cakra*, the mantra, and the Self. The fourth is Cakrāsanagatā, "having the *cakra* as a seat," while the fifth, Sarvamantrāsanasthitā, "abiding on the throne of all mantras," presides over the portion of the *śrīcakra* called Sarvārthasādhaka, "which fulfills all wishes." The sixth, Sādhyasiddhāsana, "the seat of the accomplishment of what is to be accomplished," governs the powers nearest to the Goddess, the accomplishment alluded to being the cosmic work of the Goddess as symbolized by the *śrīcakra* and the *śrīvidyā*. The seventh is the Mūrtividyā, the visible form of the Goddess. The eighth one, Āvāhinīvidyā, is the one used to invoke and keep (during worship) the presence of the Goddess. The ninth *vidyā* is Bhairavī, the Goddess herself; she is therefore the *śrīvidyā*, the *mūlamantra* of Mahātripurasundarī.[1]

> Thus, O Mistress of Kula, these nine kinds [of *vidyās*] are to be carefully placed //5// at the time of worship, in order, by the *sādhaka*.
>
> *evaṃ navaprakārās tu pūjākāle prayatnataḥ //5//*
>
> *etāḥ krameṇa nyastavyāḥ sādhakena kuleśvari /*

The term *kula*, or Kula, is often met with in the YH and the Dīpikā. It refers in a general way to the ensemble of nondualist Śaiva traditions formed by four *āmnāyas* (see the introduction, above). But it also has technical meanings. It is used to designate not only the yogic imaginal body but also the physical body or the universe conceived as a body: the grouping of diverse elements. In its usual meaning, *kula* means family or clan, notably the clan of the Yoginīs. The Goddess as "Mistress of Kula" is thus the mistress of the universe in all its cosmic or bodily aspects.

The places where these *nyāsas* are to be made are as follows:

> On the end of the feet, on the legs, the knees, the thighs, the anus, the tip of the penis. //6// On the [*mūl*]*ādhāra* is to be imposed the Mūrti[vidyā] on which is to be placed the Āvāhinī. With the Mūla[vidyā] one must do a *vyāpakanyāsa*,[2] Parameśvarī! //7//
>
> *pādāgrajaṅghājānūrugudaliṅgāgrakeṣu ca //6//*
>
> *ādhāre vinyasen mūrtiṃ tasyām āvāhinīṃ nyaset /*
>
> *mūlena vyāpakanyāsaḥ kartavyaḥ parameśvari //7//*

Once these *nyāsas* are made,

> One must, on the spots previously mentioned, namely *akula* and so forth,[3] concentrate one's thought on the nine *cakras* already enumerated, associating [each of them] with [its own] *cakreśvarī*. //8//

akulādiṣu pūrvoktasthāneṣu paricintayet /

cakreṣvarīsamāyuktaṃ navacakraṃ puroditam //8//

The adept is to evoke meditatively each of the nine constitutive *cakras* of the *śrīcakra* in each of the nine *cakras* of his yogic body. He must thus meditate intensely (*bhāvayet*), first, on the Trailokyamohanacakra, the square outer portion of the *śrīcakra*, presided over by Tripurā in the thousand-petal red *akulapadma* at the root of the *suṣumnā*. Then he meditates on the Sarvāśaparipurakacakra presided over by Tripureśī, in the *vahnyādhāra*, that is, the *mūlādhāra*, and so forth, up to the Sarvānandamayacakra, with Mahātripurasundarī, in the *bindu*, on the forehead.

In this way, the adept perceives mentally the nine parts of the *śrīcakra* and the nine deities abiding there up to the supreme Goddess as present in his body, tiered along his *suṣumnā*. This identifies him with the deity both in her diagrammatic form and in her fullness as the nine aspects she assumes in the *śrīcakra*.

> Of these I shall tell the names in their proper order. The first is the goddess Tripurā; the second is Tripureśvarī; //9// the third is the the goddess named Tripurasundarī; the fourth, a great goddess, is Tripuravāsinī. //10// The fifth is Tripuraśrī, the sixth Tripuramālinī; the seventh is Tripurasiddhi, the eighth Tripurāmbikā. //11// As for the ninth, she is the great Goddess Mahātripurasundarī. These goddesses are to be worshipped in their proper order in the ninefold *cakra* previously described. //12//
>
> *tāsāṃ nāmāni vakṣyāmi yathānukramayogataḥ /*
>
> *tatrādyā tripurā devī dvitiyā tripureśvarī //9//*
>
> *tṛtīyā ca tathā proktā devi tripurasundarī /*
>
> *caturthī ca mahādevi devī tripuravāsinī //10//*
>
> *pañcamī tripurāśrīḥ syāt ṣaṣṭhī tripuramālinī*
>
> *saptamī tripurasiddhir aṣṭamī tripurāmbikā //11//*
>
> *navamī tu mahādevi mahātripurasundarī /*
>
> *pūjayec ca kramād etā navacakre purodite //12//*

The worship prescribed here is purely mental, each of the nine Cakreśvarīs being mentally visualized and worshipped as abiding in each of the nine yogic bodily *cakras*, from the red thousand-petaled *akulapadma* to the *bindu*. This identifies the adept with these nine forms of the supreme Goddess, who appears thus as ninefold though remaining the one and supreme power, bestowing youth and immortality through identification with Śiva:

> O Parvati! The primordial One [*ādyā*] appearing thus at the time of worship under nine [different] aspects has in truth only one form, that of the primordial Power [*ādyaśakti*] bestowing eternal youth and immortality //13//
>
> *evaṃ navaprakārādyā pūjakāle tu pārvati /*
>
> *ekākārā hy ādyaśaktir ajarāmarakāriṇī* //13//

The Dī explains here that the only one who is eternally young and immortal is Śiva, and therefore, what the worshipper will now enjoy is the condition of Śiva. The reader will note that the above stanza shows that the aim of the rites described in the Tantra is the gaining of supernatural rewards or powers in addition to liberation.

The reason stanzas 1–13 of this chapter enumerate the deities of the *śrīcakra* and prescribe their *nyāsa* and worship in the *śrīcakra* is not clear, since the theme of this chapter is the expounding of the esoteric meanings of the *śrīvidyā*. We may imagine, however, that such a worship and the spiritual union with the deity are to precede and facilitate the mental exertion needed to understand the often abstruse reasoning and arcane speculations of stanzas 16–80 of this chapter, which are now expounded.

> The practice of the mantra [*mantrasaṃketaka*] of that [primordial power] can take different forms. It is only by following the tradition and the regular order of the various mantras that one can obtain [its knowledge]. //14//
>
> *mantrasaṃketakas tasyā nānākāro vyavasthitaḥ /*
>
> *nānamantrakrameṇaiva pāramparyeṇa labhyate* //14//

We have already explained the meanings of the term *saṃketa* in the introduction and chapter 1. Here the term is to be understood as the expounding and, of course, the spiritual understanding of the inner experience, the esoteric meanings of the *śrīvidyā*. As *śloka* 81 underlines, this understanding can be obtained only by following the traditional interpretation of the mantra as transmitted by the succession of the masters (*gurupārамparā*) of the Śrīvidyā school; no outside or personal interpretation is valid. Six such esoteric interpretations are given here.

The "various mantras" alluded to above are not different mantras but the various meanings given to the *śrīvidyā*, each considered a different mantra since each discloses a different understanding of it. The expression refers also to the three subdivisions, the *kūṭas* or *bījas*, of the *śrīvidyā* or to its constituting phonemes, all of which are mantras in their own right. The term may also refer to the nine Vidyās we have just seen, which are both deities and feminine mantras.

> This [practice] is sixfold, O Mistress of the Gods! I will tell it to you, O Perfect One!
>
> There is the natural meaning, the traditional one, the inner meaning, the *kaulika* meaning, //15// then the completely secret meaning, and finally the meaning according to the highest reality.
>
> *ṣaḍvidhas taṃ tu deveśi kathayāmi tavānaghe* /
>
> *bhāvārthaḥ saṃpradāyārtho nigarbhārthaś ca kaulikaḥ* //15//
>
> *tathā sarvarahasyārtho mahātattvārtha eva ca* /

As we shall see, the six symbolic interpretations of the *śrīvidyā* give mainly the esoteric meanings to be extracted from it, but they also describe meditative and yoga practices to be followed so as to experiment in mind and body the purport and power of the mantra. The interpretations given by the YH are in some cases complex and far-fetched. The most obscure and difficult to understand fully, even with the help of Amṛtānanda's (or Bhāskararāya's) commentary, are the "natural" (*bhāvārtha*) meaning (*śl.* 16–25) and the "traditional" (*saṃpradāya*) meaning (*śl.* 26–48a). The other ones are more briefly expounded.

Although the explanations given are entirely based on the syllabic pattern of the *śrīvidyā*, neither the YH nor Amṛtānanda's Dīpikā gives its syllabic composition, its "extraction" (*udhāra*)[4]. It is clear, however, that for the YH, the *vidyā* is—as we noted in the introduction—in the so-called *hādi* form, namely its fifteen syllables, shared out into three groups called *kūṭa* (or sometimes *bīja*): *HA SA KA LA HRĪṂ* • *HA SA HA KA LA HRĪṂ* • *SA KA LA HRĪṂ*.

> The natural meaning is simply the meaning of the phonemes [*akṣara*] [of the *vidyā*], O Parameśvarī! //16//
>
> *akṣarārtho hi bhāvārthaḥ kevalaḥ parameśvari* //16//

The king of mantras, O dear One! is at all times engendered by the union of Śiva and Śakti and by that of the Yoginīs, the Vīras, and the Vīrendras. //17//

Thus constituted, delighting in the utmost bliss, the Goddess, whose nature is vibration [*spanda*], of innate beauty, once known, is to be freely worshipped. //18//

yoginībhis tathā vīraiḥ vīrendraiḥ sarvadā priye /

śivaśaktisamāyogāj janito mantrarājakaḥ //17//

tanmayīṃ paramānandananditāṃ spandarūpinīm /

nisargasundarīṃ devīṃ jñatvā svairam upāsate //18//

As we will see in the following pages, the interpretation that the YH gives in stanzas 18–25 of the *bhāvārtha* of the *śrīvidyā* is anything but a description of "simply the meaning of the syllables" (*akṣarārtha*) of the *vidyā;* of all the six *arthas,* this is by far the most obscure and difficult to understand.

The above stanzas 17 and 18 describe the whole *śrīvidyā* (considered the highest and best mantra and thus called the king of mantras, *mantrarāja*) as resulting from the conjunction (*samāyoga*) of Śiva and Śakti and also from that of the pairs of male and female deities surrounding them. In this respect, too, the *śrīvidyā* is, like the *śrīcakra,* the place and the embodiment, and the result, of the "meeting" (*saṃketa*) of Śiva and Śakti.

Amṛtānanda interprets the term *Yoginī* as referring to the three goddesses Bhāratī, Pṛthivī, and Rudraṇī and to the three basic powers of Śiva, namely will, cognition, and activity (*icchā, jñāna, kriyā*); these entities, being feminine, correspond to the aspect of consciousness (*vimarśāṃśa*) of the Goddess. The Vīras, associated with the Yoginīs, are Brahmā, Viṣṇu, and Rudra, who, being male, are aspects of the light of consciousness (*prakāśāṃśa*) aspect of the supreme godhead, who is considered to be in its fullness *prakāśāvimarśamaya,* both pure conscious light and supreme active consciousness. The Vīrendras, we are told by Amṛtānanda, transcend the cosmos, their nature being pure energy, and whereas the Yoginīs and the Vīras are considered to be present in the three *kūṭas,* the three groups of syllables of the *śrīvidyā,* the Vīrendras are associated with the three *HRĪṂ* (here called *kāmakalā*) which end the three *kūṭas.*

We thus have to understand the *śrīvidyā* as pervaded by Śiva and Śakti together with their retinue of male and female ancillary deities. Being thus engendered and permeated by the united Śiva and Śakti and by their threefold divine aspects, the *śrīvidyā* is a veritable embodiment of the Goddess as united with Śiva. This the adept must "know," that is, experience, realize meditatively, the fact that the *vidyā* is the very self of the Goddess who is then to be worshipped. Neither the YH nor its commentary explains in what respect this worship is to be "freely" (*svairam*) performed. We may take it, perhaps, that it is to be performed with all the rites and offerings that will please and honor the deity and help the worshipper to identify with her.

In the next five stanzas, the YH shows, first, that the *śrīvidyā* encapsulates symbolically the creative power born from the interaction of Śiva and Śakti (that is, the Goddess surrounded by her retinue of secondary deities) (*śl.* 19–20), this interaction being visibly manifested and experienced in the *kāmakalā* (*śl.* 21). Then the supreme power is shown as abiding in the three *kūṭas* of the *vidyā* (*śl.* 22), this omnipresent Goddess (*śl.* 23a) having to be intensely meditated upon and understood.

> [The Goddess], in mantra form, is thought [*manana*], made up of the knower and the known. She abides in the eternal Brahman in the form of the conjunction of Śiva and Śakti on the plane where [Śiva] adheres to the flow of his expansion which [for him] is but an Indraic secondary trait. //19–20a//
>
> *śivaśaktyākhyasaṃghaṭṭarūpe brahmaṇi śāśvate* /
>
> *tatprathāprasarāśleṣabhuvi tvaindropalakṣite* //19//
>
> *jñātṛjñānamayākāramananān mantrarūpiṇī* /

The *śrīvidyā* is the Goddess in mantra form. She is thought (*manana*), intelligence or consciousness, a condition described as consisting of (or resulting from) the unifying interaction (*saṃghaṭṭa*)[5] of Śiva and Śakti, since the mantra is the locus of this interaction. Being divine, this interaction takes place on the supreme plane of the eternal Brahman, a plane where Śiva and Śakti, in their embrace and interpenetration, expand and transform themselves into (and therefore adhere to) the cosmos. The *śrīvidyā* is thus, like the *śrīcakra*, a symbolic form of the cosmic activity of the Goddess. This creative action of Śiva and Śakti is called "Indraic" because, bringing about the universe which is ruled by *māyā*, it is similar to the action of the god Indra, who is conceived since the Ṛgveda[6] as taking up many forms thanks to his magical power, his *māyā*. This activity, too, though important, is nevertheless, for the supreme godhead, not a main trait but a secondary one.

The supreme energy is the mother of these [deities] taken together. //20//

teṣāṃ samaṣṭirūpeṇa parāśaktis tu mātṛkā //20//

The *śrīvidyā* as supreme power (*parā śakti*) made up of the coalescence of Śiva and Śakti appears thus as the mother of all the deities and of the cosmos, which issues from her. The term describing this creative aspect is *mātṛkā*, which denotes also the fifty phonemes of the Sanskrit alphabet taken together, that is, the totality of the Word (*mātṛkā* can also designate one of these phonemes, being in that case a synonym of *varṇa* or *akṣara*).

The *śrīvidyā* is therefore described here as including, or being, both the whole pantheon and the whole universe and, implicitly, the totality of the Word: the three levels, that is, of *vāc* issuing from *paravāc* and going down to *vaikharī*.[7] This allows Amṛtānanda to end his commentary on the last half-stanza by saying: "What is expressed [*vācaka*] by the whole mantra,[8] which is made up of the [male gods] Brahma and so forth and of the [female ones] Bharatī, etc., is the total fusion [in the supreme godhead] of light [*prakāśa*] and consciousness [*vimarśa*] expanding as *paśyantī*, *madhyamā*, and *vaikharī*." The *śrīvidyā* as a whole, we are to understand, is identical with the divine power insofar as she is the Word (*vāc*). She holds within herself all the forms and planes of the Word and all the deities and all the cosmos, which we saw in chapter 1 as present in the *śrīcakra*; she is, phonetically, in a mantric form, what the *śrīcakra* is diagrammatically.

The interactive presence of Śiva and Śakti in the *śrīvidyā* is now shown as manifesting itself in a diagrammatic form as the *kāmakalā*:

[Held] between the middle *bindu* and the *visarga*, the supreme [power] in her coiled form has space and *kalā* as reflected image. //21//

madhyabinduvisargāntaḥ samāsthānamaye pare /

kuṭilārūpake tasyāḥ pratirūpe viyatkale //21//

According to Amṛtānanda (and Bhāskararāya), this stanza describes (or, rather, alludes to) the *kāmakalā* diagram (see figure 2.1). One can hardly say that the wording of this obscure stanza justifies such an interpretation, which, however, is traditionally upheld in the Śrīvidyā system. It is as follows.

The supreme power, *śakti*, in her coiled form (*kuṭilārūpaka*), is the *kuṇḍalinī*, which stretches between the "middle *bindu* and the *visarga*." This is to say that she is inscribed within an upward-pointing triangle (a masculine symbol, that

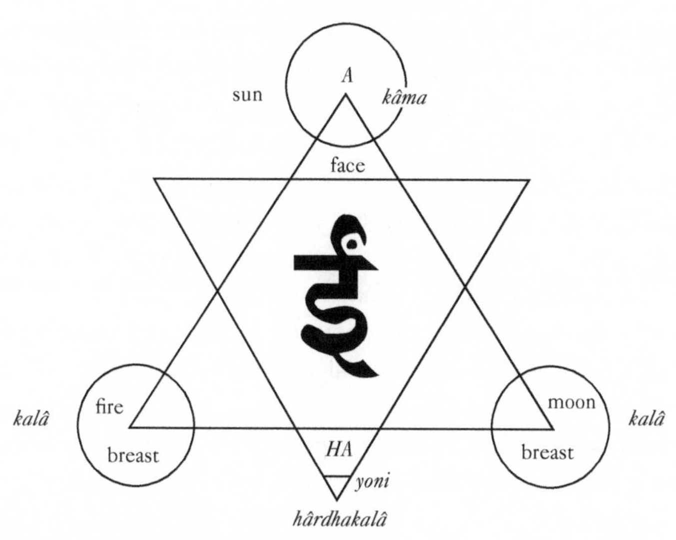

FIGURE 2.1. The *kāmakalā* diagram.

of Śiva) on whose apex is a *bindu* and on each of whose two lower angles is also a *bindu*: two *bindus*, therefore, which make up a *visarga* whose written form is that of two dots (:). The upper *bindu*, it is said, is *kāma*, desire or passion; it is considered to be made up of the coalescence of the whole Sanskrit alphabet, from *A* to *HA* and as being the Sun. The *visarga* results from the division in two of *bindu*. It is the sixteenth "vowel" of the alphabet symbolizing the creative power[9] of *vāc*, its two dots being symbolically Moon and Fire.[10] It is *kalā*, that is, active power. Between these two, between *kāma* and *kalā*, extends the *kuṇḍalinī*, which is graphically drawn as the letter *Ī* inscribed within a triangle pointing downward (a feminine symbol, that of Śakti). On the down-pointed apex of this triangle is the letter *HA*, or *hārdhakalā*, "the power of the half of *HA*" (a term that denotes also the *visarga*).

These two triangles with *kuṇḍalinī* located inside them are considered a symbol of the totality, from *A to HA*. They are also, mainly, a figure of the Goddess (sexually united with Śiva), her face being the "middle" upper *bindu*, the two lower *bindus* on the ends of the lower line of the masculine triangle being her two breasts, and the apex of the down-turned feminine triangle (where *HA* or *hārdhakalā* is) being her *yoni*. The shape of *kuṇḍalinī*, the letter *Ī* (or, rather, the *bīja ĪṂ*, since *kuṇḍalinī* is topped by the middle *bindu*), evokes her coiled form. This *kuṇḍalinī*, says the YH, is reflected by the two lower *bindus*, a statement not clearly explained by the commentators. Thus, this diagram, with *kuṇḍalinī* and the two superposed intersecting triangles, represents the co-presence of the sexually united Śiva and Śakti.[11]

The interpretation of this stanza as a description of the *śrīvidyā* embodying the *kāmakalā* diagram, however arbitrary, is confirmed by other works of the Tripurā tradition, such as Nāṭanānandanātha's commentary on the seventh stanza of Puṇyānandanātha's *Kāmakalāvilāsa* or the NṢA, 2.185–186, with the commentaries of Śivānanda and Vidyānanda. It is also to be found in the *Gandharvatantra*, 30.37–64, which prescribes a visualization of *kuṇḍalinī* shaped as the letter *ĪṂ* extending in the yogic body of the adept from the *mūlādhāra* to the *brahmarandhra*.

This is why she is described as supremely blissful and beautiful and animated by the *spanda*, the primordial vibration that creates and animates the universe.

The equally obscure next stanza is explained by the commentaries as describing the role played by the letters *A* and *HA* of the *śrīvidyā*.

> She holds herself in the central block [*piṇḍa*] of the mantra in the sky of the primordial vibration [formed by] the expansion of the central breath. Then, in the third block, //22// she flashes forth undivided in the *kūṭa* of Rahu. //23a//
>
> *madhyaprāṇaprathārūpaspandavyomni sthitā punaḥ* /
>
> *madhyame mantrapiṇḍe tu tṛtīye piṇḍake punaḥ* //22//
>
> *rāhukūṭādvayasphūrjat*

The explanation given by the Dī of the first sentence, which alludes to the middle section of the *śrīvidyā*, called *kāmarāja*, identifies the letter *HA* of this section of the mantra with the *HA* in the lower triangle of the *kāmakalā* diagram, since its says that it is placed between the two lower *bindus* of this figure. As in the *kāmakalā*, this *HA* is an aspect of the Goddess and, as such, "expands," being made up of the fulguration of the power of consciousness (*vimarśaśakti*), in the "firmament of the primordial cosmic vibration."

Then one is to imagine that in the third subdivision (*kūṭa*) of the *śrīvidyā*, the Goddess flashes in the letter *SA* of that group of phonemes made up of the letters *A* and *HA*, that is, the whole Sanskrit alphabet, which is also the totality of the Word (*vāc*).

The next two stanzas refer (in the same very obscure way) to the *śrīvidyā* as a whole, expressing the cosmic power and role of the Goddess:

> When, in a state of palpitation, she is joined to the syllables expressing what is to be expressed [that is] *dharma* and *adharma*, made of poison and nectar, She is called Omniform.

[Thus,] by meditating intensely on the primordial power, the Goddess made of three subdivisions, taking her either in her totality or in her constitutive parts, she who is the Mother, the supreme Power conjoining [in herself all] these [elements], one understands the natural sense [of the *vidyā*]. //23b–25//

calattāsaṃsthitasya tu /
dharmādharmasya vācasya viṣāmṛtamayasya ca //23//
vacakākṣarasaṃyukteḥ kathitā viśvarūpiṇī /
teṣāṃ samaṣṭirūpeṇa parāśaktiṃ tu mātṛkām //24//
kūṭatrayātmikāṃ devīṃ samaṣṭivyaṣṭirūpiṇīm /
ādyāṃ śaktiṃ bhāvayanto bhāvārtha iti manvate //25//

What is to be understood here is that the Goddess, taken to be made up of the three subdivisions (*kūṭa*) of the *śrīvidyā*, is in a state of palpitation—that is, active—because she is both the cosmos (meant here by *dharma*) and its destruction (called here *adharma*). The first of these two aspects is called poison (*viṣa*), since the *saṃsāra* is poisonous for the ordinary mortal; the other, nectar (*amṛta*, a term that, in Sanskrit, means immortality), "is the death of death whose destruction is liberation" (Dī) or immortality. Creation and destruction—*sṛśti and saṃhāra*—are the two sides of her cosmic activity symbolized by the *śrīvidyā*.

As for the two syllables expressing this double notion, they are *A*, the first letter of the alphabet usually considered to be what "expresses" Śiva, and *HA*, the last letter associated here with Śakti. This "natural sense" (*bhāvārtha*)[12] of the *śrīvidyā* is what is to be understood through intense identifying meditation (*bhāvanā*).

The second meaning will now be expounded in stanzas 26–47. It is the one transmitted by tradition (*sampradāya*), that is, the secret knowledge received by the disciple from the mouth of his spiritual master. Underlining the fact that the whole cosmic manifestation is pervaded (*vyāpta*) by the *śrīvidyā*, that is, by the united Śiva and Śakti, it shows how the phonetic elements that constitute it "express" (are the *vācakas*), that is, evoke or denote and thus bring into existence and pervade the universe made up of the thirty-six *tattvas*, the three *guṇas*, the three sorts of knowers (*pramātṛ*), the *prāṇas*, and the gods.

The *śrīvidyā* and the cosmos, in their structure and in their existence or function, are inseparably one. To understand the *vidyā* is thus to understand the universe and liberation, a knowledge obtained by *bhāvanā* (*śl.* 39), but only insofar as one receives it from an initiated master well versed in the traditional teaching, hence the name of this *artha*.

> The oral tradition is the great knowledge present in the mouth of the spiritual master. The greatness of that which spreads [thus] in the form of the universe dwells in this [mouth]. //26//
>
> *sampradāyo mahābodharūpo gurumukhe sthitaḥ* /
>
> *viśvākāraprathāyās tu mahatvaṃ ca yad āśrayam* //26//

Repeating that the ultimate knowledge is to be transmitted secretly from the mouth of the master into the ear of the disciple, the DĪ says that the knowledge thus transmitted is that of the real nature of the universe, "which results from the transformation, in the form of the three *bījas* [of the *vidyā*], of the complete fusion [of Śakti and] of the supreme Śiva, which can only be received from the mouth of the guru."

This cosmic role of the *śrividyā* is first underscored by the Tantra:

> Through the *mūlavidyā*, of which Śiva and Śakti are the primary [cause], by her, O Parameśvarī! the whole universe is permeated. Listen to this carefully, O Dear One! //27//
>
> *śivaśaktyādyayā mūlavidyayā parameśvari* /
>
> *jagatkṛtsnaṃ tayā vyāptaṃ śṛṇuṣāvahitā priye* //27//

Śiva is the letter *A*, and Śakti is *HA*; the whole universe is therefore permeated by the totality of the Sanskrit alphabet, by the totality of the word with which the *mūlavidyā*, the "basic *vidyā*," the *śrīvidyā*, that is, is identified.

> The universe made of the five elements is what [the Goddess] is made of, O Ever Eternal One! Such too is the *mūlavidyā* that I am telling you. //28//
>
> From the letter *HA* space is born, from *KA*, wind, from RA fire; from SA comes the *tattva* of water. //29// Earth is born from the letter *LA*. In this way [is made] this [reality] which contains the universe.
>
> *pañcabhūtamayaṃ viśvaṃ tanmayī sā sadā 'naghe* /
>
> *tanmayī mūlavidyā ca tat tathā kathayāmi te* //28//
>
> *hakārād vyoma sambhūtaṃ kakārāt tu prabhañjanaḥ* /

rephād agniḥ sakārāc ca jalatattvasya saṃbhavaḥ //29//
lakārāt pṛthivī jātā tasmād viśvamayī ca sā /

The Goddess and her mantra are deemed to be made of the five gross elements (the *bhūtas*) constituting the gross, concrete level of the cosmos. This is said to show that the universe as identical with the deity is metaphorically present in the *śrīvidyā*.

HA, KA, RA, SA, and *LA* are, in all traditions, considered the *bījas*, the *vācakas*, of the five gross elements. "Thus," says the Dī, "the five gross elements and the phonemes which express them are born in this way from the light and consciouness (*prakāśa* and *vimarśa*) which form the supreme Reality whose nature is the total fusion of Śiva and Śakti. The nature of this supreme *vidyā* is the total fusion of these two [aspects of the deity]. In other terms, she is made of the phonemes that compose her and of the universe [that they 'express']." The Dī then quotes stanzas 9, 10, 13, and 14 of Puṇyānanda's *Kāmakalāvilāsa*.[13]

It is said that the fifteen *guṇas* of the gross elements [are also found there]. Thus formed, she is favorable. //30//
guṇāḥ pañcadaśa proktā bhūtānāṃ tanmayī śivā //30//

There are, in fact, only three *guṇas*: *sattva, rajas,* and *tamas* (goodness, passion, and darkness). This number could be explained by the fact that there are five gross elements (*bhūtas*), which would result in 5 x 3 = 15. But the commentary explains this number by the fact that the *bhūtas* "interpenetrate mutually"; that is, the higher ones are present in those that follow, which results in 1 + 2 + 3 + 4 + 5 = 15 *guṇas*. This is a peculiar conception, not the generally admitted one of the Sāṃkhya, for whom the gross elements issue from the subtle ones (*tanmātra*). Fifteen, however is the number of the phonemes of the *śrīvidyā*. There are, therefore, two series of fifteen elements.

In any object one can say that there is energy [*śakti*]. This [energy] is the Goddess, the universal sovereign. And any object is the supreme Lord. //31//
yasya yasya padārthasya yā yā śaktir udīritā /
sā sā sarveśvarī devī sa sa sarvo maheśvaraḥ //31//

In this world, says Amṛtānanda, everything that is active is energy. And all energy is the Goddess, the universal sovereign, mistress of all

The thirty-six *tattvas* of Tantric shaivism

Śiva	
Śakti	
Sadāśiva	the eternal Śiva
Īśvara	the Lord
śuddhavidyā	pure wisdom
māyā	cosmic illusion
kalā	limitation
vidyā	(limited) wisdom; the cuirasses (*kañcuka*)
rāga	passionate attachment
niyati	necessity
kāla	time
puruṣa	Spirit, or the Lord
prākṛti	the source matter, Nature
buddhi	intellect
ahaṃkāra	"egoity"
manas	understanding (*sensorium commune*)
śrotra	hearing
tvāk	touch
cakṣus	sight; organs of perception (*buddhīndriya*)
rasana	taste
ghrāna	smell
vāk	speech
pāni	holding
pāyu	excretion; organs of action (*karmendriya*)
upaṣṭha	copulation
pāda	movement
śabda	sound
sparśa	contact
rūpa	form; subtle elements (*tanmātra*)
rasa	savor
gandha	smell
ākāśa	ether, space
vāyu	air
tejas	fire; gross elements (*bhūta*)
jala	water
pṛthivī	earth

that exists, from Śiva to the earth, whereas all that is object is the supreme Lord, the supreme Śiva. These two, he adds, take on in the *vidyā* the aspect of objects (the fifteen male *guṇas* of the five *tattvas*) and that of the fifteen (female) phonemes of the *vidyā*. The basic male-female dichotomy is therefore present in the *vidyā*. This, however, includes other elements:

> This *vidyā*, made up of the elements and the *guṇas*, is pervaded by fifteen phonemes [namely] by five, then six and four syllables. //32//
>
> *vyāptā pañcadaśārṇaiḥ sā vidyā bhūtaguṇātmikā /*
>
> *pañcabhiś ca tathā ṣaḍbhiś caturbhir api cākṣaraiḥ //32//*

These three groups of syllables are those of the three *kūṭas* of the *śrīvidyā*, which have six, then five, then four syllables. These phonemes are said to pervade the *vidyā*, since she is made up in her totality of these fifteen letters.

> If she is parceled up into vowels and consonants, she is divided into thirty-seven. If divided into thirty-seven, she is formed of the thirty-six *tattvas*, //33// her essential nature transcending the *tattvas*. This *vidyā*, one must ceaselessly meditate.
>
> *svaravyañjanabhedena saptatriṃśatprabhedinī /*
>
> *saptatriṃśatprabhedena ṣaṭtriṃśattattvarūpiṇī //33//*
>
> *tattvātītasvabhāvā ca vidyaiṣā bhāvyate sadā*

If we divide the *vidyā* into vowels and consonants, we have eleven letters in the first *kūṭa*, thirteen in the second, and nine in the third; thirty-three phonemes to which are to be added the three *bindus* which crown the three *HRĪṂ*; thirty-seven in all.[14] Divided in this way, the *vidyā* can be considered as made up symbolically of the thirty-six *tattvas* and thus to have the same nature as these cosmic divisions of the universe. The *śrīvidyā* is the Goddess in her cosmic activity, carried out by the *tattvas*, which she dominates, transcends, being in this sense a thirty-seventh *tattva*. Her essential nature, says Amṛtānanda, is that of Śiva, and it is as such that she is to be meditated (*bhāvyate*).[15]

The Dī quotes here the first twenty-seven stanzas of the *Saubhāgyasudhodaya*, which describe the cosmic creative activity of the deity as Śakti, and the divisions and aspects of this work. The passage is interesting but is too long and needs too many explanations to be quoted here.

The YH now considers again the fifteen elements and the three *guṇas* previously mentioned in *śl.* 32:

> In the elements earth, etc., each element that is above is pervading, //34// the one below is pervaded. / This is why the *guṇas* whose receptacles are the pervading [elements] are in those which are pervaded, O Goddess! being [themselves] divided into gross and subtle. //35//
>
> *pṛthivyādiṣu bhūteṣu vyāpakaṃ cottarottaram* //34//
> *bhūtaṃ tvadhastanaṃ vyāpyaṃ tadguṇā vyāpakāśrayāḥ* /
> *vyāpyeṣvavasthitā devi sthūlasūkṣmavibhedataḥ* //35//

> Thus, sound, the *guṇa* of space, pervades the [gross elements] air, etc., the fivefold sound [present in these elements] being denoted by the *bījas* of space which are in the *vidyā*. //36//
>
> Of these [five sounds], what stays in addition as [their] cause is made of *dhvani*. [The phoneme *HA*] must be [understood as being] the seed of those that carry the *guṇas* and also as that which expresses the *guṇas*. //37// The fact that they have [respectively] the nature of cause and effect shows their unity.
>
> *tasmād vyomaguṇaḥ śabdo vayvādīn vyāpyā saṃsthitaḥ* /
> *vyomabījais tu vidyāsthair lakṣayecchabdapañcakam* //36//
> *teṣāṃ kāraṇarūpeṇa sthitaṃ dhvanimayaṃ param* /
> *bhaved guṇavatāṃ bījaṃ guṇanām api vācakam* //37//
> *kāryakāraṇabhāvena tayor aikyaṃ vivakṣayā* /

What is to be understood here seems to be that each subtle element is present in the corresponding gross element but also that a gross element may be present in another one becoming subtle with regard to it.[16] The so-called *bījas* of space (*vyomabīja*) denoting the five elements are the five letters *HA* present in the three sections of the *śrīvidyā*. The element added to these five *HA* is, according to Amṛtānanda, the sixth *HA* of the *vidyā*, that is, the *HA* of the third *kūṭa*, placed between the *KA* and the *LA* of the *kāmarājakūṭa*. This *HA* is, for some reason, considered to be "made of *dhvani*," that is, embodying a subtle form of sound, which would explain why it is the cause of the five other ones.

The YH continues by expounding the links that exist between the *guṇas*, the gross elements (*bhūta*), and the letters deemed to "express" them:

> One must meditate intensely, O Goddess! on the apparition of the [elements] air, fire, water, and earth, distinguishing the gross from the subtle ones, and on that of [the *guṇas* of] contact [which pervade them] as originating all from the three Mahāmāyā and from the *bindu* which is their origin. //38b–39//
>
> *mahāmāyātrayeṇāpi kāraṇena ca bindunā //38//*
>
> *vāyvagnijalabhūmīnāṃ sparśanāṃ ca catuṣṭayam /*
>
> *utpannaṃ bhāvayed devi sthūlasūkṣmavibhedataḥ //39//*

The Mahāmāyās are the letters *Ī* of the three *HRĪṂ* of the *śrīvidyā*, the *bindus* being the three *Ṃ*s.

> The three [*guṇas*] of [the *tattva* of] form [*rūpa*] are to be meditated on in the same manner using the three *RA*. Their essential part has the form of fire. [They are] indeed engendered by this *bīja*. //40//
>
> *rūpāṇāṃ tritayaṃ tadvat tribhī rephair vibhavitam /*
>
> *pradhānaṃ tejaso rūpaṃ tadbījena tu janyate //40//*

These three *guṇas* are those found in the *tattvas* of earth, water, and fire. *RA*, to be used to meditate them, is the *bīja* of fire, since their essential part is fire. This implies the presence of form in these three *tattvas*.

According to the Dī: "The three *guṇas* of form, which is the *guṇa* of fire, having been [described as] denoted by the phonemes which are the *vācaka* of fire, the *guṇa* of water is now described by the phonemes that are the *vācakas* of that element."

> Taste, both subtle and gross, is evoked through the lunar *bījas* present in the *vidyā*. In this world also one knows the association of *rasa* and *amṛta*. //41//
>
> *vidyāsthaiṣ candrabījais tu sthūlaḥ sūkṣmo rasaḥ smṛtaḥ /*
>
> *saṃbandho vidito loke rasasyāpi amṛtasya ca //41//*

The lunar *bījas* are the letters *SA* of the three *kuṭas* of the *śrīvidyā*, the letter *SA* often being given the name *candra* (moon). Taste is the *guṇa* of water. It is therefore in its natural gross form in the *tattva* of water, which is taken to be pervading; in the *tattva* of earth, which is pervaded, it is subtle, the Dī explains. It also explains (more comprehensibly) that according to the Purāṇas, the *amṛta* appeared from the water of the ocean when it was churned by the gods and the *asuras*. Hence the link between these two elements.

> The *guṇa* of the earth is smell. Its letter is that which expresses smell. The threefold nature [of this letter] is to the result of the link existing between the three worlds, O Maheśvarī! //42//
>
> *vasundharāguṇo gandhas tallipir gandhavācikā* /
>
> *bhuvanatrayasaṃbandhāt tridhātvaṃ tu maheśvari* //42//

The *bīja* of earth is *LA*, and it is denoted by one *LA* only, whereas there are three *LA* in the *śrividyā*. If one were to object to this fact, the DĪ answers: there are three worlds (*lokatraya*) in the universe, which are mutually supporting and supported, and, because of that, the earth is also considered triple though being one.

> The other body in the three [sorts of] conscious subjects—pure, impure, and mixed—is manifested by the triple *krodhīśa* present in the *vidyā*. //43//
>
> *aśuddhaśuddhamiśrāṇāṃ pramātṛṇāṃ paraṃ vapuḥ* /
>
> *krodhīśatritayenātha vidyāsthena prakāśyate* //43//

The triple *krodhīśa* are the three letters *KA* of the *śrīvidyā*. They denote the three sorts of conscious subjects (*pramātṛ*), which represent three different levels or modes of consciousness. They are, says Amṛtānanda, the *vijṇānākalā*, who suffer only the *āṇavamalā*, the innate impurity of the soul (the *aṇu*), their minds being already purified and in essence like Śiva; then the *pralayākala*, bound souls who will be endlessly reborn to "burn" their *karman* till the next *pralaya*; and the *sakala*, who are bound by all the fetters of this world.[17]

> Just as the ten *śrīkaṇṭhas* are that which expresses the nonmanifested, O Goddess! so the eleventh remains in the form of breath, the other one //44// is the *puruṣa*: being unique, he becomes multiple.
>
> *śrīkaṇṭhadaśakaṃ tadvad avyaktasya hi vācakam* /
>
> *prāṇarūpaḥ sthito devi tadvad ekādaśaḥ paraḥ* //44//
>
> *ekaḥ sann eva puruṣo bahudhā jāyate hi saḥ* /

The ten *śrīkaṇṭhas* are the ten letters *A* of the twelve syllables that form the *śrīvidyā* (which are twelve if one excludes the three *HRĪṂ*). The non-manifest (*avyakta*) which these the letters express is, says the Dī, the vital principle, the *jīva*, of the human individual bound by the senses linked to the inert, insentient (*jaḍa*), not illuminated by divine Consciousness. The other one, linked to the two other *A*, is the *puruṣa*, the supreme soul, Śiva, who is, in fact, unique but becomes multiple by his infinite appearances and by being present in the vital breath of all living beings.

> The deities named Rudra, Īśvara, and Sadeśa, limited [divine] forms, are invoked by the three *bindus*. The totally unlimited forms, those of Śanti, Śakti, and Śambhu, are denoted by the three *nādas*. //45b–46//
>
> *rudreśvarasadeśākhyā devatā mitavigrahāḥ* //45//
>
> *bindutrayeṇa kathitā amitāmitavigrahāḥ* /
>
> *śāntiḥ śaktiśca śambhuś ca nādatritayabodhanaḥ* //46//

The Dī, referring for that to the *Svacchandasaṃgraha*, expatiates on the role of the deities enumerated in this stanza. Rudra, it says, presides over the *tattva* of fire, in which are the five *tattvas* from *puruṣa* to *māyā*, the *tattvas śuddhavidyā*, *sadāśiva*, and *īśvara* depending from the *tattva* air. Being linked to *tattvas*, these three deities are limited in time and scope. They are invoked by the three *bindus* which "crown" the *M* of the three *HRĪṂ* of the *śrīvidyā*. The three unlimited divine forms, Śānti, Śakti, and Śambhu (Śiva), are denoted (have for *vācaka*) three *nādas*. Śānti is thus the not-manifest subtle sound (*avyaktadhvani*) produced in the *brahmarandhra cakra*, where all the highest energies are deemed to be appeased; one thus shifts here from syllables of the mantra to the body of the adept. Śakti is the highest aspect of *śaktitattva*, Śambhu being the *śivatattva*.

The YH concludes the section on the *bhāvārtha* as follows:

> As the threads of a net are gathered in its initial thread, in the same way the mantras are all found together in the *vidyā*. //47//
>
> *vāgurāmūlavalaye sūtrādyāḥ kavalīkṛtāḥ* /
>
> *tathā mantrāḥ samastāś ca viyāyām atra saṃsthitāḥ* //47//

The Dī explains that the net alluded to here is a net for catching fish, the threads of whose mesh are gathered at their "root" in a metal ring from which they, as it were, issue forth. In the same way, the *vaikari*, manifested form of the word, of all uttered mantras, and, of course, the *śrīvidyā* when made use of, is gathered initially in the supreme, *parā*, plane of the Word, *vāc*.

Then comes the so-called traditional meaning (*saṃpradāyārtha*), which is transmitted through the (oral) teachings of the succession of spiritual masters of the Śrīvidyā school (*gurūpadeśakrameṇa*). In this respect, this *artha* does not bring anything new, as appears from its being expounded in one half-*śloka*:

> [The meaning] that one can attain through the succession of spiritual masters is called the traditional meaning.
>
> *gurukrameṇa saṃprāptaḥ sampradāyārtha īrithaḥ* /

The Dī quotes here a long (unidentified) passage from the *Svacchandabhairavatantra* which describes how the teaching issuing from the supreme "transmental" (*unmanā*) plane of the divinity or of the Word (*vāc*) goes through several lower divine planes down to the god Śrīkaṇṭha, who then reveals it to human masters. Śrīkaṇṭha, we note here, is not one of the five masters of the *divyaugha*, the "flow of divine masters" of the Śrīvidyā tradition in the *pāraṃparas* given by Śivānanda, Vidyānanda, and Amṛtānanda. This can be explained by the fact that the *Svacchandabhairava*, which is often referred to in the Dī, is not—if we identify it with the *Svacchandatantra*—a Tantra of the Śrīvidyā. Concluding on the subject, Amṛtānanda says: "Whoever who, ignorant of the exact meaning of the words and of the tradition, would, without attending the teaching of a master, try to discover alone the meaning of the words as one can do for the stanzas of the Purāṇas and so forth, shall never be able to find it."

The next meaning is the inner or secret (*nigarbha*) one. It is not merely alluded to but briefly considered:

> As for the inner meaning, O Great Goddess! it is an experience (or perception) of Śiva, the spiritual master and the self. //48//
>
> *nigarbho 'pi mahādevi śivagururātmagocaraḥ* //48//

This sense is secret and/or inner (*nigarbha*)[18] insofar as Śiva is transcendent, unattainable by thought and word. The spiritual master considers Śiva his own inner transcendent self, this same omnipresent self being also the self of the disciple, who is to have a personal inner experience of this full omnipresent pure divine Consciousness, "all his fetters having been destroyed by the compassionate gaze of the guru" (DĪ, p. 174). This "sense"—this experience, that is—of the *vidyā*, concludes the DĪ, consists in "the concentration of the mind [*anusandhāna*] on the experience of the unity of Śiva, the master, and the self." But how is one to concentrate on this unity? The answer is:

> I give you only a mere indication of how it is done, O Mistress of the gods! [A fusion] of this sort results from the one-pointed attention on the unity of Śiva, the guru, and the self. //49//
>
> *tatprakāraṃ ca deveśi diṅmātreṇa vadāmi te /*
>
> *śivagurvātmanāṃ aikyānusandhānāt tadātmakam //49//*

Namely:

> Having understood that there is no division within Śiva and that the spiritual master has the same quality, the [disciple], bent down in devotion, unsullied by the presence of contraction, must realize thanks to the power of the gaze of his master that he has himself the nature of Śiva. //50–51a//
>
> *niṣkalatvaṃ śive buddhvā tadrūpatvaṃ guror api*
>
> *tannirīkṣaṇasamarthyād ātmanaś ca śivātmatām //50//*
>
> *bhāvayed bhaktinamraḥ san śaṅkonmeṣākalaṅkitaḥ /*

The general meaning of this stanza is clear. The term "contraction" (*saṃkoca*) may, however, surprise the reader. The DĪ explains that it is the condition of a person whose mind is attached to the life in this world, this condition being revealed (*unmeṣa*) by the pleasure one finds in "such external objects as wife, son, and the like." More philosophically, it is the state of the soul that has lost its original omnipresence and freedom.

The saving power of the gaze (*nirīkṣaṇa*) of the master which "falls" (*katākṣapāta*) on his disciple—one also says *dṛṣṭipāta*—is a common theme. The practice is also used ritually: *nirīkṣaṇa* is one of a group of four purifying rites in Śaiva ritual.

We may also note here the attitude of devotion (*bhakti*), both mental and bodily, prescribed to the adept: a *tāntrika* is not merely a ritualist and a yogin; he is also a devotee.

The next *artha* is expounded in the next seventeen stanzas. Although it is complex, it is not difficult to understand:

> I will now tell you the *kaulika* meaning: it is the unity of the *cakra* and the deity, //51// the *vidyā*, the spiritual master, and the self. What this [unity] consists of will be shown.
>
> The four-sided lines [are born] from the letters *LA*. The two lotuses, which are fire and moon and are accompanied by a triple circle, are born from [the phonemes of] energy, O Dear One! From the letters numbering nine which form the three *hṛllekhā* //53// [when] joined to three *bindus* is born the *cakra* with nine *yonis*, O Dear One!
>
> The *cakra* that is in contact with the triple circle and which is fire and energy //54// is born only from the triple *bīja* of space. Accompanied by the triple subject, associated with the three "intoxicatings," will, knowledge, and activity, //55// is the throne of Sadāśiva, O Goddess! constituted by the *mahābindu*, supreme. This is why the nature of the *cakra* is that of the mantra.
>
> *kaulikaṃ kathayiṣyāmi cakradevatayor api //51//*
> *vidyāgurvātmanāṃ aikyam tatprakāraḥ pradarśyate /*
> *lakāraīścaturasrāṇi vṛttatritayasaṃyutam //52//*
> *saroruhadvayaṃ śāktair agniṣomātmakaṃ priye*
> *hṛllekhātrayasaṃbhūtair akṣarair navasaṃkhyakaiḥ //53//*
> *bindutrayayutair jātaṃ navayonyātmakaṃ priye /*
> *maṇḍalatrayayuktaṃ tu cakraṃ śaktyanalātmakam //54//*
> *vyomabījatrayeṇaiva pramātṛtritayānvitam /*
> *icchājñānakriyārūpamādanatrayasaṃyutam //55//*
> *sadāśivāsanaṃ devi mahābindumayaṃ param /*
> *itthaṃ mantrātmakaṃ cakram*

In these stanzas, the YH goes on describing the mutually interwoven condition and interdependence of the *śricakra* and the *śrīvidyā*. This is shown by saying that the different parts of the *cakra* are born from different letters of the *vidyā*. The four-sided figure is the external square enclosure of the *cakra* made of three lines—hence the plural (*caturasrāṇi*) form used. The "energy phonemes" are the letters *SA* of the three *kūṭas*, this being justified by a quotation from a Tantra: "Śiva is *HA*, Śakti is *SA*."

As for the two lotuses, the outer one with sixteen petals is *soma*, a usual designation of the moon, the number sixteen being a lunar number.[19] The letters numbering nine are the three letters *H, R, Ī* of each of the three *HRĪṂ* (here called *hṛllekhā*, "the letter *HRĪṂ*"), the *bindu* joined to them being the *Ṃ* of *HRĪṂ*.

We have seen the *navayoni cakra* in chapter 1. The *cakra* that is in contact with the triple circle is the *cakra* of twelve triangles inside which are the two other *cakras* of, respectively, fourteen and ten triangles, all three being deemed to issue from the three *bījas* of space, that is, the three *HA*. The throne of energy is the central triangle, the three "intoxicating" (or maddening) phonemes being the letters *KA* deemed to be the phonetic aspect of the subjects submitted to the powers of will, knowledge, and activity.

But if the *cakra* is identical with the mantra, it is also, fundamentally, an aspect of the Goddess. The YH, therefore, says:

It is the other body of the deity. //56//

devatāyāḥ paraṃ vapuḥ //56//

The Dī refers here to stanza 55 of the first chapter, which says that the *cakra* is "the cosmic body of the Goddesss all surrounded by the sparkling waves of her multitudinous power." This cosmic aspect of the Goddess (which we will find again in the third chapter, beginning at *śl.* 9, where the Gaṇeśas, etc., are placed by *nyāsa* on the body of the worshipper) consists of deities (Gaṇas, Yoginīs, Ḍākinīs, etc.), breaths, and aspects of the word, shown as linked to different parts of the *vidyā*. The mantra brings together all these inseparably divine and human realities.

That the Goddess could, while always supreme and unique, appear as so many different epiphanies should not surprise us. The multiple aspects of deities go back to the Veda; it gives an expression to the diversity of their power. This multiplication, which implies the multiplication of sanctuaries, concretizes (today and in the past) the omnipresence of a deity on the Indian soil, sacred space being delimitated by their sanctuaries.

This totality is shown as follows:

In addition, since her nature is that of one hundred and eleven deities, the Great Goddess has the supremacy over the *gaṇas*; further, because of the fact that will, cognition, and activity, together with moon, sun, and fire, are associated with the three *guṇas*, this Goddess has a planetary aspect. //56b–58a//

ekādaśādhikaśatadevatātmatayā punaḥ /

gaṇeśatvaṃ mahādevyāḥ sasomaravipāvakaiḥ //57//

icchājñānakriyābhiś ca guṇatrayayuktaiḥ punaḥ /

graharūpā ca sā devī

The one hundred and eleven deities—called "troups" (*gaṇas*)[20]—are those surrounding Tripurasundarī, abiding in the nine parts of the *śrīcakra*, from Kāmeśvara and Kāmeśvarī, in the center, to the Mudrās and Siddhis, in the outer square. We have already met them in the first chapter and will see their worship in chapter 3. The Goddess, says Amṛtānanda, is both the deities of the *cakra* and the totality of the deities, of the Godhead. As such, she is the three basic energies, will, knowledge, and activity, in the powers symbolized by the three luminaries (*dhāman*),[21] moon, sun, and fire, and is also the nine planets, the *grahas*.[22]

Her aspect as constellations comes from the senses of apperception and action as well as from their objects, O Mistress of the gods! from the internal organs, from *prakṛti* and from the *guṇas* and from the self and the state of *pumān*. //58b–60a//

jñānakarmendriyair api //58//

tadarthair eva deveśi karaṇair āntaraiḥ punaḥ /

prakṛtyā ca guṇenāpi puṃstvabandhena cātmanā //59//

nakṣatravigrahā jātā

The Goddess as mantra takes on the aspects or nature of the twenty-seven constellations (*nakṣatra*);[23] these astral aspects are correlated, in the *vidyā*, with the *tattvas*, enumerated here going from the five faculties of action (speech, grasping, evacuation, copulation, movement), the five senses of apperception (hearing, contact, seeing, taste, smell), their ten objects (the subtle and gross elements: the five *tanmātras* and the five *bhūtas*), and then the internal organs, *manas, ahamkāra, buddhi,* plus *prakriti* and *puruṣa* and the *guṇas*. The Dī concludes: "It is because these twenty-seven [elements] make up her constitutive parts that the Goddess appears as the constellations, an aspect she takes on of her own free will."

> [Her] nature of Yoginī is now expounded. Because of the Ḍākinis, etc., mistresses of the body elements, the skin, etc., she is associated with the eight Yoginīs presiding over the eight groups of phonemes. Assuming the condition of the Yoginīs, she shines forth, having the world as her form. //60a–61//
>
> *yoginītvam athocyate* /
>
> *tvagādidhātunāthābhir ḍākinyādibhir apy asau* //60//
>
> *vargāṣṭakaniviṣṭābhir yoginībhiś ca saṃyutā* /
>
> *yoginīrūpam āsthāya rājate viśvavigrahā* //61//

The elements that constitute the human body (*dhātu*) number traditionally seven: skin, blood, flesh, fat, marrow, semen, bones. The DĪ quotes only six, omitting bones. Their number does not coincide with that of the Yoginīs which are, says Amṛtānanda, Ḍākinī, Rākinī, Lākinī, Kākinī, Śākinī, and Hākinī. These deities, generally collectively called Ḍākinīs, are traditionally associated with the bodily elements. Here they come together with the eight Yoginīs, which are, in fact, the eight Mothers (Mātṛ or Mātṛkā), Brahmī, and so on, traditionally considered the regents of the eight groups of phonemes of the Sanskrit alphabet.[24] Together, these Yoginīs, says the DĪ, embody or stand for the totality of the cosmos. It adds: "the Goddess plays in the form of these Yoginīs."

Then follows another aspect taken up by the Goddess:

> [The ten breaths,] *prāṇā*, *apāna*, *samāna*, *vyāna*, *udāna*, *nāga*, *kūrma*, *kṛkāra*, *devadatta*, and *dhanañjaya*, along with the individual soul and the supreme Self—it is through them that she assumes a zodiacal nature. //62–63a//
>
> *prāṇāpānau samānaścodānavyānau tathā punaḥ* /
>
> *nāgaḥ kūrmo 'tha kṛkaro devadatto dhanañjayaḥ* //62//
>
> *jīvātmaparamātmā cety etair rāśisvarūpiṇī* /

This series of ten vital breaths (*prāṇa*) is a current one. Together with the individual soul, or vital principle (*jīvātman*), and the supreme soul, *paramātman*, they number twelve, like the signs of the zodiac, which are the same in India as in the West, from which they were borrowed by the Indians.

The next aspect is less evident:

The great *vidyā* made of supreme Word and of the other [three levels of the Word], having as nature the triple group [of phonemes] *A*, *KA*, *THA*, and the other ones, becomes mistress of the *gaṇas*, starting with the third [of these groups]. //63b–64a//

akathāditripaṅktyātmā tārtīyādikrameṇa sā //63//

gaṇeśo 'bhūn mahāvidyā parāvāgādivāṅmayī /

The Sanskrit alphabet, from *A* to *HA*, is the totality of the Word (*vāc*) which—in the view of most Tantric traditions—is considered as existing on four levels: *parā*, the supreme; *paśyantī*, the visionary; *madhyamā*, the intermediate; and the plane of the gross, empirical speech, of discursive thought, *vaikharī*.[25] *A* here designates the sixteen vowels, the first of which is *A*; *KA* stands for the sixteen consonants from *KA* to *TA*; *THA* is for the sixteen letters from *THA* to *SA*. The *A* group is considered to be included in the last *kūṭa* of the *śrīvidyā*, the *śaktibīja*; the *KA* group is in the middle *kūṭa*, *kāmarāja*; and the *THA* group is in the first *kūṭa*, *vāgbhava*. The totality of the alphabet is thus present in the whole *śrīvidyā*.

When in the three *kūtas* [in the form] of *bīja*, *bindu*, and *dhvani*, she takes on the nature of the planets. //64b//

[When made of her] syllables numbering fifteen: the three *hṛllekhas* and the twelve other phonemes, her form is that of the constellations. //65//

bījabindudhvanīnāṃ ca trikūṭeṣu grahātmikā //64//

hṛllekhāttrayasaṃbhūtais tithisaṃkhyais tathākṣaraiḥ /

anyair dvādaśabhir varṇair eṣā nakṣatrarūpiṇī //65//

Since there are three elements, *bīja*, *bindu*, and *dhvani*, in each of the three *kūṭas*, the total is nine, which is the number of the *grahas*. *Bīja*, the commentary explains, is the *HRĪ* of the three *kūṭas*, *bindu* being the *Ṃ* and *nāda* the subtle phonic vibration that ends the *HRĪṂ*.

As for the *nakṣatras*, which number twenty-seven, this number is obtained by counting first the fifteen phonemes of the *śrīvidyā* (fifteen being also the number of the lunar days, the *tithis*),[26] then its twelve phonemes without the three *HRĪṂ*. "Thus," concludes the DĪ, "the *vidyā* in the form of constellations being formed by fifteen and twelve phonemes, we get twenty-seven in all."

The state of Yoginī of the *vidyā* [results from] six syllables: [those of] energy and those preceding the energies that are present in the *vidyā*.

Its zodiacal state [arises] when one removes those that are at the end. //66//

vidyāntarbhūtaśaktyādyaiḥ śāktaiḥ ṣaḍbhis tathākṣaraiḥ /

yoginitvaṃ ca vidyāyā rāśitvaṃ cāntyavarjitaiḥ //66//

The syllables of energy are the three *HRĪṂ*; what precedes them are the three letters *LA*, the total of six being reached if one counts the *HRĪṂ* as one syllable only. The aspect of energy of the Goddess is that of the six Yoginīs, Ḍākinī, and so on, that we have already seen.

For the twelve signs of the zodiac, one counts the syllables of the *vidyā* without the three *HRĪṂ*.

Maheśvarī [when] in the form of the *cakra* [has] in the same way a cosmic aspect. //67a//

evaṃ viśvaprakārā ca cakrarūpā maheśvarī /

The *śrīcakra*, along with the *śrividyā*, is the Goddess in her cosmic activity. All the forms we have just seen taken over by her as the *vidyā*—as mistress of the *gaṇas*, and so on—she also assumes when in the form of the *cakra*. The Dī tells which parts of the *śrīcakra* are to be associated with the different aspects (*gaṇas*, planets, constellations, etc.) quoted in stanzas 57–66:

[All the aspects just] described as in the body of the Goddess [are to be found] in the same way in the body of the spiritual master, and, through his grace, the disciple will also shine in this form. //67b–68a//

devyā dehe yathā prokto gurudehe tathaiva hi //67//

tatprasādāc ca śiṣyo 'pi tadrūpaḥ saṃprakāśate /

The body of the Goddess Tripurasundarī, says Amṛtānanda, is the one she has assumed, in her play, of her own free will (*svecchāgṛhīta-līlāvigraha*). The nature of the guru, he adds, being that of the deity's body, the deity is also in his body. And this is also to be found in the body of the disciple, who "having benefited from the grace of his master, shines, like him, like the deity." We note here again the importance always given in Tantric traditions to the grace bestowed by the spiritual master, which replicates on the human level the movement of the divine grace (*anugraha*), also called "descent of the [divine] energy" (*śaktipāta*).

> Thus is said the *kaulika* meaning, O Perfect One! Celebrated by the heroes. //68//
>
> I will tell you also the most secret of all meanings, O Perfect One!
>
> *ity evaṃ kaulikārthas tu kathito vīravandite* //68//
>
> *tathā sarvarahasyārthaṃ kathayāmi tavānaghe* /

This interpretation of the *śrīvidyā* is the most secret one, says the Dī, because thanks to it, the disciple may attain the supreme (*para*). It is, in fact, a yogic practice.

> The *vidyā* having taken on, in the *mūlādhāra*, the condition of the *vāgbhava*, similar to lightning, //69b// her body being made of fifty phonemes associated with thirty-eight *kalās*, in the form of the *kuṇḍalinī*, pierces the three *maṇḍalas*. //70// Shining like ten million flashes of lightning, shaped like a lotus fiber, she attaches herself to the *maṇḍala* of the moon of the inner sky, her nature being that of a flow of nectar //71// of which she pervades the whole universe, her nature being constant bliss. The thought: "this energy is my own self," such is the secret meaning, O Maheśvarī! //72//
>
> *mūlādhāre taḍidrūpe vāgbhavākāratāṃ gate* //69//
>
> *aṣṭatriṃśatkalāyuktapañcāśadvarṇavigrahā* /
>
> *vidyā kuṇḍalinīrūpā maṇḍalatrayabhedinī* //70//
>
> *taḍitkoṭinibhaprakhyā bisatantunibhākṛtiḥ* /
>
> *vyomendumaṇḍalāsaktā sudhāsrotaḥsvarūpiṇī* //71//
>
> *sadā vyāptajagatkṛtsnā sadānandasvarūpiṇī* /
>
> *eṣā svātmeti buddhis tu rahasyārtho maheśvari* //72//

The term *vāgbhava* here does not designate the first *kūṭa* of the *śrīvidyā* but the condition (*bhava*) of the Word (*vāc*) whose fourfold division we have seen above (*śl.* 63). The *vidyā* is thus identified with the totality and the full power of the Word. This explains why her body (in the shape of the *kuṇḍalinī*) is "made of fifty phonemes," the Sanskrit alphabet being, as we have seen, the totality of the Word.

Going upward, from the *mūlādhāra*, in the body of the adept, the *vidyā* as *kuṇḍalinī* pierces three *maṇḍalas* not otherwise identified by the YH and its commentary, except (by the DĪ) as being those of the fire, the sun, and the moon, traditionally considered to have, respectively, ten, twelve, and sixteen divisions called *kalās*, totaling thus thirty-eight. These *kalās* are cosmic and divine entities with which are associated the fifty Sanskrit phonemes; here, too, is the totality of the Word. The moon, called *soma* (the sacred beverage of the Veda), is traditionally associated with the *amṛta*, the nectar, which, when this center is pierced by the *kuṇḍalinī*, flows over and fills up the universe and, evidently, the body and mind of the adept, who is then identified with the divine *śakti*, saying, "This energy is my own self."

"The thought [*buddhi*] that 'this *kuṇḍalinī śakti* made of consciousness [*cinmayī*] is my own self' [*svātmeti*], that is to say, the total fusion by identification [*tadātmatayā samāveśaḥ*] with this form [of power], such is the sense of the secret meaning," says the DĪ, which also says that *kuṇḍalinī*, having pierced the moon *maṇḍala*, enters the *akula* center.[27]

The experience described here is therefore both cosmic and bodily. The DĪ quotes a stanza from the *Svacchandasaṃgraha* which says that the supreme sky (*paraṃ vyoman*) is placed on the head between the forehead and the summit of the head (between the *brumadhya* or *bindu* and the *brahmarandhra*).

Then comes the next meaning:

> The meaning [relating to] the highest reality, I will tell you, O Goddess.
>
> It [consists in] uniting oneself with the indivisible, supreme, subtle, imperceptible, with no concrete existence, the reality supreme, above the inner sky, light and bliss, both transcending the universe and identical with it. //73–74//
>
> *mahātattvārtha iti yat tac ca devi vadāmi te* /
>
> *niṣkale parame sūkṣme nirlakṣye bhāvavarjite* //73//
>
> *vyomātīte pare tattve prakāśānandavigrahe* /
>
> *viśvottīrṇe viśvamaye tattve svātmaniyojanam* //74//

This stanza heaps up terms to describe the indescribable divine Absolute. The DĪ explains the terms, but the passage does not really need to be interpreted. It underlines the total transcendence of the Absolute, adding, "but this supreme reality is also identical with the universe [*viśvamaya*]"; it manifests itself through the infinite diversity of the world. Quoting the Upaniṣadic saying *tat tvam asi*, "This thou art,"[28] the Dī concludes: "Such is the supreme truth. And the meaning relating to the highest reality is to identify oneself totally with it, that is to say, to unite one's self, whose pure essential nature is awakened by the spiritual master, with the supreme Śiva, giver of the supreme *vidyā* brimming with this supreme meaning."

But how are we to know this nature of our self? The answer is:

> Since luminosity is the state of things that are luminous and also that of those that are dark, there is therefore a necessary and essential connection between the universe and the [highest reality]. //75//
>
> *tadā prakāśamānatvaṃ tejasāṃ tamasām api /*
>
> *avinābhāvarūpatvaṃ tasmād viśvasya sarvataḥ //75//*

Commenting on this stanza, the Dī gives a summary of some of the main tenets of the nondualist Śaiva vision of the deity and the cosmos: "Even as Śiva shines in the mind [*citte*] of all living beings, in the same way the self is united to the senses and these to the objects; thus the state of luminosity exists in luminous things, such as the sun, etc., and also in those that are insentient, dark, such as pots and pans and the like. It shines first in consciousness, in the supreme Śiva, who is the Self of consciousness [*cidātman*], then through the play of sense organs; the perception of reality shines also on the plane of the diversity of objects. As the Revelation says: 'Everything shines as a reflection of His Light, by His brightness this [world] shines' (Katha Upaniṣad, 5.15)."

This vision of the cosmos as something that shines (*prakāśate*) as a reflection of the divine light (a theme developed notably by Abhinavagupta in the *Tantrāloka*, chapter 3) is stated again in the next half-stanza:

> The highest reality shines, O Flame of the essence of the divine play! //76a//
>
> *prakāśate mahātattvaṃ divyakrīḍārasojjvale /*

This play (*krīḍā*) of the Goddess is the unlimited power of divine Consciousness (*cicchakti*), a power whose work is to manifest and animate the universe: "Thou, O Goddess! art the blazing light bursting forth from this action, being [for us and in us] the intuitive comprehension [*pratīti*][29] eternally fastened on the total union of Śiva and Śakti."

The secret meaning, [the attainment of which is] preceded by the stability of the spirit that appears when all volition and all doubt are banished, is completely hidden. It gives immediate certainty. //76b–77a//

nirastasarvasaṃkalpavikalpasthitipūrvakaḥ //76//

rahasyārtho mahāguptaḥ sadyaḥ pratyayakārakaḥ /

The state of mind necessary to have this mystical experience of the highest reality is the complete nakedness, or void, of consciousness, without any will to act or any doubt about what is to be done. Once this state is present, the certainty flashes forth that "I am Śiva" (*śivo 'ham*), says the commentary.

It is seen in the ocean of the high knowledge. There, no doubt [survives], O Pārvatī! //77b// Giver of divine powers, it is present in the [three *kūṭas*] composing the seat [*pīṭha*] of the *vidyā*. //78a//

mahājñānārṇave dṛṣṭaḥ śaṅkā tatra na pārvati //77//

vidyāpīṭhanibandheṣu saṃsthito divyasiddhidaḥ /

Amṛtānanda explains the term *vidyāpītha*, saying that the Śrīvidyā is herself the *pīṭha*, since she is the place where Śiva and Ṣakti rest together. This seat is made up of the three constitutive parts (the *kūṭas* or *bījas*) of the *śrīvidyā*, whose meaning or spiritual import is to be experimentally realized by following the phonic process that extends from the first syllable of each *kūṭa* to the ultimate phonic vibration of the *HRĪṂ* that ends each of them: the phonic plane of *unmanā*, the "transmental."[30]

As for the divine powers (*divyasiddhi*), they are defined as consisting of the total knowledge and understanding of the supreme reality, not as the possession of supernatural powers, which is the usual meaning of the term *siddhi*—a meaning that is, however, given to it in stanzas 203–204 of the last chapter: Amṛtānanda, as we know, interprets the YH according to the Śaiva nondualist tradition, insisting on its metaphysical and spiritual aspects, not the magical ones.

Will enjoy this, O Goddess! those who follow the practice of Kula and who meditate on the feet of the Master, who take part zealously in the meetings with the Yoginīs, who have received the divine unction, are free from the stain of doubt, their spirit ceaselessly joyful and well versed in the secret meaning known through the uninterrupted succession [of masters]. //78b–80//

kaulācāraparair devi pādukābhāvanāparaiḥ //78//
yoginīmelanodyuktaiḥ prāptadivyābhiṣecanaiḥ /
śaṅkākalaṅkavigataiḥ sadā muditamānasaiḥ //79//
pāraṃparyeṇa vijñātararahasyārthaviśaradaiḥ /
labhyate

"The *kaulas*," says the Dī, "are those who know that *kula* is the body and that it can have a very great use."[31]

Concerning the meditation on the feet of the Master, the Dī quotes the following stanza: "One is the shape of Śiva, luminous by himself [*prakāśa*]. [One, too,] is the 'being' or essence [*tanu*] which is its awareness [*vimarśa*]. The supreme, total fusion of these two aspects [of the supreme deity], such is the imprint of the feet [of the Master]. It is in essence the supreme Śiva." The supreme godhead is, in the nondualist Śaiva traditions, both light (*prakāśa*) and free consciousness (*vimarśa*), a reality that only those who are devoted to the feet of the Master will enjoy.

The "meeting with the Yoginīs" (*yoginīmelana*) is a collective *kula* ritual in which participants, by pair, male and female, under the guidance of their guru, worship the deity, the ritual usually including the sexual union of the participating couples. The Dī underlines the festive, joyful atmosphere of the rite, in which the adepts, fully instructed according to the traditional teaching, free from doubt, enjoy the union with the deity.

[So it is and] not otherwise, I promise you, O Goddess, Beauty of the Family! //80// Those who, deprived of the tradition, are infatuated with their own science, since they transgress the rule, the rays [of consciousness] destroy them. //81//

nānyathā devi tvāṃ śape kulasundari //80//
pāraṃparyavihīnā yejñānamātreṇa garvitāḥ /
teṣāṃ samayalopena vikurvanti marīcayaḥ //81//

The infatuated adepts are those who, being without an initiated guru, do not benefit from the teachings of the Tantras, do not know the meanings expounded here, and therefore do not understand the full meaning and import of the *śrīvidyā* and of its constituting syllables: the rules of utterance (*uccāra*) of the mantras, and so forth.

The rays of consciousness (*cinmarīci*), the DĪ explains, are the Mothers of Kula (*kulamātaraḥ*), the goddesses Brahmī, and so on, along with the deities of the bodily elements (*dhātudevatā*)[32], the Ḍākinīs. These divine rays destroy the bodies of the bad adepts by causing a disequilibrium of these elements.

> But he who experiences consciously the joy of the divine essence, staggering in the bliss of alcohol, propitiates the rays [of consciousness] at all times and especially in the morning, on lunar days, and on those of the constellation of the deity, obtains the fullness of [awakened] consciousness. //82–83//
>
> *yas tu divyarasāsvādamodamānavimarśanah /*
>
> *devatātithinakṣatre vāre 'pi ca vivasvataḥ //82//*
>
> *marīcīn prīṇayaty eva madirānandaghūrṇitaḥ /*
>
> *sarvadā ca viśeṣeṇa labhate pūrṇabhodhatām //83//*

The yogin who follows the practices of Kula (*kaulācāra*) is deemed to be always united with Śiva. His experience is that of "the uncreated flashing bliss of the intense absolute consciousness [*parāmarśa*] of his unity with the supreme Śiva." Then, says the DĪ, having partaken of the ritual offerings (*arghya*) to the Goddess (which include meat and alcohol), he staggers.

The particular times and days mentioned here are those when occasional mandatory rituals, prescribed in Tantric manuals of worship, are to be practiced by the adept.

> O Mistress of the gods! such a state [of mind] made of highest knowledge is immediately obtained by human beings thanks to the grace of the best of spiritual masters. //84//
>
> *evaṃbhavas tu deveśi deśikendraprasādataḥ /*
>
> *mahājñānamayo devi sadyaḥ saṃprāpyate naraiḥ //84//*

The chapter concludes:

Thus, the knowledge that gives all this, which is attained through the science of the phonemes of the *vidyā*, O Goddess! and is secret, has been explained to you in six ways, O Durgī! because of my love [for you]. He who understands this becomes immediately lord of the circle of heroes. //85//

evam etatpradaṃ jñānaṃ vidyārṇāgamagocaram /

devi guhyaṃ priyeṇaiva vyākhyātaṃ durgi ṣaḍvidham /

sadyo yasya prabodhena vīracakreśvaro bhavet //85//

The lord of the circle of heroes, says the Dī, is the supreme Śiva, which means that the initiated adept who has obtained the knowledge of the six meanings is identified with Śiva.

3

Encounter in the Worship

PŪJĀSAṂKETA

THIS CHAPTER IS also called *saṃketa*, since wherever male and female principles or deities are present in couples during the *pūjā*, Śiva and Śakti can be held to be present in conjunction: they meet and/or fulfill their promise (*saṃketa*) to be there. The worship, too, although it is that of Tripurasundarī, is aimed at the supreme godhead, which both includes and transcends the masculine and the feminine. Since the chapter describes ritual practices, the term *saṃketa* could also be translated as "practice," which is one of the meanings of this Sanskrit word.

This chapter is the longest. With 204 stanzas, it accounts for more than half of the *Yoginīhṛdaya*. It does not describe precisely the visible aspect of the Goddess, although she is to be visualized as clearly and precisely as possible during the worship, which is performed on a *śrīcakra*, without any material icon, the deities to be worshipped being placed immaterially by *nyāsa*, using their mantras, on the different parts of the *cakra*,[1] where they are to be visualized and imagined as present. The fact that the YH consists of instructions given by Bhairava to Tripurasundarī may explain why she is not described. The main reason, however, for the lack of practical informations is that the YH is not a mere ritual manual to be read and used privately by any person. It is a revealed text to be transmitted by word of mouth to a chosen disciple by a master who would give him all necessary information for understanding the doctrine and performing the sometimes very complicated prescribed ritual actions.

The *pūjā* is to be performed using a *śrīcakra* diagram, usually drawn ritually and according to precise rules, with colored powders, and adorned as mentioned in stanzas 95b–97. But if this geometrical figure is the necessary material basis of the worship of Tripurasundarī, the *pūjā*, its performance appears (as is, in fact, the case in all Tantric ritual worship) to consist more in evoking mental images and uttering (audibly or mentally) mantras than in concrete visible actions. At some points, the officiating adept is to concentrate intensely and/or follow the ascent of his *kuṇḍalinī*. He is therefore intensely and completely implicated, immersed, in what he is doing, The *śrīcakrapūjā* is (or ought to be) a total—bodily, mental, spiritual—divinizing experience. This aspect appears from the start, in the first stanzas of this chapter, and is continuously underlined by the Dī.

> Now, O Incomparable One! I will tell you the practice of the worship whose mere knowledge causes the liberated in life to exult. //1//
>
> Your worship, eternally present and manifest, is threefold, O Gaurī! It is supreme, nonsupreme, and thirdly, supreme-nonsupreme. //2//
>
> *pūjāsaṃketam adhunā kathayāmi tavānaghe /*
>
> *yasyaprabodhamātreṇa jīvanmuktaḥ pramodate //1//*
>
> *tava nityoditā pūjā tribhir bhedair vyavasthitā /*
>
> *parā cāpy apara gauri tṛtīyā ca parāparā //2//*

The Sanskrit term used to characterize the ritual worship of the Goddess is *nityodita*, which means eternally (*nitya*) appearing or arising (*udita*), being eternally present. The term is often used by Jayaratha in his commentary on the *Tantrāloka* as the characteristic of the divine Consciousness, which is ever present, active, manifested. It is applied here to the *pūjā* because the supreme deity is deemed to be ceaselessly worshipped in the heart of her devotees, a worship made in the luminous center of nonduality (*advaya dhāmni*), "in the grandeur of the inner void," says Amṛtānanda. The non-supreme worship is the ordinary ritual worship, which will be described in this chapter. The supreme-nonsupreme one consists in "intense meditation [*bhāvanā*], absorption in the absolute Consciousness, in nonduality and in the nondualistic element present in the dualistic worship."[2]

The main traits of these three types of worship are now shown:

> The domain of the first [type of worship] is the activity of all [senses] insofar as they remain in the condition of nonduality. //3a//
>
> *prathamādvaitabhāvasthā sarvaprasaragocarā /*

This worship is purely spiritual. The Dī quotes here stanzas 116–117 of the *Vijñānabhairava*, the first of which states: "Wherever the mind goes, toward the exterior or the interior, there is the state of Shiva. Since he is omnipresent, where can [the mind] go to avoid [Him]?" There is no way to evade the omnipresence of the supreme deity.

> The second one, the worship of the *cakra*, is ceaselessly performed by me. //3//
>
> *dvitiyā cakrapūjā ca sadā niṣpadyate mayā //3//*

We may well wonder how Bhairava would ritually worship Tripurasundarī. He says this, however, in spite of his being omniscient, in order to help the devotees understand nonduality.

> The third one, O Goddess! consists in [placing] that which arises by itself in what is pure knowledge. //4a//
>
> *evaṃ jñānamaye devi tṛtīyā svaprathāmayī /*

This practice is "supreme-nonsupreme" (*parāpara*) in that it consists (insofar as we can understand the YH and the Dī), for the adept, in seeing mentally by an intense meditation of nonduality (*advaitabhāvanā*) all the rites he performs—the worship of all the deities abiding in the *śrīcakra*, that is—as immersed in the Absolute. The Dī quotes: "With the offering, I throw the mental constructions of the limited being, and all such elements, into the fire which is a compact mass of consciousness, just as one pours clarified butter into the sacrificial fire." We will see later several ritual acts interpreted metaphysically in the same way.

> The highest is known as the supreme one. Listen now to how it must be done. //4//
>
> Having evoked mentally within the *vāgbhava* placed in the forest of the great lotus the footprint of the [divine] Master which fills the form of the universe by pouring down the supreme ambrosia, //5// [the adept] totters, intoxicated with the realization of nonduality with the supreme.
>
> *uttamā sā parā jñeyā vidhānaṃ śṛṇu saṃpratam //4//*
>
> *mahāpadmavanāntasthe vāgbhave gurupādukām /*
>
> *āpyāyitajagadrūpāṃ parāmṛtavarṣiṇīm //5//*
>
> *saṃcintya paramādvaitabhāvanāmadaghūrṇitaḥ /*

This practice is considered supreme because it implies a complete fusion of the adept with the Absolute.

Vāgbhava, here as in stanza 69 of chapter 2 (see above), designates not the first *kūṭa* of the *śrīvidyā* but the place where the four planes of the Word (*vāc*) are situated (*bhavanti*). This totality of the Word is to be visualized by the adept as shining in the "forest of the great lotus," that is, the *akulapadma*, which, as we have seen in chapter 1, is, in this system, a white thousand-petaled lotus located on the summit of the *suṣumnā*, where the *vyāpinī kalā* of the *uccāra* of the mantra is located, pouring incessantly a flow of ambrosia (*amṛta*). The Dī explains that this flow of ambrosia is "the flow of the essence of the undivided divine Consciousness." The adept is to have an intimate direct awareness (*svātmatayā vimṛśya*) of this. Note that the above visualizations are to be mentally "seen" in the yogic body of the adept; yoga and worship are inseparable.

The footprint of the Master is the presence in this world of the supreme Śiva. Amṛtānanda quotes again the first stanza of his *Cidvilāsastava*: "One is the form of Śiva, luminous by himself. One [also] is the 'being' [*tanu*] which is the awareness of this. The supreme [reality], total fusion of these two [elements], such is the footprint of [the Master]: it is in essence the supreme Śiva."

On the realization of nonduality, the Dī adds: "The mystical realization of the absence of all duality with Him consists in being totally absorbed in the [awareness of] 'This, verily, I am' [*saivāham asmīti samāveśa*], a state called intoxication since it makes one [divinely] intoxicated; and it is because of the state thus caused that the [adept], full of joy, totters."

> He must turn away from the chatter of discursive thought, being entirely devoted to the contemplation of the *nāda* which arises inside the Small One. //6//
>
> *daharāntarasaṃsarpan nādālokanatatparaḥ //6//*
>
> *vikalparūpasaṃjalpavimukhaḥ*

To define the Small One (*dahara*), the Dī quotes the *Mahānārāyana Upaniṣad*: "The Small One, without defects, residence of the supreme Lord, lotus of the heart abiding in the center of the citadel." It is therefore the space in the center of the lotus of the heart: "In this Small One is the inner space" (*daharo'sminn artarākāśaḥ*), says the *Chāndogya Upaniṣad*. The adept must therefore contemplate, meditate, this symbol of the supreme, concentrating on the *nāda*, the inner subtle vibration he feels in his heart, leaving therefore aside such discursive activity as the recitation of mantras.

The adept must meditate (*dhyānaṃ kuryāt*) as follows:

> Ceaselessly looking inward, [he participates] in the intense beauty that is the destruction of contraction by the shining forth of the power of consciousness. //7//
>
> *antarmukhaḥ sadā* /
>
> *citkalollāsadalitasaṃkocas tvatisundaraḥ* //7//

The actual, material worship is now described in the 156 stanzas that follow:

> The worship of oneself must be done with elements that are pleasing to the senses. //8a//
>
> *indriyaprīṇanair dravyair vihitasvātmapūjanaḥ* /

The worship to be done is not of the self of the worshipper but of the deity that is the very essence—the deity of one's self (*svātmadevatā*)—of the worshipper. The Dī quotes here a text that says: "To worship in a natural fashion the deity that is one's own self by using perfumes etc. to which the doors of the senses are opened, such is the great sacrifice of one who knows." And it adds: "as has been said, the highest sort of *pūjā* consists in attaining a complete fusion [*sāmarasīkaraṇa*] thanks to the great felicity born from the experience of the sounds, etc., perceived by the ears and the other senses of the worshipper." The identification of the worshipper with the deity being worshipped, which is the aim of the Tantric *pūjā*, is considered in all Tantras as being more easily achieved when helped by the beauty and charm of the ritual.

The description of the "nonsupreme" (*apara*) *pūjā* begins now, with the preliminary rite of *nyāsa*, which is very complex, a large number of elements having to be ritually imposed on the body of the officiant in order to purify and divinize it: identifying it with the mantra, the *śrīcakra*, and the deities abiding in it. Seventy-nine stanzas (8–87) are devoted to this rite.

Impositions (nyāsa)

Four series of *nyāsas* are to be performed: first, the "sixfold imposition" (*ṣoḍhānyāsa*), *śl.* 8–40; second, the imposition of the *śrīcakra, śl.* 41–68; third, the imposition of the deities abiding in the *śrīcakra*, *śl.* 69–79. Then come four series of placings: the purification of the hands (*karaśuddhi*), an imposition of the *śrīvidyā*, then another *karaśuddhi*, and finally a group of impositions of the throne (*āsana*) and of several entities. Finally this is completed (*śl.* 85–86) by a *tritattvanyāsa* on the whole body deemed to achieve the total "cosmicization" and divinization of the officiating *sādhaka*.[3]

> One must [first] perform the placing of mantras on the body starting with the sixfold placing. //8//
>
> *nyāsaṃ nirvartayed dehe ṣoḍhānyāsapuraḥsaram //8//*

> The first placing [must be done] with the Gaṇeśas, the second one with the planets, the third with the *nakṣatras*, the fourth with the Yoginīs, //9// the fifth with the signs of the zodiac, and the sixth with the *pīṭhas*. The sixfold *nyāsa* [now] told to you is said everywhere to be invincible. //10// The one whose body is touched in this way is worthy of being worshipped by all yogins. In the worlds there is no [being, even his] father, mother, etc., that he should revere. //11// He alone is to be venerated by all [for] he is himself the supreme Lord. If he were to bow in front of someone who has not received the sixfold *nyāsa*, O Parvatī! //12// he would soon die and go to hell.
>
> *gaṇeśaiḥ prathamo nyāso dvitīyas tu grahair mataḥ /*
> *nakṣatraiśca tṛtīyaḥ syād yoginibhiś caturthakaḥ //9//*
> *rāśibhiḥ pañcamo nyāsaḥ ṣaṣṭhaḥ pīṭhair nigadyate /*
> *ṣoḍhānyāsas tvayaṃ proktaḥ sarvatraivāparājitaḥ //10//*
> *evaṃ yo nyastagātras tu sa pūjyaḥ sarvayogibhiḥ /*
> *nāsty asya pūjyo lokeṣupitṛmātṛmukho janaḥ //11//*
> *sa eva pūjyaḥ sarveṣāṃ sa svayaṃ parameśvaraḥ /*
> *ṣoḍhānyāsavihinaṃ yaṃ praṇamed eṣa pārvati //12//*
> *so 'cirān mṛtyum āpnoti narakaṃ ca prapadyate /*

The sixfold *nyāsa* (*ṣoḍhānyāsa*, sometimes called *mahāṣoḍhānyāsa*, the "great sixfold *nyāsa*"), which imposes on the body of an adept or officiant six aspects or forms of a deity, is described in many Tantric texts and even in some *purāṇas*. It is considered particularly effective in pervading the body of the adept with divine power. The divinization of the officiant of the worship is a necessity, for it is only after having shed his human ordinary condition and becoming divine that an adept is permitted to approach a deity and to perform its ritual worship, the *pūjā*. As the saying goes, "One should worship God [after] having become god" (*devaṃ bhutva devaṃ yajet*). This is the paradox of the Tantric *pūjā* that it aims at the divinization of an officiating person who, to be permitted to reach this goal, must first be already divinized. The paradox—the ritual redundancy—is all the greater since, as we shall see, the *ṣodhānyāsa* is followed by other impositions: those of the *śrīcakra* and of the deities that abide in it.

> I will tell you how to do the sixfold placing, O Perfect One! //13//
>
> *ṣodhānyāsaprakāraṃ ca kathayāmi tavānaghe* //13//
>
> First is described the *nyāsa* of fifty-one Gaṇeśas, enumerated as follows:
>
> Vighneśa and Vighnarāja, Vināyaka and Śivottama, Vighnakṛt, Vighnahartā and Gaṇarāja, Gaṇanāyaka, //14// Ekadanta and Dvidanta, Gajavaktra, Nirañjana, Kapardavān, Dīrghamukha, Śaṅkukarna, Vṛṣadhvaja, //15// Gaṇanātha and Gajendra, Ṣurpakarṇa, Trilocana, Lambodara and Mahānāda, Caturmūrti, Sadāśiva, //16// Āmoda and Durmukha, Sumukha and Pramodaka, Ekapāda and Dvijuhva, Sūra, Vīra and Ṣaṇmukha, //17// Varada and Vāmadeva, Vaktratuṇḍa, Dvituṇḍaka, Senānī, Grāmaṇī, Latta, Vimatta, Mattavahana, //18// Jāṭī, Muṇḍī and Khaṅgī, Vareṇya, Vṛṣaketana, Bhakṣyapriya and Gaṇeśa, Meghanāda, Ganeśvara. //19// These [gods] have three eyes, the face of an elephant; they are like the rising sun. They hold in their hands the noose and the hook and make the gestures of granting wishes and of fearlessness. They are accompanied by their *śaktis*. //20// One must place them on the body as one does for the imposition of the *mātṛkā*, O Dear One!
>
> *vighneśo vighnarājaś ca vināyakaśivottamau* /
> *vighnakṛd vighnahartā ca gaṇarāḍ gaṇanāyakaḥ* //14//
> *ekadanto dvidantaś ca gajavaktro nirañjanaḥ* /
> *kapardavān dīrghamukhaḥ śaṅkukarṇo vṛśadhvajaḥ* //15//
> *gaṇanātho gajendraś ca śurpakarṇas trilocanaḥ* /
> *lambodaro mahānādaś caturmūrtiḥ sadāśivaḥ* //16//
> *āmodo durmukhaś caiva sumukhaśca pramodakaḥ* /

ekapādo dvijihvaś ca sūro vīraś ca ṣaṇmukhaḥ //17//
varado vāmadevaś ca vaktratuṇḍo dvituṇḍakah /
senānīr grāmaṇīr matto vimatto mattavāhanaḥ //18//
jaṭī muṇḍī thatā khaṅgī vareṇyo vṛśaketanaḥ /
bhaksyapriyo gaṇeśaś ca meghanādo gaṇeśvaraḥ //19//
taruṇāruṇasaṃkāsān gajavaktrān trilocanān /
pāśānkuśavarābhītīhastān śaktisamanvitān //20//
etāms tu vinyased dehe mātṛkānyāsavat priye /

That there could be fifty-one Gaṇeśas should not surprise the reader. Tantric deities tend to multiply: there are nine Durgās, sixteen Nityās, eighteen (or fifty-one) Rudras, even six hundred forty million Yoginīs (*śl.* 193); the supreme deity manifests thus the omnipresence of its power. Since there are fifty-one Gaṇeśas, to be placed by *nyāsa* on the same places as the phonemes of the *mātṛkā*, the latter must be made up of fifty-one letters, including therefore the so-called Vedic *ḷ*, which is not usual.

Being Tantric, these Gaṇeśas are accompanied by their consorts, fifty-one *śaktis*, enumerated in the DĪ. In iconography, they are shown sitting on the Gaṇeśas' left thighs, sometimes holding his erect *liṅga*. The adept, when performing their *nyāsa*, is probably supposed to visualize these couples as he utters or evokes mentally the mantra of each of these gods. The names of the Gaṇeśas and of their *śaktis* are not exactly the same in all Tantras.

The *nyāsa* of other deities or entities is then described, starting with the planets (*graha*):[4]

> One must impose Sūrya below the heart accompanied by the vowels, //21// the Producer of Nectar on the place of the *bindu* with the four phonemes *YA*, etc.; on the eyes, the Son of the Earth presiding over the group of the gutturals, O Dear One! //22// Then, on the heart, one must place Venus, regent of the group of palatals; above the heart one will impose Mercury, regent of the cerebrals. //23// On the region of the throat, Bṛhaspati, who presides over the dentals, O Dear One. On the navel, Saturn, master of the *pavarga*, O Mistress of the Gods! //24// Then one must impose Rahu accompanied by the four phonemes *ŚA*, etc., on the face, and Ketu accompanied by the letter *KṢA* on the anus, O Mistress of the Gods! //25//
>
> *svaraistu sahitaṃ sūryaṃ hṛdayādhaḥ pravinyaset //21//*

bindusthāne sudhāsutiṃ yādivarṇacatuṣṭayaiḥ /
bhuputraṃ locanadvandve kavargādhipatiṃ priye //22//
hṛdaye vinyasecchukraṃ cavargādhipatiṃ punaḥ /
hṛdayopari vinyaset ṭavargādhipatiṃ budham //23//
bṛhaspatiṃ kaṇṭhadeśe tavargādhipatiṃ priye /
nābhau śanaiścaraṃ caiva pavargeśaṃ sureśvari //24//
vaktre śādicaturvarṇaiḥ sahitaṃ ṛahum evaca /
ksākarasahitaṃ ketuṃ pāyau deveśi vinyaset //25//

The constellations (*nakṣatra*) are then to be imposed:

Then, on the forehead, the right and left eye, the two ears, the lobes of the nose, the throat, the shoulders, //26// then on the elbows and on the wrists, on the nipples and on the area of the navel, on the hips and lastly //27// on the thighs and the knees, the ankles and the feet [are to be placed the *nakṣatras*] Aśvinī and the others who shine like the blazing fire [destroyer] of time, their hands making the gesture of granting of wishes and of reassurance //28// and that of salutation and who are wearing all the ornaments. One must impose them on those places, O Goddess honored by the gods![5] //29//

lalāṭe dakṣanetre ca vāme karṇadvaye punaḥ /
puṭayor nāsikāyāś ca kaṇṭhe skandhadvaye punaḥ //26//
paścāt kūrparayugme ca maṇibandhadvaye tathā /
stanayor nābhideśe ca kaṭibandhe tataḥ param //27//
uruyugme tathā jānvor jaṅghayoś ca padadvaye /
jvalatkālānalaprakhyā varadābhayapāṇayaḥ //28//
natipāṇyo 'śvinīpūrvāḥ sarvābharaṇabhūṣitāḥ /
etās tu vinyased devi sthāneṣveṣu surārcite //29//

The Yoginīs are then to be placed:

One must impose the deities Ḍā, etc., mistresses of the constituent elements of the body, on the *viṣuddha*, heart, navel, *svādhisthāna*, *mūl*[*ādhāra*], and *ājñā* [*cakras*]. //30// They are to be visualized exactly through meditation on the feet and on the *liṅga* and the

> belly, on the heart and on the root of the arms, associating them with Amṛtā, etc., O Mistress of the gods! //31//
>
> *viśuddhau hṛdaye nābhau svādhiṣṭhāne ca mūlake /*
>
> *ājñāyāṃ dhātunāthāśca nyastavyā ḍādidevatāḥ* //30//
>
> *amṛtādiyutāḥ samyag dhyātavyāś ca sureśvari /*
>
> *pāde liṅge ca kukṣau ca hṛdaye bāhumūlayoḥ* //31//

The "deities Ḍā, etc." are a group of secondary goddesses, or Yoginīs, the name of the first one beginning with *ḍa*. They are: Ḍākinī, Rākinī, Lākinī, Kākinī, Sākinī, and Hākinī. They are traditionally considered the regents of the *dhātus*, the seven constituent elements of the body, of which the commentary here quotes only six: skin, blood, flesh, fat, marrow, and semen,[6] because the YH associates them with six bodily *cakras* only.

Amṛtā is the first of a group of sixteen *śaktis* or Mothers (*mātṛkās*); their names are enumerated in a passage of the *Svacchandasaṅgraha* quoted in the DĪ (p. 238).

All these deities are placed mentally on the imaginal body of the officiating adept by an *āntaranyāsa*, an inner imposition, which is a mental rite; this is explained in the commentary, which also says that the *dhyāna*, the mental visualization of all the deities, can be found "in another *āgama*."

> Starting with the right foot and ending with the left foot, one must impose the signs of the zodiac, Aries, etc., with the phonemes [of the *mātṛkā*], O Parvatī! //32//
>
> *dakṣiṇaṃ padam ārabhya vāmapādāvasānakam /*
>
> *meṣādi rāśayo varṇair nyastavyā saha pārvati* //32//

For this *nyāsa*, the fifty phonemes of the Sanskrit alphabet are distributed in twelve groups, beginning with the group of the vowels and ending with *KṢA*.

Finally to be placed on the body of the officiant are the fifty seats of power (*pīṭha*) of the Goddess, that is, the fifty places on the Indian subcontinent to which the pieces of the dismembered body of Śiva's wife, Satī, fell from his shoulders while he roamed, desperate, after her death when she had jumped into the sacrificial fire of Dakṣa:[7]

> Then, O Goddess, one must impose the *pīṭhas* on the places where the *mātṛkanyāsa* [is made]. Their names are [now] given. Listen carefully, O Dear One! //33//:

Kāmarūpa, Vāraṇasī, Nepāla, Pauṇḍravardhana, Purasthira, Kānyakubja, Pūrṇaśaila and Arbuda, //34// Amrātakeśvara, Ekāmra, Trisrotas, Kāmakoṭaka, Kailāsa, Bhṛgunagara, Kedāra and Pūrṇaścandraka, //35// Śrīpīṭha, Omkārapīṭha, Jālandhra, Mālava, Utkala, Kulānta, Devīkoṭṭa, Gokarṇa, Maruteśvara, //36// Aṭṭahāsa and Viraja, Rājagṛha, Mahāpatha, Kolāpura, Elāpura, Kāleśa and Jayantikā, //37// Ujjayinī, Vicitra and Kṣīraka, Hastināpura, Oḍḍiśa, the one named Prayāga, Ṣaṣthī then Māyāpuri, //38// Jaleśa, Malayaśaila and the Meru, the best of all mountains, Mahendra and Vāmana, then Hiraṇyapura, //39// Mahālakṣmīpura and Uḍyāna and, lastly, Chāyāchatra. [Thus are] enumerated these *pīṭhas* [which are to be imposed] on the same places as the *mātṛkā*. //40//

pīṭhāni vinyased devi mātṛkāsthānake punaḥ /
teśāṃ nāmāni kathyante śrnusvāvahitā priye //33//
kāmarūpaṃ vārāṇasīṃ nepālam paundravardhanam /
purasthiraṃ kānyakubjaṃ pūrṇaśailaṃ thatārbudam //34//
āmrātakeśvaraikāmre trisrotaḥ kāmakoṭakam /
kailāśaṃ bhṛgunagaraṃ kedārapūrṇacandrake //35//
śrīpīṭhaṃ oṃkārapīthaṃ jālandhraṃ mālavotkale /
kulāntaṃ devikoṭṭaṃ ca gokarṇaṃ māruteśvaram //36//
aṭṭahāsaṃ ca virajaṃ rājagṛhaṃ mahāpatham /
kolāpuraṃ elāpuraṃ kāleśaṃ tu jayantikā //37//
ujjayinī vicitraṃ ca kṣīrakaṃ hastināpūram /
oḍḍīśaṃ ca prayāgākhyaṃ ṣaṣṭhī māyāpurī tahtā //38//
jaleśaṃ malayaṃ śailaṃ meruṃ girivaraṃ tathā /
māhendraṃ vāmanaṃ caiva hiraṇyapuram eva ca //39//
mahālakṣmīpuroḍyāṇe chāyāchatram ataḥ param /
ete pīṭhāḥ samuḍḍiṣṭhā mātṛkārūpakāḥ sthitāḥ //40//

We have seen in chapter 1 (*śl.* 41–43) the four main *pīthas* of the Tripurā tradition. Enumerated here are the fifty *śākta* ones, the list of which varies according to different texts. The list given here is perhaps ancient, but this is not certain. Some *pīṭhas* can be identified (Kāmarūpa, Nepal, and Varaṇasi, for instance), others not. Attempts have been more or less convincingly made at locating all of them geographically. They seem to spread out all over India but not to include Kashmir.

The Dī explains that each phoneme is to be uttered distinctly when placing it on the body, together with the name of the *pīṭha* concerned.[8]

> The sixfold [*nyāsa*] having thus been done, the imposition of the *śrīcakra* is then to be performed. Listen, O Dear One! to the imposition of the *cakra* of the venerable Tripurasundarī //41// which has never been told to anyone, purifies the body, and is supreme.
>
> *evaṃ ṣodhā purā kṛtvā śrīcakrancakrayāsam ācaret /*
>
> *śrīmattripurasundaryās cakranyāsaṃ śṛṇu priye //41//*
>
> *yan na kaścid ākhyātaṃ tanuśuddhikaraṃ param /*

The Dī here extols the *nyāsa* of the *cakra* of the supreme goddess Tripurasundarī, who is "the supreme dynamism of consciousness (*paracitkalā*), the object of supreme love (*parapremāspada*), her *cakra* being made up of all the *tattvas* from Śiva down to the earth, which is the place where she reveals herself. The process of this *nyāsa* is to be kept secret. It purifies the body and is supreme." This, says the Dī, is to say that "it transforms the body made of the thirty-six *tattvas* by bringing it up to the level of the supreme essence"; this is why this imposition is superior to all others.

> First, while saying "Praise to the first line of the square," one must make a pervasive imposition on the right side: on the back of the shoulder, the extremity of the hand, the hip, and the toes and, on the left side: on the toes, the hip, the extremity of the hand, and the back of the shoulder //43// and also on the base and the back of the head, O Beautiful One!
>
> *caturasrādyarekhāyai nama ity ādito nyaset //42//*
>
> *dakṣāṃsapṛṣṭhapāṇyagrasphikkapādāṅgulīśvathā /*
>
> *vāṃāṅghryaṇguliṣu sphikke pāṇyagre cāṃsapṛṣṭhake //43//*
>
> *sacūlīmūlapṛṣṭheṣu vyāpakatvena sundari /*

The imposition to be made here is called a *vyāpakanyāsa*, a term we translate as "pervasive" imposition or placing. This practice, very often prescribed, consists of touching the body on several places according to the usual rules of *nyāsa*, the effect of these several placings being conceived as spreading from one point to the other in order to (in the present case) trace on the body the lines of the *śrīcakra*. A *vyāpakanyāsa* may also be made with the two hands, which rub or stroke the body to pervade it with the power of a mantra.

One may well wonder how a square structure with circles inside it can, even in imagination, actually be placed on a human body. The idea, however, is not so much to place a structure on the body of the adept as to place there all the deities abiding in the *śrīcakra*, thus pervading him with the divine elements, which are in, and constitute, this diagrammatic supremely energetic form of the supreme Goddess.

> On the same ten locations, one must impose the ten Siddhis, Aṇimā, and the others.[9] //44// Then, back from these, one is to impose [the second line of the square, conceived] as stretching along the body, with the mantra "Praise to the middle line of the square," O Dear One! as well as the energies Brahmāṇī, etc., on eight locations of this line: on the big toes of the feet, on the right side, then on the other side of the head, //46// on the left and right knees, then on the outsides of the two shoulders.
>
> What is to be imposed [next] must be placed with [the mantra] "Praise be to the inside line of the square" //47// as stretching along[10] the body behind the points just described.
>
> On ten points of this [line], one will impose the ten Mudrās. //48// Eight of them must be imposed on the eight locations of Brahmaṇī, etc., and the last two on the *dvādaśānta* and on the big toe. //49//
>
> *atraiva sthānadaśake aṇimādyā daśa nyaset //44//*
> *siddhīḥ tadantaṣ ca tanuvyāpakatvena sundari /*
> *caturasramadhyarekhāyai nama ityapi vallabhe //45//*
> *vinyaset tasyāḥ sthāneṣu brahmāṇyādyās tathāṣṭasu /*
> *pāḍaṅguṣṭhadvaye parśve dakṣe mūrdhno 'nyapārśvake //46//*
> *vāmadakṣiṇajanvoś ca bahiraṃsadvaye tathā /*
> *nyastavyāś caturasrāntyarekhāyai namā ityapi //47//*
> *vinyased vyāpaktevena pūrvoktāntaś ca vigrahe /*
> *tasyāḥ sthāneṣu daśasu mudrāṇāṃ daśakaṃ nyaset //48//*
> *brahmāṇyādyasṭhānāntas tāsām aṣṭau nyaset tataḥ /*
> *śiṣṭe dve dvādaśānte ca pādāṅguṣṭhe ca vinyaset //49//*

The Mudrās are the deity aspects of the ten *mudrās* we have seen in chapter 1, *śl.* 56–71, which are hand gestures but are also forms of divine power and deities.

The *dvādaśānta,* the "end of twelve," is the *cakra* considered to be located over the head twelve finger-breadths above the *brahmarandhra.* It is the highest of the *cakras.* The *Svacchandasamgraha* identifies it with the sky of consciousness, the *vyoman.*[11]

Then is told the *vyāpakanyāsa* of the sixteen-petaled lotus:

> Inside this [square], after having imposed the mantra "Praise to the sixteen-petaled lotus," one must impose on these petals Kāmākarṣinī and the other [powers]. //50// The petals are considered as being, on the right side, on the back of the ear, on the shoulder, the elbow, the back of the hand, the thigh, the knee, the ankle, and the sole of the foot, //51// and, on the left side, on the symmetrical [spots], but starting from the sole of the left foot.
>
> *tadantaḥ ṣoḍaśadalapadmāya nama ity api /*
>
> *vinyasya taddale kāmākarīṇyādyāś ca vinyaset //50//*
>
> *dalāni dakṣiṇaśrotrapṛṣṭhaṃsaṃ ca kūrparam /*
>
> *karapṛṣṭhaṃ corujānugulphapādatalaṃ tathā //51//*
>
> *vāmapādadalādy evam etad evāṣṭakaṃ matam /*

Now, the *vyāpakanyā* of the eight-petaled lotus:

> Thereafter, on this [lotus], after having made an imposition using the mantra "Praise to the eight-petaled lotus," //52// one must place the eight energies Anaṅgakusumā, etc., on these petals, on the right temple, collarbone, thigh, and ankle and on the left ankle, thigh, collarbone, and temple. //53–54a//
>
> *tadantare cāṣṭadalapadmāya nama ity api //52//*
>
> *vinyasya taddaleṣveṣu dakṣaśaṅkhe ca jatruke /*
>
> *ūrvāntargulphorujatruśaṅkhe ca vāmataḥ //53//*
>
> *anaṅgakusumādyās tu śaktir aṣṭau ca vinyaset /*

The commentary gives the names of these eight minor goddesses, which all begin with Anaṅga. They are Guptatarayoginīs, "very secret Yoginīs." Their worship is described in *śl.* 131–135 of this chapter.

The preceding ones, Kāmākarṣinī, and so on, to be placed with the imposition of the sixteen-petaled lotus, are Guptayoginīs, "secret Yoginīs" (ritual described in *śl.* 120–130).

Then follow (*śl.* 54–80) the impositions (all of which are pervasive, *vyāpakanyāsa*) of the circles of triangles that are inside the lotuses and surround the Goddess; the deities abiding in theses *cakras* are also placed on the body of the officiant:

> Having made an imposition inside this [lotus] with [the mantra] "Praise to the *cakra* with fourteen [tri]angles," //54// one must impose on these [tri]angles the fourteen energies Sarvasaṃkṣobhinī,[12] etc. These [tri]angles, I will tell you [where to impose them]. //55// [They are to be imposed] on the right side of the forehead, on the middle of the right cheek and of the shoulder, on the [right] side, on the inside of the right thigh and the right leg. Then on the left cheek, and so forth, O Pārvati! //56// on the left thigh, the left side, the left shoulder, the left side of the forehead, and on the back [of the head]. //57//
>
> After this, one must also [make an imposition with the mantra] "Praise to the *cakra* with ten [tri]angles," O Pārvati!
>
> The [tri]angles [of this *cakra* are to be placed] on the right eye, at the root of the nose and on the left eye, on the northeast and the northwest angles of the trunk, the knees, and the anus, then on the angles of the trunk named *nairṛti* and *vahni*. //58–59a//
>
> *tadantaś caturdaśāracakrāya nama ity api* //54//
> *vinyasya tasya koṇeṣu nyasecchaktīś caturdaśa* /
> *sarvasaṃkṣobhinyādyās tu tasya koṇāni vacmyaham* //55//
> *lalāte dakṣabhāge ca dakṣagāṇḍāṃsamadhyataḥ* /
> *pārśvāntarūrujaṅghāntarvāmajaṅghādi pārvati* //56//
> *vāmorau vāmapārśve ca vamāṃse vāmagaṇḍake* /
> *lalāṭavāmabhāge ca tathā vai pṛṣṭha ity api* //57//
> *tato daśāracakrāya nama ity api pārvati* /
> *tasya koṇāni dakṣākṣināsikāmūlanetrake* //58//
> *kukṣīśavāyukoṇeṣu jānudvayagudeṣu ca* /
> *kukṣinairṛtivahnyākhyakoṇeṣveṣu*

Even for a reader able to follow the Sanskrit text, the two last stanzas are not very clear. The commentary explains, therefore, that the constituent triangles of this *cakra* are to be mentally visualized (*bhāvanīyāni*). The term *kukṣi*, which we translate as "trunk," means usually the belly, but it is explained by the commentary to mean "the part of the body which extends from the thighs to the arms," that is, the trunk. The upper portion of the trunk is considered to be on the east side, the lower part on the west, the left and right sides respectively on the south and the north. The "angles" of the trunk would then be where the arms and the thighs begin. "Thus," the DĪ concludes, "the root of the left arm will be in the northeastern angle [*īśa*], the left groin will be in the northwest [*vāyu*], the right groin in the southwest [*nirṛti*], and the root of the right arm in the southeastern[13] angle."

> Then he shall impose //59// the ten energies Sarvasiddhipradā, etc., O Dear one!
>
> Then, having made the imposition with [the mantra] "Praise to the first *cakra* with ten [tri]angles" in that [inner *cakra* of ten angles], //60// one is to place Sarvajñā, etc., on its angles. [These are to be placed] on the right nostril, the right corner of the mouth, the right breast, the [right] testicle, the scrotum, the left testicle, the left breast, the corner of the mouth and nostril, and the tip of the nose. Such are, one should know, the ten [tri]angles. //62//
>
> *nyaset punaḥ //59//*
>
> *sarvasiddhipradādīnāṃ śaktināṃ daśakaṃ priye /*
>
> *tadantaśca daśārādicakrāya nama ity api //60//*
>
> *vinyasya tasya koṇeṣu sarvajñādyāṣ ca vinyaset /*
>
> *dakṣanāsā sṛkkiṇī ca stanaṃ vṛśaṇam eva ca //61//*
>
> *sīvanīvāmamuṣkaṃ ca stanaṃ sṛkkininasike /*
>
> *nāsāgraṃ caiva vijñeyaṃ koṇānāṃ daśakaṃ tathā //62//*

Now is described the pervasive imposition of the eight-triangle *cakra*:

> Having imposed inside that one [the mantra] "Praise to the originating *cakra* with eight [tri]angles," one must impose on its angles the eight energies Vaśinī, etc. //63//
>
> *tadantar aṣṭakoṇādicakrāya nama ity api /*
>
> *vinyaya tasya koṇeṣu vaśinyādyaṣṭakam nyaset //63//*

We may take the Vāgdevīs mentioned here to be the eight Mātṛkās, regents of the *vargas* of the alphabet.

> The chin, the throat, the heart, and the navel are considered as forming the right side [of this *cakra*]; the *maṇipūra*, etc., being the foursome of the left side, //64// the whole forming the [*cakra*] with eight [tri]angles.
>
> *cibukaṃ kaṇṭhahṛdayanābhīnāṃ caiva dakṣiṇam /*
>
> *jñeyaṃ pārśvacatuṣkaṃ ca maṇipūrādi vāmakam //64//*
>
> *catuṣṭayaṃ ca pārśvānāṃ etat koṇāṣṭakaṃ punaḥ /*

The *cakra* of eight triangles is considered "originating" because the three larger *cakras* encircling it, which we have just seen, are deemed to issue from it. This is consistent with the inner movement of the *śrīcakra*, which goes from the center to the periphery. The central position of this *cakra*, encircling the central triangle within which is the *bindu*—the place of the Goddess—is underlined by the fact that it is imposed on four places along the axis of the body, one of which is not a part of the physical body but is the *maṇipūracakra*, a center of the yogic imaginal body[14] situated on the level of the navel (as the Dī explains). The weapons (*āyudha*)[15] that the Goddess holds in her four hands are then to be imposed:

> One must impose on the outside, in the four directions, around [this] triangle which is in the heart, the arrows, the bow, the noose, and the goad. //65//
>
> *hṛdayasthatrikoṇasya caturdikṣu bahir nyaset //65//*
>
> *śaracāpau pāśasṛṇi*

> Then, having done the imposition with the mantra "Praise to the triangle," one must impose on the angles [of this triangle], in front, to the right and to the left, //66// the Goddesses Kāmeśvarī, etc., and, in the middle, the Goddess.
>
> *trikoṇāya namas tathā /*
>
> *vinyasya tasya koṇeṣu agradakṣottareṣu ca //66//*
>
> *kāmeśvarādidevīnāṃ madhye devīṃ ca vinyaset /*

The central triangle of the *śrīcakra* being, as it were, its heart is, quite naturally, to be imposed on the heart of the officiating adept—the heart being, as is well known, the spiritual, mystical center of the human being. The lines of this triangle (to be placed by a *vvāpakanyāsa*, whose efficacy spreads along all of the outside lines) are to be imposed with the mantra *trikoṇāya namaḥ*. To avoid any misunderstanding, the DĪ explains that the heart is "in the middle of his breast." Three goddesses are to be imposed there—Kāmeśvarī, Vajreśvarī, and Bhagamālinī—on the three points of the triangle and, on its center, on the *bindu* (also called *baindavacakra*), the Goddess. The weapons, it is explained, are those of Kāmeśvara and Kāmeśvarī,[16] two different deities that are the male and female aspect of the Goddess; eight *āyudhas* are thus to be placed.

> Thus, O Goddess! I have told you the imposition, a most secret procedure. //67// It is indeed to be performed by you most secretly, O Praised by the heroes! It is to be entrusted to those [only] who follow the rule [of Kula], never to anyone who is not the [initiated] disciple [of a master of this tradition]. //68//
>
> This [ritual] is more secret than any secret I have revealed to you today.
>
> *evaṃ mayodito devi nyāso guhyatamakramaḥ //67//*
> *etad guhyatamaṃ kāryaṃ tvayā vai vīravandite /*
> *samayasthāya dātavyaṃ nāśiṣyāya kadācana //68//*
> *guptād guptataraṃ caitat tavā 'dya prakaṭīkṛtaṃ /*

The extreme importance given to secrecy is, as we have already said, a characteristic Tantric trait. Amṛtānanda gives here a metaphysical reason for this secrecy. He says, speaking for Śiva: "All this I have revealed to you because you are my beloved, your nature being that of the light of consciousness which is a portion of myself" (*madaṃśabhūtavimarśātmikā*). The supreme godhead is indeed *prakāśavimarśamāya*, both conscious light and absolute Consciousness, a supreme truth not to be revealed to unbelievers.

> After this, one must do an imposition beginning with the originating Goddess and ending with Aṇimā. //69//
>
> *mūlādevyādikaṃ nyāsam aṇimāntaṃ punar nyaset //69//*

After having described the placing of the circles of deities abiding in the *śrīcakra*, going from Aṇimā to the Goddess (called here *mūladevī*, "root-goddess," since she is the originating cause of the whole universe),[17] the YH now prescribes the imposition of the same deities in the reverse order, from the Goddess to Aṇimā. This is to be done as follows:

> On the triangle of the head, one must impose, starting from the east [the goddesses] Kāmeśvarī, etc.
>
> One must impose—on the right and on the left—the arrows on the eyes, the two bows on the eyebrows, //70// the nooses on the ears, the goads on the tip of the nose.
>
> *śirastrikoṇe pūrvādi kāmeśvaryādikā nyaset* /
>
> *bāṇān netre bruvoś cāpau karṇe pāśadvayaṃ nyaset* //70//
>
> *sṛṇidvayam ca nāṣāgre dakṣiṇāgraṃ tu vinyaset* /

The "triangle of the head" is probably the place of the fontanel. The Dī describes it: "there is on the center of the head a triangular place, which is easily seen, being very fragile, on small children." The deities accompanying Kāmeśvarī are Vajreśvarī and Bhagamālinī. The officiant is to imagine on the top of his head a triangular place where he imposes the Goddess surrounded by her three first *āvaraṇadevatās.*[18] The "weapons" (*āyudha*) to be imposed on the left and the right of this triangle are those held by Kāmeśvara (on the right) and Kāmeśvarī (on the left).

> Along a rosary placed on the head, one must impose the eight Vāgdevatas. //71//
>
> *muṇḍamālākrameṇaiva nyased vāgdevatāṣṭakam* //71//

These eight deities of the word, also named Mātryaṣṭaka, or Aṣṭamātarāḥ, "the eight Mothers," presiding over the eight groups (*varga*) of phonemes of the Sanskrit alphabet are usually Mahālakṣmī (or Brahmī),[19] and so on. The Dī says they are "Vaśinī, etc.," a list proper to the Śrīvidyā, however, not given. They are also considered to form a group of eight *siddhayoginī*, as we will see later (3.154).

> The *cakra* of the *bindu* and the other ones are [the only elements now] to be imposed, O Beautiful One! on the inside and outside corners of the eye, then in front and in the back of the ear. //72// In front of the tuft[20] one must impose the half [of these deities], the other half being imposed on the tuft behind the ear, in front of the ear, and on the inner and outside corners of the eye. //73//

baindavādīni cakrāṇi nyastavyāni varānane /
netramūle tvapāṅge ca karṇapūrvottare punaḥ //72//
cūḍādike 'rdhanimne 'rdhaṃ śeṣārdhaṃ karṇapṛṣṭhake /
karṇapūrve tvapāṅge ca tasya mūle ca vinyaset //73//

The deities of the retinue of the Goddess, surrounding her, are now to be imposed on the body of the officiant:

> One must then impose the [Yoginīs] Sarvasiddhi[pradā], etc., on the neck, going from the right to the left. Then on the heart, in the same way, the energies abiding in the *cakra* of fourteen triangles. //74//
>
> The lotus with eight petals is to be imposed on the navel; this, however, is made on the spine, on the left, then on the other side of the belly, this for the first group of four [*śaktis*]. //75// The other group of four [*śaktis*] is imposed between the spine and the left side, etc.
>
> *sarvasiddhyādikaṃ kaṇṭhe prādakṣiṇyena vinyaset /*
> *hṛdaye manukoṇasthāḥ śaktayo 'pi ca pūrvavat //74//*
> *nābhāvaṣṭadalaṃ tat tu vaṃśe vāme ca pārśvake /*
> *udare savyapārśve ca nyased ādicatuṣṭayam //75/*
> *vaṃśavāmāntarālādi nyased anyaccatuṣṭayam /*

The exact places on the body on which to impose all these deities are explained in the commentary. For instance, "in front of the tuft" is explained as the forehead. Since our readers are not expected to practice this *pūjā*, we do not believe it is necessary to clarify the text.

The two next impositions are to be made on two *cakras*; they are to be imposed by *nyāsa* on the parts of the body corresponding to the *cakras*. For the *svādhiṣṭhāna*, the group of four deities is to be placed circularly on four places on the lower part of the belly. As for the ten Mudrās to be imposed on the *mūlādhāra*, they are, in fact, to be imposed there and (according to the DĪ) on the right and the left of the spine:

> On the *svādhiṣṭhāna* one must impose, starting from the east in front of oneself and finishing in the south, //76// the [energies] in groups of four, successively, in the four directions of space.
>
> The best of *sādhakas* must impose the ten Mudrās on the *mūlādhāra*. //77// Then [impose] again the ten Mudrās on the spine, on the left and the right, in between and above and below.

svādhiṣṭhāne nyaset svasya pūrvād dakṣāvasānakam //76//

catasras tu catasras tu caturdikṣu kramān nyaset /

mūlādhāre nyasen mudrādaśakaṃ sādhakottamaḥ //77//

punar vaṃśe ca savye ca vāme caivāntarālake /

ūrdhvādho daśamudrāṣ ca

According to the commentary, the ten Mudrās, after having been imposed on the body where the *mūlādhāra* is situated, are to be imposed on the right and the left sides of the spine, four in places corresponding ideally to the four directions of space, the nadir and the zenith (these two directions meant by "above and below").

> [The locations] above and below being excluded, //78// one will impose the eight [energies, or Mothers] Brahmaṇī, etc., on the right leg, this being done as [was described] previously. Then, beginning by the left leg, //79// one must impose eight Siddhis, starting from the left, on the same locations, and two others on the soles of the feet.
>
> *ūrdhvādhovarjitaṃ punaḥ //78//*
>
> *brahmāṇyādyaṣṭakaṃ dakṣajaṅghāyāṃ tās tu pūrvavat*
>
> *vāmajaṅghāṃ samārabhya vāmādikramato 'pi ca //79//*
>
> *siddhyaṣṭakaṃ nyaset teṣu dvayaṃ pādatale nyaset*

"Brahmanī, etc.," are the eight Mothers (*mātṛkā*) who preside over the eight groups of phonemes (*varga*) of the Sanskrit alphabet. They are called Vāgdevatā, "Goddesses of the Word" (*śl.* 71), and Vāgdevīs (*śl.* 84).

The ten Siddhis, which are deities or Yoginīs *and* supernatural human powers, have already been mentioned above (*śl.* 44).

The YH now concludes on the nature and role of *nyāsa*:

> The imposition spreads from its cause as a lamp, it is said, [is lighted] from [another] lamp. //80// [Thus,] who has performed the imposition in this way, O Mistress of the Gods! will consider himself as not different from the Self.
>
> *kāranāt prasṛtaṃ nyāsaṃ dīpād dīpam evoditam //80//*
>
> *evaṃ vinyasya deveśi svābhedena vicintayet /*

As the DĪ explains, this stanza is to be understood metaphysically. What is the "cause," or, better, what is at the root of the imposition of the *śricakra* (together with the Goddess and the deities abiding in it), is the total fusion of the light and the act of consciousness (*prakā śvimarśasāmarasya*):[21] the supreme deity insofar as it is identical with the totality of the universe (*akhilajagadrūpa*), which, as we have seen, is the real nature of the *śrīcakra*. By imposing on the body of the officiant, section by section—as lamps are lighted going from one lamp to another—all the constitutive parts and all the deities of the *śrīcakra*, the adept's body becomes progressively, part after part, identified with this cosmic Absolute in its several aspects and in its totality. To quote the DĪ: "Having meditated and made mentally appear [*vibhāvya*] all the parts of the *śrīcakra* together with their energies as not different from the various parts of his body [on which they are imposed, the adept] must meditate and realize mystically [*bhāvayet*] that there is no distinction between himself and the supreme [Goddess] presiding over this [*cakra*]."

This identification once obtained, the adept must still perform a few other preliminary rites:

> Then [the officiant] must do the impositions of purification of the hands, etc., his mind being fully concentrated. //81// He must impose the *vidyā* on the head, the sex organs, and the heart, on the three eyes, on the ears, O Goddess! then on the mouth and on the arms, //82// on the back, on the knees, and on the navel. After this, he must perform the purification of the hands, then impose the throne, the six *aṅgas* //83//, Śrīkaṇṭha, etc., and the Vāgdevīs. Then he must impose the *cakras* of fire, etc., on the [*mul*]*ādhāra*, the heart, the tuft, and on the place of the *bindu*. //84//
>
> *tataś ca karaśuddhyādinyāsaṃ kuryāt samāhitaḥ* //81//
> *mūrdhni guhye ca hṛdaye netratritaya eva ca* /
> *śrotrayor yugale devi mukhe ca bhujayoḥ punaḥ* //82//
> *pṛṣṭhe janvośca nābhau ca vidyānyāsaṃ samācaret* /
> *karaśuddhiṃ punas caiva āsanāni ṣaḍaṅgakam* //83//
> *śrīkaṇṭhādiṃśca vāgdevīḥ ādhāre hṛdaye punaḥ* /
> *śikhāyāṃ baindavasthāne tvagnicakrādikā nyaset* //84//

The imposition of the *vidyā* is that of the three *bījas* (or *kūṭas*) of the *śrīvidyā*, the *vāgbhavabīja* being imposed on the head, the *kāmarājabīja* on the sexual organs, and the *śaktibīja* on the heart.

The Dī does not identify the throne. The six *aṅga* are the six "limbs" of Śiva: *hrdaya* (heart), *śiras* (head), *śikha* (tuft), *kavaca* (cuirass), *netra* (eyes), and *astra* (weapon), which are, in fact, not limbs of the body but attributes or powers of the god (or of any other deity). The *nyāsa* of Śrīkaṇṭha is an imposition of fifty Rudras, of which Śrīkaṇṭha is the first. The eight Vāgdevīs, as we have seen, are the Mātṛkās, Kāmeśvarī, and so on, mistresses of the *vargas* of the Sanskrit alphabet.

The imposition of "the *cakras* of fire, etc." is a complex procedure. First to be imposed are the *cakras* of the three luminaries (*dhāman*), Fire, Moon, and Sun; then the four main *pīṭhas* of the Śrīvidyā, Oḍḍiyāna, Kāmarūpa, Jālandhara, and Pūrṇagiri, with their regents, powers, and attendant goddesses. The details of this process are given in the Dī.

Then a last imposition is to be made:

> Having made a general imposition of the three *tattvas* [separately] and together, accompanied by the three *bījas* of the *vidyā*, from the feet to the navel, the neck, and the head, //85// then having identified himself with the Supreme, [the officiant of the rite] must offer to the Goddess a libation whose liquids are the nectars of moon and fire. //86//
>
> *tattvatrayaṃ samastaṃ ca vidyābījatrayānvitam* /
>
> *pādādinābhiparyantam āgalaṃ śirasas tathā* //85//
>
> *vyāpakaṃ caiva vinyasya svātmīkṛtya paraṃ punaḥ* /
>
> *saṃtarpayet punar devīṃ saumyāgneyāmṛtadravaiḥ* //86//

The three *tattvas* (*tritattva*) are Śiva, *śakti*, and *nara* (God, the energy, and man), the three components of the cosmos, each being imposed while uttering one of the three parts of the *śrīvidyā*, the cosmic divine totality being thus imposed on the adept before he begins the ritual of the *pūjā*.

According to the Dī, the moon is the "half-*kalā* of *HA* without second" (*anuttara*), that is, *Ḥ*, which is in the triangle at the center of the thousand-petaled lotus placed at the base of the *kuṇḍalinī*, whereas the fire is the letter *S* in the triangle at the center of the four-petaled lotus of the *mūlādhāra*. (The mantra to be imposed is therefore *SAUḤ*, the *bījamantrra* of Paṛā, the supreme goddess of the Trika.) From there, a flow of nectar issues, resulting from the fusion of the *amṛtakuṇḍalinī* of moon and the *agnikuṇḍalinī* of fire, one flowing downward and the other upward, assuming the double (sexual) aspect of the union of *yoni* and *liṅga*.

> It is thus, O Worshipped by the Gods! that the fourfold imposition is to be performed. The sixfold *nyāsa*, O Dear One! that of Animā, etc., and that of the *mūladevī*, and so forth, //87// and also that of the purification of the hands [must be performed completely] by the adept in order to completely effect his object.
>
> *evaṃ caturvidho nyāsaḥ kartavyo vīravandite /*
>
> *ṣoḍhanyāso 'ṇimādyaś ca mūladevyādikaḥ priye //87//*
>
> *karaśuddhyādikaś caiva sādhakena susiddhaye /*

This object, says the Dī, is liberation, not the possession of supernatural powers, since these are already possessed by the adept who is a *sādhaka*.

> They are to be performed each separately in the morning, at the time of the ritual worship, during the rite of *homa* //88/ and the *japa*; or the best of adepts will do all of them during worship.
>
> *prātaḥkāle tathā pūjāsamaye homakarmaṇi //88//*
>
> *japakāle tathā teṣāṃ viniyogaḥ pṛthak pṛthak /*
>
> *pūjākāle samastaṃ vā kṛtvā sādhakapuṅgavaḥ //89//*

The commentary explains that the sixfold *nyāsa* is to be done in the morning, at the time of the worship, the *nyāsa* of the Siddhis, Animā, and so on; the imposition of the Goddess, and so on, taking place with the *homa* and the *karaśuddhinyāsa*, and so on, having to be performed when doing *japa*. Otherwise, all the impositions can be performed before beginning the *pūjā*, as prescribed here.

Other preliminary rites

> Having imagined the throne [of the Goddess] as going up to the thirty-sixth *tattva*, [the officiant] must offer a *bali*[22] with a mantra to the secret Yoginīs and to the other ones //90//
>
> *ṣaṭtriṃśattattvaparyantam āsanaṃ parikalpya ca /*
>
> *guptādiyoginīnāṃ ca mantreṇātha baliṃ dadet //90//*

The Goddess dominates the universe; her throne is therefore made up of all the *tattvas* that constitute it, from the *tattva* of earth to that of Śiva. One would be tempted to imagine this throne as rising up from the central *bindu* of the *śrīcakra*. The commentary, however, says that it is the whole *śrīcakra* that is to be imagined as the throne of the Goddess, "because it is the receptacle of the rays of light of consciousness [*cinmarīci*],[23] of the deities, that is, who abide in the *śrīcakra*." Regarding the mantra and the ritual action to be performed, a stanza is quoted as stating: "One must, while meditating in one's heart the *tattvas* from earth to Śiva, cause the throne to appear by throwing lotuses on which the phoneme *SAU*[24] has been recited." (How and on what the lotuses are to be thrown is not said.)

The "secret Yoginīs" (*guptayoginī*), says the Dī, are not hidden but are all those that are manifested (*prakaṭa*). The other ones form seven groups: Guptatara (very secret), Sampradaya (traditional), Kulakaula, Nigarbha, Rahasya (hidden), Atirahasya (very hidden), and Parāpararahasya. This makes eight groups in all, which are to be found, under the same or under different names, in many Tantric Śaiva traditions. We shall meet these Yoginīs later, in *śl.* 113–155 of this chapter, distributed in the different parts of the *śrīcakra*, from the outer square to the central triangle

The Dī adds that since the adept must first perform an inner, purely mental worship, he must meditate on the *śrīcakra* "made of all the *tattvas*" as being his own body and perform a worship on his head with the *mūlamantra* of the Yoginis.

He will then proceed by removing the internal obstacles:

> Since they are shared out among the [centers named] *piṇḍa, rūpa, pada,* and *granthi,* the [internal] obstacles [are destroyed] by the imposition of the *vidyā* on the secret place,[25] the heart, the face, and the head, O Beautiful One! //91//
>
> *piṇḍarūpapadagranthibhedanād vighnabhedanam /*
>
> *guhyahṛnmukhamūrdhasu vidyānyāsena sundari //91//*

Pinda, rūpa, pada, and *granthi* are places or elements of the structure of the yogic body that are also bodily centers of focused awareness, normally tiered along the *suṣumnā*. As such, they represent stages of (bodily) experience in the ascending movement toward liberation. They are proper to the Kula traditions, notably the Kubjikāmata. The internal obstacles to be destroyed are mental or sensual dispositions that tend to block the way toward liberation and, in the present case, to prevent the officiant from reaching the state of purity necessary for the inner worship he is now to perform.

How to destroy these obstacles ritually is now described:

> He who knows the mantras, driving away the obstacles in the temple of the sacrifice, will expel the obstacles that are on the earth by a kick with the heel, those in the atmosphere by clapping the hands, //92// and with the *astramantra* and the casting of a glance those that are in the sky.
>
> *yāgamandiragāṃścaiva vighnān utsārya mantravit /*
>
> *pārṣṇighātena bhaumāṃśca tālena ca nabhogatān //92//*
>
> *astramantreṇa dṛṣṭyā ca divyān vighnān apohayet /*

Tantric rites can only be performed in a place or an area that is perfectly pure, free from all impurities and (more) all evil, dangerous, or impure forces, hence this threefold rite, whose pattern is customary. The casting of a glance (*īkṣaṇa* or *nirīkṣaṇa*) is used in many circumstances in the Hindu world for ritual or spiritual reasons.

> [Thereafter] one must visualize mentally with precision the form of a great fire [shining] in all directions, above and below. //93//
>
> *dikṣvadhordhvaṃ mahāvahniprākāraṃ paribhāvayet //93//*

The Dī, true to its metaphysical interpretation of the YH, says that this great fire is nothing other than the Supreme Consciousness flashing forth everywhere. This fire, it adds, must be impassable so that none of the obstacles resulting from dualistic thought may enter the consecrated area of the sacrifice or the mind of the officiating adept who has mentally constructed this luminous image.

> O mistress of the gods! one is to perform with the common *arghya* the worship of Mārtaṇḍa accompanied by the energy of light. He is of a red color, resplendent, //94// surrounded by the Seizers, and others, manifesting the brilliance of the universe.
>
> *sāmānyārghyeṇa deveśī mārtaṇḍaṃ paripūjayet /*
>
> *prakāśaśaktisahitam arūṇākalpam ujjvalam //94//*
>
> *grahādiparivāraṃ ca viśvatejo 'vabhāsakam /*

Mārtaṇḍa is a name of the sun god, Sūrya. The worship of the sun (*sūryapūjā*) is the first item of the daily mandatory (*nitya*) ritual worship (*pūjā*) of Śiva. The sun is generally considered golden but is also seen as red, especially in the Āgamas or Tantras. When represented in human form, he is often white with a red garment. Red is the color of the Goddess; it is also the color of passion, attachment, and *vimarśa*, self-consciousness, while *prakāśa*, light, is white, the color of Śiva. Insofar as Mārtaṇḍa manifests the universe, he is on the side of *vimarśa* and redness.

The Seizers (Graha), who number nine, are, as we have seen before (see chapter 2, *śloka* 58), the planets, but they are also demonic, dangerous supernatural beings who "seize" their victims. The planets, too, are seizers insofar as they "seize," or influence, human beings. The "others" (*ādi)* are the six "limbs" (*aṅga*) of Śiva, *hṛdaya, śiras, śikha,* and so on,[26] according to the Dī; but *ādi,* in *grahādi,* can also be understood as "the sun being the first (*ādi*)" (of the Seizers).

Arghya—there is no satisfactory translation of the term—is the specially prepared water offered as oblation to a deity.[27]

The sun worship having been performed (neither the YH nor the Dī describes it), the worship of the Goddess can begin:

> O Goddess! one must make appear in the right manner the king of *cakras* [drawing it] with orpiment, agalloche, and kunkuma mixed with lunar and igneous [substances] while reciting the *mūla*[*mantra*] of the Yoginīs. //95–96a//
>
> *saumyāgneyayutair devi rocanāgurukuṇkumaiḥ* //95//
>
> *mūlam uccārayan samyag bhāvayec cakrarājakam* /

By "in the right manner," the YH means "following carefully the instructions given by an expert." Orpiment (*rocana*, also called *gorocana*) is a mineral form of arsenic, of a yellow color. Agalloche is also a yellow stuff, as is kunkuma (turmeric). The lunar (*saumya*) substance is camphor, which is white, like the moon; while the igneous or fiery one is saffron, "for it looks like a flame," says the Dī, which also explains that these items are to be mixed "with nectar," *sudha*, a term usually synonymous with *amṛta*. It may, however, also mean powder; *maṇḍalas* to be used only once are most often drawn with powders. The Dī explains, too, that the *śrīcakra* is to be drawn on a sheet of gold "or another" (*ādi*) material with a needle of gold. It adds that some experts say that the diagram may be drawn "with musk, saffron, camphor, sandal, and nectar."

The *mūlamantra* to be recited is that of the manifest Yoginīs (*prakaṭayoginī*), says the Dī; see our commentary on *śl.* 90 above.

> Then one must throw on it flowers held in one's joined hands. //96// Or [one may adorn it] with gems and coral while [reciting] the *mūlavidyā* backward One must, in all cases, ensure that [the *cakra*] is not empty, [for] if it were empty, the obstacles would be innumerable. //97//
>
> *yoginīmūlamantreṇa kṣipet puṣpāñjaliṃ tataḥ* //96//
> *maṇimuktāpravalair vā vilomaṃ mūlavidyayā* /
> *aśūnyaṃ sarvadā kuryāt śūnye vighnās tvanekaśaḥ* //97//

The rule that the *cakra* or the chalice used for the ritual worship of a Tantric deity must never be empty of the prescribed offerings is a general rule. In the case of Bhairava, the Tantrāloka says that if the chalice were empty, the god, always furious and voracious, would immediately devour the adept. More sedately, the Dī says that if the *cakra* were empty of these offerings during the worship, the ritual would be fruitless.

> [The *sādhaka*] must place the *arghya* between the *śrīcakra* and himself on [a figure] of six angles inside a square, O Beloved of the gods! //98// where, after having worshipped the six *āsanas* and having honored successively inside the triangle the four *pīṭhas* Kā, Pū, Jā, O, //99// he must sacrifice on the place of the *arghya* to the ten *kalās* of Fire.
>
> *śrīcakrasyātmanaś caiva madhye tvarghyaṃ pratiṣṭhayet* /
> *caturasrāntarālasthakoṇaṣaṭke sureśvari* //98//
> *ṣaḍāsanāni saṃpūjya trikoṇasyāntare punaḥ* /
> *pīṭhāni caturo devi kā pū jā o iti kramāt* //99//
> *arcayitvā 'rghyapāde tu vahner daśa kalā yajet* /

The Dī describes the diagram in which a six-angled figure with a small triangle in its center is inscribed in a circle, which is inside a square. The chalice into which the *arghya* has been poured (the *arghyapātra*) is to be placed on this inner small triangle. The Dī gives the names of the six *āsanas* who seem to be throne deities (or deities of the throne), sacralizing, as it were, the "throne," the place of the *arghyapatra*.[28]

Kā, Pū, Jā, and O are the initials of the names of the four main *pīthas* of the Ṣrīvidyā tradition, Kāmarūpa, Pūrṇagiri, Jālandhara, and Oḍyāna, as we have already seen in chapter 1, (*ślokas* 41–43).

The *kalās* are energies associated with a deity and formed (or symbolized) by letters of the Sanskrit alphabet. Fire as a deity (Agni) has ten *kalās* associated with the last letters, from *YA* to *KṢA*.[29]

> Once the *arghyapātra* is placed, [the officiant] must perform there a sacrifice to the twelve *kalās* of the Sun. //100// He will [thus] worship on the chalice the *kalās* of the Sun [associated with the letters] *KA-BHA*, etc. Then, with clarified butter and [another] substance, he will offer a sacrifice to the sixteen *kalās* of the Moon. //101//
>
> *arghyapātraṃ pratiṣṭhāpya tatra sūryakalā yajet //100//*
>
> *pātre sūryakalāś caiva kabhādi dvādaśārcayet /*
>
> *vighṛte tu punar dravye ṣoḍaśendukalā yajet //101//*

The *sādhaka* is to worship a (mental) image of the sun god in the center of the chalice by invoking its image in his heart while uttering its mantra and worshipping its twelve *kalās*, associating each with one of twelve letters of the Sanskrit alphabet from *KA* to *THA* and from *BHA* to *ḌA*, while uttering their names, this being done with an offering of perfumed water. The sixteen *kalās* of the moon are worshipped in the same way, with the sixteen first letters of the alphabet, from *A* to *visarga*,[30] and sprinkling of clarified butter associated with "another substance," which, according to the Dī, is wine (*madya*).[31]

> And in its center he must meditate intensely on Amṛteśī with the Navātma[mantra]. Then, with the Navātman, O Goddess! he must make a libation of the goddesses of the constituent elements [of the body] //102// and to Ānandabhairava with [a mantra] ending with *vauṣaṭ*.
>
> *amṛteśīṃ ca tanmadhye bhāvayed ca navātmanā /*
>
> *navātmanā tato devi tarpayed dhātudevatāḥ //102//*
>
> *ānandabhairavaṃ caiva vauṣaḍantena tarpayet /*

Amṛteśī, "the Mistress of the Nectar," is a goddess who pours *amṛta* on the world, thus helping and stimulating it. The Navātmamantra is usually given as *HSKṢMLVRYŪṂ*. It is an important mantra of the Trika.

It is also the mantra form of the beautiful god Navātma, the consort of the crooked goddess Kubjikā, the main deity of the Tripurā tradition of the Kula. We translate the verb *bhāvayet* as "meditate intensely," which implies a mental concentration so intense as to create in the mind of the adept a precise image of the deity. Anandabhairava is a form of the god Bhairava. The mantra ending with *vauṣaṭ* is the Navātmamantra to which is added *ānandabhairavāya vauṣaṭ*.[32]

> The best of *sādhakas* must also prepare carefully, in the same way, the special *arghya*. //103//
>
> Having worshipped the sandals of the [succession of] masters, he must then offer this *arghya* to Bhairava. Being impelled by the latter's order, he must offer it to the succession of masters. //104//
>
> *tathaivārghyaṃ viśeṣeṇa sādhayet sādhakottamaḥ* //103//
>
> *gurupādālim āpūjya bhairavāya dadet punaḥ* /
>
> *tadājñāpreritaṃ tacca gurupaṅktau nivedayet* //104//

The sandals or footprints (*pādukā*) of the gurus are those of all the masters of the tradition of Tripurā, from Śiva to one's own guru. These *pādukas* are metaphysically the imprint, the trace of the presence of the supreme deity in this world; to worship them is therefore to worship the deity as present in this world. The *gurupūjā* is a mandatory element of the first part of the Tantric *pūjā*.

In this tradition, the succession of the gurus is deemed to go through three stages, called flows (*ogha*). First, the divine (*divya*) flow, starting with Śiva followed by four masters, one for each of the four cosmic cycles, the *yugas* from *Kṛtayuga* to *Kaliyuga*; then the flow of perfect or accomplished masters (*siddhaugha*); and finally, the human ones (*mānavaugha*), the succession of the masters of this world, going from the first revelation of the doctrine to our days. The DĪ tells how to worship them: the *arghya* is to be elevated three times up to his head by the officiant, then offered to Bhairava, who, as the Master, is in a triangle in the center of the "forest of the great lotus," which, as we have seen (*śl.* 3–5), is on the *brahmarandhra*.

> Having collected what remains of it, one must perform [with it] an oblation in the fire of desire where the whole universe is burning while reciting the *mūlavidyā* and the [formula of worship of] the sandals of the Master. //105//

tadīyaṃ śeṣam ādāya kāmagnau viśvatastviṣi /
pādukāṃ mūlavidyāṃ ca japan humaṃ samācaret //105//

As is underlined at length by the DĪ, this oblation is not so much a material as a symbolic rite. Actual pouring may take place, but the process is a mental, spiritual one. The officiant, namely, is to imagine the Master as standing on his head, and, as the Master (the godhead) orders, he is to offer mentally in the "fire of consciousness," that is, to the supreme godhead in her aspect of cosmic destruction, the whole creation together with his own mental constructions. It is an oblation consisting of symbolically throwing duality into the fire of consciousness in order to burn it entirely.

In spite of the symbolic nature and meaning of the oblation, what remains of it after it has been offered to the deity is supposed to be absorbed by the officiant.

The YH explains further its metaphysical value:

> One must pour in oblation, together with the internal organ or intellect, the activity of the rays of light in the great light [located] in the mouth of Kuṇḍalī, where the resorption and vomiting forth of the cosmic flow take place. //106//
>
> *mahāprakāśe viśvasya saṃsāravamanodyate /*
> *marīcivṛttir juhuyān manasā kuṇḍalīmukhe //106//*

The YH pursues the metaphysical aspect of the oblation:

> Conceiving the unity of I-ness and objectivity as being in the ladle *srùc*, which is *unmanī*, what is born there through the intensity of the rubbing is the great oblation. //107// Pouring and pouring himself the oblation, [the adept] becomes spontaneous bliss.
>
> *ahantedantayor aikyam unmanyāṃ sruci kalpitam /*
> *mathanodrekasambhūtaṃ vasturūpaṃ mahāhaviḥ //107//*
> *hutvā hutvā svayaṃ caivaṃ sahajānandavigrahaḥ /*

The ladle *srùc* is one of the two ladles used since Vedic times for offering the ritual oblation in the fire, the *homa*. This ladle, in the present case, is not a material object. It is the "transmental" (*unmanī*), the highest plane of consciousness.[33] It is on this level that the oblation takes place;

it consists of pouring (in spirit) all the aspects of the cosmic manifestation in the central, both human and divine, void of consciousness. This is why a "spontaneous" (that is, uncaused) bliss arises in the officiating adept. The Dī says: "Having poured again and again the full oblation (both human and divine) of clarified butter, which in reality is the total fusion of the objectivity and the I-ness (*ahāntā*)[34] born from the rubbing of the *araṇis* of the mantra, [one reaches] the supreme fulgurating bliss. Such is the internal oblation."

According to a passage of the Dī (which also quotes stanza 72 of the Vijñānabhairava), the oblation may be made of *amṛta* and may even include an alcoholic substance—a possibility the Dī mentions again when, commenting the next half-*śloka*, it says that a wise man is somebody who, because he drinks alcohol, keeps his mind concentrated in a single intent. From this concentration (*dhāraṇā*), meditation (*dhyāna*) is born: "without concentration, the worship is fruitless." Thus, having offered to the Masters, Śiva, and so forth, alcohol transformed into nectar (*amṛta*) and having poured it in offering into the fire of the self, the spirit of the adept will become perfectly stable, and he will experience the supreme, blazing bliss. The practice is mental, spiritual, rather than actually performed with an alcoholic beverage.

Thus, as stated in the next half-*śloka*:

> The wise [adept] must then perform the worship of the *śrīcakra*, the form that the expansion of his consciousness takes as it spreads out. //108//
>
> *svaprathāprasarākāraṃ śrīcakraṃ pūjayet sudhiḥ* //108//

The *śrīcakra* can be said to be the form taken by the adept's consciousness as it spreads out, because in the nonduality of consciousness (*saṃvidadvaya*) of Kashmir Shaivism, there is no difference between human consciousness and the deity's absolute consciousness. To quote the Dī: "What shines (i.e., appears) as the *śrīcakra* is nothing else than the cosmic expansion of the godhead who is his (the adept's) consciousness, an expansion formed by the fourfold *antahkarana*, the inevolute (*avyakta*), the *mahant*, and the *ahaṃkāra*, along with the subtle elements (*tanmātra*), the ten senses (*indriya*), their ten activities, their objects, the *puryaṣṭaka*, and the expansion [which goes down] to the gross elements (*dhātu*) and [forms] the sixteen 'evolutes' (*vikāra*)."[35]

Now comes the description of the *śrīcakra pūjā* proper, *ślokas* 109–168.

The śrīcakra pūjā

This *pūjā* consists of the worship of Tripurasundarī and her retinue of ancillary deities: of the several deities abiding in the *śrīcakra*, from those in the outer square section to the Goddess in the central triangle. The worship is followed by the *japa* of the *śrīvidyā* and a final offering in the fire, a *homa*.

> A sacrifice[36] to Gaṇeśa and to Dūtarī, to the Master of the Field, and to Dūtī is to be performed, O Goddess! as also, on the external door, to the goddesses headed by Svastikā. //109//
>
> *gaṇeśaṃ dūtarīṃ caiva kṣetreśaṃ dūtikāṃ tathā /*
>
> *bāhyadvāre yajed devi devīśca svastikādikāḥ* //109//

The Dī explains that the ritual worship of the first group of deities is to be performed "on the frame of the door" of the outer square section of the *śrīcakra*. The Master of the Field, Kṣetreśa or Ksetrapāla, is the god Baṭuka, an aspect of Bhairava; Dutī is his consort. The goddesses headed by Svastikā, worshipped on the external part of the door, number five; they are "singing goddesses" (*gāyikā*), deemed to delight Tripurasundarī with their songs.

> Then the line of masters, which abides, threefold, in the inner triangle is also [to be worshipped].
>
> *tataś cāntastrikoṇe 'pi gurupaṅktiṃ tridhā sthitam /*

The succession of the masters of the Tripurā tradition is said to be threefold because, as we have seen (*śl.* 104), starting from Śiva, it is divided into three groups: divine, perfect, and human gurus. This succession is secret, says the Dī. It is not to be found in books but learned by word of mouth.

> and in this [*baindavacakra*] he will worship, after having invoked her, the great Goddess //110// who holds herself in the forest of the great lotus, resting against my side, her body [filled with] the joy of the "cause": You, Goddess, who gives the fruits that the will desires! //111//
>
> [This] worship is to be performed with offerings of food, etc., of which you are yourself formed.
>
> *tadantaś ca mahādevīṃ tām āvāhya yajet punaḥ* //110//
>
> *mahāpadmavanāntasthāṃ kāraṇāndavigrahām /*

madaṅkopāśrayāṃ devīm icchākāmaphalapradām //111//
bhavatīṃ tavanmayair eva naivedyādibhir arcayet /

The "Forest of the Great Lotus," as we have seen (*śl.* 5), is the *akula* lotus of one thousand petals on the summit of the *suṣumnā*. It is therefore on a spot of his own yogic body that the adept is to mentally perform this worship. The ritual process of the *pūjā* appears here—as it will do again later—as a total process, both bodily and mental. The Goddess is seen in this lotus leaning against Bhairava, on whose left thigh she is sitting.

As for the "cause" (*kāraṇa*)[37] that fills her with joy, it is an alcoholic beverage, as is appropriate in a Tantric ritual. This, says the DĪ, when drunk by the Goddess, becomes nectar and fills her body with joy, her body being henceforth pure, supreme, luminous bliss.

The offerings of "food, etc.," are the usual ritual offerings of perfume, food, lights, incense, and flowers, each corresponding to one of the five constitutive gross elements of the cosmos and of the body: earth, water, fire, air, and space, elements of which the Goddess is also constituted insofar as she is identical with the cosmos.

The DĪ expatiates at length on the metaphysical symbolic interpretation of these offerings; as interesting as they are, these developments are too long and complex to be reported here.

Then, on the triangle, [one must worship] the reflected forms of her flashing forth, //112// the Nityās made of all the *tithis*, their aspects being those suitable for optional rites.

trikoṇe tatsphurattāyāḥ pratibimbākṛtīḥ punaḥ //112//
tattattithimayīr nityāḥ kāmyakarmānurūpiṇīḥ /

This worship is to be performed on the three lines of the central triangle. The Nityās (the Eternal Ones) are ancillary deities numbering sixteen, identified with the phonemes of the *śrīvidyā*, which surround the Goddess. They are also identified with the *tithis*, the lunar days, which are divine entities and also number sixteen.[38] The *śrīcakrapūjā* being performed to attain a desired (*kāmya*) goal, all the rites it includes are so-called optional or desiderative (*kāmya*) rites; the mentally visualized forms of all the deities must therefore be adapted to that type of worship.[39]

There, in the Trailokyamohana[cakra], are the manifested Yoginīs. //113// Because they are gross forms of the *mātṛkā*, these Yoginīs pervade the skin, etc. They are known as manifest for they are [located in a *cakra*] whose nature is to support the gross world. //114//

tatra prakaṭayoginyaś cakre trailokyamohane //113//

mātṛkāsthūlarūpatvāt tvagādivyāpakatvataḥ /

yoginyaḥ prakaṭā jñeyāḥ sthūlaviśvapradhātmani //114//

The skin is one of the seven constituent elements of the organic body which are therefore gross (*sthūla*), a character shared by the so-called manifest Yoginīs, who, appropriately, abide (and are worshipped) in the outer square part of the *śrīcakra* (also named *bhūgṛha*, "underground room"), a part that can be said to support the world, since it is the section of the diagram that is metaphysically on the level of the manifested universe. It is also the plane of *vaikharī*, the lowest, gross level of the Word (*vāc*).

[There, too,] abide the eight *siddhis* Aṇimā and the others, O great Goddess! They are deep red in color; their hands make the gesture of propitiation and protection. //115// They hold the great fabulous gem and thus give the fruit one desires.

aṇimādyā mahādevi siddhayo 'ṣṭau vyavasthitāḥ /

tās tu raktatarā varṇair varābhayakarās tathā //115//

dhṛtacintāmahāratnā manīṣitaphalapradāḥ /

We have already seen the *siddhis* (*śl.* 44). The "great fabulous gem" is the *cintāmaṇi* (or *mahācintamaṇi*) supposed to fulfill all desires of its possessor. It is mentioned in many Sanskrit works.

There also one must worship, in order, Brāhmī, etc., O Dear One. //116//

Brahmāṇī, yellow in color and adorned with four faces, her hands in the *varadā* and *abhaya mudrās*, holds a jug and a rosary, radiant. //117//

Māheśvarī, white in color, having three eyes and holding in her hands the trident, the skull, the antelope, and the axe, O Dear One! //118//

Kaumārī must be visualized as being yellow in color, carrying a spear and a javelin, [her two other] hands displaying the *varadā* and the *abhaya* [*mudrā*], O supreme Mistress! //119//

Vaiṣṇavī, dark in color, carrying in her hands the conch, the discus, the mace, and the lotus and adorned with divine jewels. //120//

Vārāhī, dark in color, her face as the blazing snout of a boar, carrying in her hands the plow, the mace, the sword, and the shield. //121//

Aindrī, dark in color, holding in her hands the lightning bolt and the shining lotus. //122//

Cāmuṇḍā, dark blue, holding in her right hands trident and ḍamaru, a sword, and a vetāla and in her other [hands] a shield, a serpent and a bell, along with a skull. //123//

As for Mahālakṣmī, supreme mistress, of shining yellow color, she holds two lotuses, a mirror, and the fruit of the wild lemon tree.[40] //124//

brāhmyādyā api tatraiva yaṣṭavyāḥ karmaśaḥ priye //116//
brahmāṇī pītavarṇā ca caturbhiḥ śobhitā mukhaiḥ /
varadā 'bhayahastā ca kuṇḍikākṣasragujjvalā //117//
māheśvarī śvetavarṇā trinetrā śūladhāriṇī /
kapālam eṇaṃ paraśuṃ dadhānā pāṇibhiḥ priye //118//
kaumārī pītavarṇā ca śaktitomaradhāriṇī /
varadābhayahastā ca dhyātavyā parameśvari //119//
vaiṣṇavī śyāmavarṇā ca śaṅkhacakragadābjakān /
hastapadmais ca bibhrāṇā bhūṣitā divyabhuṣanaiḥ //120//
vārāhī śyāmalacchāyā potrivaktrasamujjvalā /
halaṃ ca musalaṃ khadgaṃ kheṭakaṃ dadhatī bhujaiḥ //121//
aindrī śyāmalavarṇā ca vajrotpalalasatkarā /
cāmuṇḍā kṛṣṇavarṇā ca śūlaṃ ḍamarukaṃ tathā //122//
khaḍgaṃ vetālaṃ caiva dadhānā dakṣiṇair bhujaiḥ /
nāgakheṭakaghaṇṭākhyān dadhānānyaiḥ kapālakam //123//
mahālakṣmīs tu pītābhā padmau darpanaṃ eva ca /
ṃatuluṅgaphalaṃ caiva dadhānā parameśvarī //124//

All these goddesses, being feminine aspects of male gods, carry the attributes and bear the colors of these gods, Brāhmaṇī having four faces like Brahmā, Maheśvarī carrying Śiva's (Maheṣvara's) attributes, Vaiṣṇavī those of Viṣṇu, and so on.

> Having thus visualized [these goddesses], one must worship them, then [worship] Tripurā, mistress of the *cakra*.
>
> Because she purifies the organs of action, she is called She Who Accomplishes the Purification of the Hands; //125// and there is found the *siddhi* Aṇimā arising from the purification of the hands.
>
> *evaṃ dhyatvā yajed etāś cakteśīṃ tripurāṃ tataḥ /*
>
> *karmendriyāṇāṃ vaimalyātkaraśuddhikarī smṛtā //125//*
>
> *kāryaśuddhibhavā siddhir aṇimā cātra saṃsthitā /*

The purification of the hands (*karaśuddhi*) is a mandatory preliminary ritual, since in order to perform ritual acts of worship of a deity, the hands of the officiant must be perfectly pure. This rite normally consists of imposing on the hands the *astra* (weapon) mantra. Here it is the Goddess who is symbolically deemed not only to purify but also to cause the *siddhi* goddess Aṇimā to exist. But why Aṇimā? Because, says the DĪ, the *siddhi aṇimā* (and thus the goddess Aṇimā) reduces the self, the living being (of the officiating adept), to its finest, most subtle state.

The worship in the second *cakra*, the sixteen-petaled lotus, is then described:

> In the group of sixteen vibrations, the *kalās* whose nature is wonder //126// are what animate the sixteen vital breaths, *prāṇa*, etc. They are seeds because their nature is that of vowels; they have the form of seeds because they incite. //127// Because they are internal, the Yoginīs who abide [there] are hidden. They are Kāmākarṣaṇā, etc. Since they dominate in emanation, O Dear One! //128// they are to be worshipped [going from right] to left in the *cakra* called Sarvāśāpūraṇa.
>
> *ṣoḍaśaspandasaṃdohe camatkṛtimayīḥ kalāḥ //126//*
>
> *prāṇādiṣoḍaśānāṃ tu vāyūnāṃ prāṇanātmikāḥ /*
>
> *bījabhūtāḥ svarātmatvāt kalanād bījarūpakāḥ //127//*
>
> *antaraṅgatayā guptā yoginyaḥ saṃvyavasthitāḥ /*
>
> *kāmākarṣaṇarūpādyāḥ sṛṣṭeḥ prādhānyataḥ priye //128//*
>
> *sarvāśapūraṇākhye tu cakre vāmena pūjayet /*

These stanzas must be explained. The Yoginīs that abide in the sixteen-petaled lotus of the *śrīcakra* are identified with an aspect of the cosmic vibration that animates the universe, the *spanda*. This *spanda* is said, in the present case, to be sixteen-fold, being identified with the sixteen "vowels" of the Sanskrit alphabet, which, in Ṣaiva cosmogonies, are the sixteen *kalās*, limiting energies, of Bhairava when he manifests the cosmos. Their nature is described as "wonder" (*camatkāra*), by which is meant that they are pervaded with consciousness (*cit*), that is, subtle. They are also identified with the vital breaths, *prāṇa, apāna, udāna*, and so on, which, in fact, are usually considered to number only ten, not sixteen: "the names of the six others can be found in other *āgamas*," says the Dī, without quoting any reference. These *kalās*, being active, are "seeds" (*bīja*), which is the case of the "vowels."[41]

The Yoginīs abiding in this inner portion of the *śrīcakra* are called Guptayoginīs (see above, *śl.* 90). This, says the Dī, is because they are evolutes that are pervaded with consciousness. They are to be worshipped in the reverse order, starting from the right, not simply because they are Tantric deities but, says the Dī, because they are associated with the emanation that is done by "vomiting" (*vāmena*,) the universe.

> They hold the noose and the goad; they are red and clothed in red. //129// The *siddhi* of he who enjoys [them] is lightness, made of the purification of the breaths. Tripureśī, mistress of the [*śrī*]*cakra*, must be worshipped with all the ritual services. //130//
>
> *pāśāṅkuśadharā hyetā raktā raktāmbarāvṛtāḥ* //129//
>
> *prāṇaśuddhimayī siddhir laghimā bhoktur ātmanaḥ* /
>
> *tripureśī ca cakreśī pūjyā sarvopacāraiḥ* //130//

Since the aspect of pure, nondiscursive consciousness pervades this *cakra*, *laghimā*, the supernatural power of lightness (the *prāṇas* being also purified), it is, quite naturally, the power deemed to be given by these secret Yoginīs to the adept who worships them.

This part of the worship ends with a renewed ritual worship of the main Goddess to which all the prescribed ritual services (*upacāra*) are to be offered. The lists of *upacāras* vary, going from five to thirty-six; they are offerings of lights, incense, food, flowers, clothes, jewels, and so forth, all that can be offered to a distinguished guest. In a Tantric context, the variety of the *upacāras*, pure or impure, is very great.

Now comes the worship in the third *cakra*, the eight-petaled lotus:

> Linked to the enjoying *puryaṣṭaka* absorbed in the experience of the body, subtle, associated with the eightfold *vāgbhava*, having for essence the classes of phonemes, //131// all these Yoginīs, Anaṅgakusumā, etc., are very hidden [and are to be worshipped] in the [*cakra*] Sarvasaṃkṣobhana. They are adorned with red cuirasses, //132// beautiful, their braids of hair hanging down, carrying bow and arrows.
>
> *kaulikānubhavāviṣṭabhogapuryaṣṭakāśritāḥ* /
>
> *vāgbhavāṣṭakasaṃbaddāḥ sūkṣmā vargasvarūpataḥ* //131//
>
> *tās tu guptatarāḥ sarvāḥ sarvasaṃkṣobhaṇātmake* /
>
> *anaṅgakusumādyās tu raktakañcukaśobhitāḥ* //132//
>
> *veṇīkṛtalasatkeśāś'cāpabāṇadharāḥ śubhāḥ* /

The *puryaṣṭaka*, "the eight in the body," is the subtle transmigrating body, a nonmaterial, all-pervading soul, which, while the person lives, is absorbed in the experience (the enjoyment, *bhoga*) of the body it animates. The "eightfold *vāgbhava*" is the phoneme *AI* repeated eight times with the eight Yoginīs whose essence (*svarūpa*) is constituted by the classes (*varga*) of consonants of the Sanskrit alphabet. The very hidden (*guptatara*) Yoginīs are one of the several categories of Yoginīs of the Śrīvidyā tradition.

> Parameśvarī, mistress of this *cakra*, is purification of the intellect. The quality she possesses is beauty. //133// She rests on the planes of *piṇḍa*, etc., of the Lord, the subject who enjoys all that can be enjoyed, which is to say, the intellect and the variety of all [that the intellect perceives]. //134// Her nature is the supernatural power of growing at will. She must be worshipped with all the ritual offerings and services.
>
> *tattadākārabuddhyātmabhogyabhoktur mahīśituḥ* //133//
>
> *piṇḍādipadaviśrāntisaundaryaguṇasaṃyutā* /
>
> *cakreśvarī buddhiśuddhirūpā ca parameśvarī* //134//
>
> *mahimāsiddhirūpā ca pūjyā sarvopacarākaiḥ* /

To say that Parameśvarī is purification of the intellect means that the intellect is purified when it reaches her level. The intellect (*buddhi*) is the plane of consciousness that grasps the objects of the senses whose savor is enjoyed by the supreme subject, Śiva, who, as the Dī says, is therefore called the "knower of the field" (*kṣetrajña*) of perception.

The expression "planes of *piṇḍa*, etc.," refers to the conception of the subtle body as including four ascending planes called *piṇḍa, pada, rūpa*, and *rūpātīta*, planes also conceived of as tiered along the *suṣumnā*; the highest of these, *rūpātīta*, is on the consciousness level of *turīya*, where one attains liberation.[42]

To say that the nature (*rūpa*) of Parameśvarī is the supernatural power of growing at will is to say that she bestows that *siddhi*.

> [This worship is to be performed] by a penetration, going up to the extreme point of the *visarga*, of consciousness, which flashes forth while piercing the twelve knots after experiencing energy. //135b–136a//
>
> *dvādaśagranthibhedena samulasitasaṃvidaḥ* //135//
>
> *visargāntadaśāveśācchāktānubhavapūrvakam* /

The Dī explains this obscure stanza as follows. Consciousness here is, in fact, the *kuṇḍalinī*, which ascends following the path of the *suṣumnā* along which are tiered twelve subtle centres (*granthi*)—the usual six *cakras* and six "knots" placed between them—and goes up to a center called *ṣoḍaśānta* ("end of sixteen"), probably to be imagined as sixteen fingers-breadths above the head. This ascending energy within the body of the adept, being Consciousness, is luminous; it flashes forth. The same movement was described previously in chapter 2, *śl.* 71 of the YH: "Shining like ten million flashes of lightning,... she attaches herself to the maṇḍala of the moon of the inner sky". This was said above about the inner ascent of the *śrīvidyā*; the same experience is taking place here. Here the maṇḍala of the moon is not mentioned, but with sixteen being a lunar number,[43] the *ṣoḍaśānta* is also a "lunar" center. This ascent is described as "going up to the *visarga*," because the *visarga* is the sixteenth "vowel" of the Sanskrit alphabet; saying *visarga* is therefore equal to saying "sixteen."

While performing this worship, the adept is to cause his *kuṇḍalinī* to go up to this center. This is one of the cases in which a yogic process is to take place during a ritual action. As we know, in Tantra, yoga and rites cannot be entirely separated; they are two aspects of the total, both bodily and mental, active experience of ritual.

[The worship is to be done] with [what is born] from the expansion of the energy of awakening, the predominance of the energy of will, //136// and with the four phonemes formed by her unifying interaction with *akula*, [then] with the phonemes the main of which is *SA*, vapor of the knowable, and with those that are produced by the mixed energy of will, //137// accompanied by the two phonemes corresponding to the absorption in the energy of *kula*. [Thus,] by the expansion of the essence of the energy, O Maheśvarī, //138// [is to be performed] in the Sarvasaubhāgyadāyaka *cakra* [the worship of the Yoginīs] received through traditional transmission.

unmeṣaśaktiprasarair icchāśaktipradhānakaiḥ //136//
tathaivākulasaṃghaṭṭarūpair varṇacatuṣṭyaiḥ /
vedyuṣmarūpasādyarṇair miśrecchābhāvitair api //137//
kulaśaktisamāveśarūpavarṇadvayānvitaiḥ /
śakteḥ sāramayatvena prasṛtatvān maheśvari //138//
saṃpradāyakramātās cakre saubhāgyadāyake /

The worship, progressing toward the center, is to be done now in the next three *cakras*: the first of fourteen angles and the two others of ten angles. The practice is based on the so-called *bhūtalipi*, the "writing—*lipi*—of the elements,"[44] of forty-two letters. We saw previously the place of yoga in ritual; we see now the role of the letters. The Sanskrit alphabet (as we have said before) is divine, appearing first, and being eternally present, in the supreme godhead and thus the source and origin of the whole cosmic manifestation.

The above stanzas first enumerate the letters of the *bhūtalipi*. These are to be visualized by the adept as present in the so-called *akula* white, thousand-petaled lotus turned downward placed on the *brahmarandhra-cakra*, on the top of the head. There is the first letter of the alphabet, *A*, which is the supreme Śiva. It is in "unifying interaction" (*saṃghaṭṭa*) with the energies of will (*icchā*, hence *I*) and of awakening (*unmeśa*, hence *U*); we have thus *A* +*I* = *E*, *A* + *U* = *O*. *Akula*/*A* now interacts with *E* and *O*, which gives *AI* and *AU*. The process goes on in the same way in order to produce all forty-two letters of the *bhūtalipi*. The "phonemes of which the main is *SA*" are the sibilants *ŚA ṢA SA* and the aspirate *ḤA*, usually called vapor (*ūṣman*), and so forth. We cannot decrypt here the whole procedure to produce all the letters.

The last stanza underlines the fact that the expansion of the energy of will (*icchāśakti*) realized in the ascent of the *kuṇḍalinī* is the effective element of this worship of the Yoginīs present in this *cakra*. These are said to be "received through traditional transmission," not because they are more received than the other ones by the tradition transmitted by the gurus but because they are called Sampradāyayoginīs, "traditional Yoginīs."[45]

These Yoginīs are now described:

> O goddess! the [Yoginīs] having at their head Sarvasaṃkṣobhiṇī, magnificent, looking like Aṇimā, [are those to be worshipped] in the *cakra* whose name agrees with what it is, by uniting oneself to the force of the beauty that spreads without interruption. //140// The *siddhi* Īśitva, also, purifier of the body, the senses, etc., in the triple city already described, to be realized, [along with] Tripuravāsinī, by destroying the original impurity of the conjunction [with duality]. //141// All these [deities], O Goddess, must be worshipped with all the offerings.
>
> *nirantaraprathārūpasaubhāgyabalayogataḥ* //139//
> *anvarthasaṃjñake devi aṇimāsadṛśāḥ śubhāḥ* /
> *sarvasaṃkṣobhinīpūrvā dehākṣādiviśuddhidā* //140//
> *īśitvasiddhir api ca proktarūpe puratraye* /
> *yogādikleśabhedena siddhā tripuravāsinī* //141//
> *etāḥ saṃpūjayed devi sarvāḥ sarvopacārakaiḥ* /

The name of the *cakra* is Sarvasaubhāgyadāyaka, "the giver of all felicities," which agrees with its nature, since it is deemed to bestow on the adept all forms of felicity. The Yoginīs, Sarvasaṃkṣobhinī, and so on, look like Aṇimā, and so on, since, like these, they are clothed in red and bear the same ornaments. The "force of the beauty that spreads without interruption" with which the worshipper is to unite is the power born from the uninterrupted intense meditation on the nonduality from Śiva (*śivādvaitabhāvanā*):[46] this mental state is apparently to be maintained by the adept during the worship of the Yoginīs of this *cakra*.

The Siddhi Īśitvā, also worshipped there, gives the adept the state of Śiva, which implies, says the Dī, the purification of the body and of the senses of the adept and also of the objects. This threefold purification gives to the adept the state of Īśvara. To say that it takes place "in the triple city" (*pūratraye*) means that "the knower, knowledge, and the known," the perceiving person and what he perceives—man and the world he perceives—are "purified," (mentally) deified, understood *sub specie aeternitatis.*

Worship in the fifth (ten-angled) *cakra,* Sarvārthasādhaka, is as follows:

> [The energy of the Goddess in the fifth *cakra*] takes on the nature of the eternal *nādas* abiding in the nine apertures, //142// along with a general and common aspect while being made of distinct sounds. [She is manifested] by ten phonemes, shadows of the movable and immovable objects of knowledge. //143// They are the Kulakaulikāyoginīs who bestow all the powers or perfections.
>
> *sadātanānāṃ nādānāṃ navarandhrasthitāṭmanām* //142//
>
> *mahāsāmānyarūpeṇa vyāvṛttadhvanirūpiṇī* /
>
> *asthtirasthiravedyānāṃ chāyārūpair daśārṇakaiḥ* //143//
>
> *kulakaulikayoginyaḥ sarvasiddhipradāyikāḥ* /

Here, too, the Yoginīs to be worshipped are identified with phonetic aspects of the divine energy experienced by the officiant as present in his body, a spirit-mind-body experience.

Nāda is a subtle form of sound, a stage in the process of dissolution of uttered sound or phonemes into the silence of the Absolute. It is not audibly perceptible; it is "unstruck," *anāhata,* sound, being a form of *śabdabrahman,* the cause of the apparition and of the efficacy of the phonemes. In spite of this unique and absolute nature, *nāda* is sometimes considered divisible, divided in eight, nine, or ten *nādas,* often associated with different parts of the yogic body; such is the case here. The nine apertures (*randhra*) are nodal points, *cakras,* of the yogic body. The Dī describes them as parts of the inner space (*gaganabhāga*) of the *suṣumnā* and enumerates them: "*mūlādhāra, svādhisthāna, maṇipūra, anāhata,* then above these *vajrapadma, kaṇṭha, laṃbikā, viṣuddha,* and *ājñā,*" of which only the first four and the last three are the usual *cakras* of this system. As the Dī also explains, the Goddess, in addition to these "distinct sounds," is present in the body in a general way as an indistinct sound (*nirviśeṣadhvani*). The ten phonemes that manifest her are the cerebrals and the dentals. They are "shadows" of the various objects of knowledge in that they are deemed to manifest these objects. The long commentary of the Dī on this stanza is rich and interesting but too abstruse to be given here.

> White, clothed in white, wearing white ornaments, //144// the [Kulakaulayoginīs] Sarvasiddhipradā, etc., are in the

Sarvārthasādhaka *cakra*, whose name agrees with what it is because of the expansion of the proper nature of the mantras that takes place [there]. //145//

śvetāmbaradharāḥ śvetāḥ śvetābharabhūṣitāḥ //144//

mantrāṇāṃ svaprathārūpayogād anvarthasaṃjñake /

sarvasiddhipradādyās tu cakre sarvārthasādhake //145//

The "expansion of the mantras," according to the DĪ, means that they help the officiant to realize that the true nature of his self is the same as that of the "absolute I" of Śiva (*śivāhambhāvabhāvanā*). Because such a mystical realization takes place in this *cakra*, it is called Sarvārthasādhaka, "fulfiller of all wishes," the highest of which is, of course, the wish for union with Śiva, which is precisely being fulfilled in this *cakra* (says the DĪ).

The Mistress of the *cakra* is Tripurāśrī, O Great Sovereign! [named thus] because she is the cause of the prosperity of the three worlds. In addition, born from the purification of the mantras, //146// it is said [that she gives] the power of subjugation. All these [deities] must be worshipped.

lokatrayasamṛddhīnāṃ hetutvāc cakranāyikā /

tripurāśrīr maheśāni mantraśuddhibhavā punaḥ //146//

vaśitvasiddhir ākhyātā etāḥ sarvāḥ samarcayet /

Tripurāśrī means "prosperity of the three cities," that is, of the three worlds—of the universe, in other words. The purification of the mantras, it is explained, results from the prolongation of their utterance (*uccāra*)—in the case of *OṂ, HRĪṂ*, etc.—from the final *Ṃ* to the transmental (*unmanā*) plane, where the utterance disappears in the utter silence of the Absolute. If the adept is able to ascend to such a supreme level, he acquires the supernatural power to subjugate all beings (*īśitva*).

Worship in the sixth (ten-angled) *cakra*, Sarvarakṣākara, is as follows:

O Goddess! the phonemes *KA*, etc., as they expand, are manifested by the *kuṇḍalinī* facing upward and [then] downward //147// when she externalizes herself by the will of Kula. They are manifested by the supreme interior Yoginīs, Sarvajñā, etc., located in the Sarvarakṣākara *cakra*, which, being totally absorbed in its own inner

> nature, brings about total absorption. These [Yoginīs] carry a book and a rosary. //148–149//
>
> *ūrdhvādhomukhayā devi kuṇḍalinyā prakāśitāḥ* //147//
>
> *kulecchayā bahirbhāvāt kādivarṇaprathāmayāḥ* /
>
> *nigarbhayoginīvācyāḥ svarūpāveśarūpake* //148//
>
> *sarvāveśakare cakre sarvarakṣākare parāḥ* /
>
> *sarvajñādyāḥ sthitāḥ etāḥ saha pustāksamālikāḥ* //149//

The divine energy, *kuṇḍalinī*, facing first upward, reaches the supreme; then, facing downward, coiling back in the *mūlādhāra*, she manifests the universe through the phonemes *KA*, and so on, the consonants. This she does by the will of Kula, the deity, as identical with the cosmos (or, as the Dī says, holding in herself the thirty-six *tattvas*, together with the phonemes).[47] These are manifested by the ten Nigarbha ("interior") Yoginīs whose names begin always with Sarva, abiding as they do in the *cakra* Sarvarakṣākara ("causing total protection").

In this *cakra*, the officiant, is supposed to be absorbed in his own nature or essence (*svarūpāveśa*), thinking, "I am the supreme Śiva." "Through this absorption," says the Dī, "the deity shines without duality in the sixth *cakra*, which produces in the worshipper a total absorption in Śiva," while the *cakra* protects him from everything that could hinder his spiritual search.

> Nourishing the [three] cities of the knowing subject, the knowable, and knowledge, the mistress of this *cakra*, magical enchantress of this world, is called Tripurāmālinī. //150//
>
> *mātṛmānaprameyāṇāṃ purāṇāṃ pariposinī* /
>
> *tripurāmālinī khyātā cakreśī sarvamohinī* //150//

We have already seen the triad of knowing subject, knowledge, and known (*mātṛmānaprameya* or *mātṛ, māna, meya*) used to designate the totality of the world, which the Goddess both nourishes by her *śakti* and deludes by her *māyā*.

> The supernatural power that is purification of the energy of the *vidyā* is called *prākāmya*. All these goddesses must be worshipped with all the ritual services. //151//

vidyāśaktiviśuddhiṃ ca siddhiṃ prākāmyasaṃjñitām /
etāḥ sarvopacāreṇa pūjayed devatāḥ kramāt //151//

The energy of the *śrīvidyā*, says the Dī, is "expressed," that is, manifested, by her phonemes. It is in reality the power of the all-powerful Supreme Consciousness. The *siddhi* given here is therefore quite naturally *prākāmya*, irresistibility. The adept who acquires it can transform himself or act freely everywhere, like Śiva.

Now comes the worship in the seventh, eight-triangled *cakra*, Sarvarogahara, destroyer of all illnesses, with all the mental constructions that go with it:

> As the knots open because of the unifying interaction of the vital breaths when becoming immobile, [the energy] extending from the root-*granthi* to the heart, where consciousness is, as the void subtle transmigrating body, [one must worship] the goddesses, the secret Yoginīs, Vaśinī, etc., abiding, O Beloved of the heroes, in the Sarvarogahara *cakra*, in the blazing fire of destruction of the *saṃsāra*, by following the groups of consonants touched by the *kalās* of the vowels, which are seeds. //152–154a//
>
> *niruddhavāyusaṃghaṭṭasphuṭitagranthimūlataḥ* /
> *hṛdayāntarasaṃvittiśūṇyaṣṭakātmanā* //152//
> *bījarūpasvarakalāspṛṣṭavargānusārataḥ* /
> *rahasyayoginīr devīḥ saṃsāradalanojjvale* //153//
> *sarvarogahare cakre saṃsthitā vīravandite* /

The worship in this case consists, for the officiating adept, of making his *kuṇḍalinī* go up from the "root-*granthi*," the *mūlādhāra*, that is, to the heart *cakra*, the *cakras* (or *granthis*) between these two points being "opened," awakened, by the conjunction (*saṃghaṭṭa*)—which consists, in fact, of their immobilization—of the *prāṇa* and *apāna* vital breaths. These two breaths stop in the central void of the heart, which is where the subtle transmigrating body (the *puryaṣṭaka*) is generally supposed to stay. Therefore, there arises in the adept a subtle, "void" state of mind.

The Dī expresses this as follows: "meditating on [the *kuṇḍalinī*] as a snake whose brightness is made to palpitate by the syllable *HUṂ*, one makes it go upward together with the ascent of the breath and the thought. Thus, the *kuṇḍalinī* rises up from the *mūlādhāra*. As an expert master says: 'then one must meditate in the lotus of the heart the blazing power of consciousness,' the adept's consciousness, blazing in his heart, being the self which is consciousness itself (*cidātman*)."

This mental process also has a phonetic aspect, the Yoginīs to be worshipped there being associated with the sixteen "vowels," from *A* to *visarga* (also called here *kalās*) associated with the groups (*varga*) of consonants, *KA*, *CA*, and so on, these syllables being what brings about the presence of the secret—Gupta—Yoginīs who are to be worshipped. Their subtlety, says the Dī, explains why they are in the Sarvarogahara *cakra* where the fire of cosmic destruction is deemed to be present, its fire being able to destroy the "illness" (*roga*) of the *saṃsāra*, "impermanent, stained, and impure."

> The Yoginīs endowed with supernatural powers, Vaśinī, and so forth, are red in color, [their hands] forming the gesture of protection and of reassurance and holding the book and the rosary. //154b–155a//
>
> The *siddhis* of enjoyment and the *siddhi* of pure knowledge, O Maheśvarī, //155// [and] Tripurasiddhi, mistress [of this *cakra*, all these deities] are to be worshipped by the offering of drops [of *arghya*].
>
> *vaśinyādyāḥ raktavarṇā varadābhayamudritāḥ* //154//
>
> *pustakaṃ japamālāṃ ca dadhānāḥ siddhayoginīḥ* /
>
> *śuddhavidyāviśuddhiṃ ca bhuktisiddhiṃ maheśvari* //155//
>
> *īśvarīṃ tripurāsiddhim pūjayed bindutarpaṇaiḥ* /

Pure knowledge (*śuddhavidyā*), says the Dī, is the consciousness of the nonduality of the subject and the object: all is pure, unique, divine Consciousness. The realization of the nonduality of consciousness (*saṃvidadvaita*), of the nonduality with Śiva, is the highest, liberating knowledge. "Thus, the supernatural power of enjoyment [*bhukti*] is the great power to enjoy the whole diversity of the world gained by the adept when worshipping in this seventh *cakra*." This he does, adds the Dī, "by offering drops of *arghya*, together with unhusked grains of barley corn (*akṣata*) and flowers, with the *mudrā* of union of Śiva and Śakti made by joining the thumb and the little finger."

The *pūjā* in the eighth (three-angled), Sarvasiddhimāyā, *cakra* is now described:

> O Goddess! [the Yoginī] whose nature is that of the three energies, auspicious, splendid, and powerful flow of consciousness, //156// forms of the fire of cosmic destruction, supremely secret, are the cause of the supernatural power whose nature is fullness and nonfullness, O Sureśvarī! In the *cakra* called Sarvasiddhimaya, adorned by the divine weapons, are the four deities of the *pīṭhas* with Kāmeśvarī at their head. //158//
>
> *śaktitrayātmikā devi ciddhāmaprasarāḥ śivāḥ* //156//
>
> *saṃvartāgnikalārūpāḥ paramātirahasyakāḥ* /
>
> *pūrṇāpūrṇasvarūpāyāḥ siddher hetuḥ sureśvari* //157//
>
> *sarvasiddhimayākhye tu cakre tvāyudhabhūṣite* /
>
> *sthitāḥ kāmeśvarīpūrvāś catasraḥ pīṭhadevatāḥ* //158//

The deities in this *cakra* are, by their nature, nearer to the Goddess than the Yoginīs we saw previously. They are more important ones.

The three energies are the three basic energies of Śiva: will, knowledge, and action (*icchā, jnāna, kriyā*). Consciousness, says the Dī, is the Supreme Consciousness named Ambikā, the Mother; her splendor (*dhāman*) is made of light rays (*kiraṇa*) whose expansion (*prasara*) is the cosmic vibration (*spanda*) produced by the three regents of the cosmos identified here with the three energy goddesses Vāmā, Jyeṣṭhā, and Raudrī. The four regents of the ages of the world (the *yuganāthas*) are also there.

All these entities form the first circle of deities surrounding the Goddess. They are said to be forms of the fire of destruction (*saṃvartāgni*), for when one approaches the Goddess, the world tends to disappear. The power they bestow is fullness, because it is the complete absorption (*samāveśa*) in the supreme Śiva. It is also nonfullness, because it includes the totality of the cosmic manifestation. The Siddhi present here, having these two aspects, gives liberation in life (*jīvanmukti*).

The *pīṭhas* are the four sacred seats of the Goddess, the ritual and spiritual (more or less mythical) centers of this tradition. They are Kāmarūpa, Pūrṇagiri, Jālandhara, and Oḍḍīyāna, as we have already seen.[48] Kāmeśvarī is the first of a group of four goddesses; the three others are Vajreśvarī,

Bhagamālinī, and Tripurasundarī. Only the first three are in this *cakra*, Tripurasundarī residing in the next, central, *cakra*.

> As for the weapon deities, shining with an intense red brilliance, each carrying its weapon on its head, their hands making the gesture of reassurance and protection, they are to be worshipped. They give the fruit desired by those who visualize them in meditation. //159// They are yours and mine and bestow power on men and women.
>
> *āyudhās tvatiraktābhāḥ svāyudhojjvalamastakāḥ* /
>
> *varadābhayahastāśca pūjyā dhyātṛphalapradāḥ* //159//
>
> *tvadīyāśca madīyāś ca puṃstrīvaśyavidhāyinaḥ* /

All Tantric deities are represented as holding in their hands objects called weapons (*āyudha*), which are sometimes arms (bow and arrows, for instance), sometimes tools (such as a goad) or various symbolic objects. Although objects, *āyudhas*, being elements of a divine figure, are considered deities, *devatās*, and may in such cases be represented (or, as is the case here, be visualized by *dhyāna*) as human figures bearing their "weapons" on their heads. They are then to be worshipped as deities, bestowing boons on their worshipper. They can also be associated with phonemes or mantras.

> O Sureśvarī! these arrows of yours are associated with the second vowel, their nature being that of [the constituent elements of the body,] skin, blood, flesh, fat, and with what follows bone and marrow. //160b–161a//
>
> *tvagasṛṇmāṃsamedo 'sthimajjārṇāntāḥ sureśvari* //160//
>
> *dvitīyasvarasaṃyuktā ete bāṇās tvādīyakāḥ* /

We are to understand here that the arrows are associated with the mantras of the *dhātus*, the constituent elements of the body, which are formed by the second vowel, *Ā*, of the Sanskrit alphabet and by one of five consonants and ending with *Ṃ*. These consonants are the four semivowels, *YA* for the skin, *RA* for the blood, *LA* for the flesh, *VA* for fat, and "what follows bone and marrow," which is *SA*, for semen, which is designated in this way because, in the lists of the *dhātus*, *semen* (*śukra*) usually follows bone and marrow. The mantras of the five arrows to be used in the worship to invoke them are (as given in the Dī): *YĀṂ, RĀṂ, LĀṂ, VĀṂ,* and *SĀṂ.*

[The Mistress of this *cakra* is] Tripurāmbikā, who generates the three cities Vāmā, etc., //161// These [deities], O Lovely-faced Woman, are to be worshipped with all the ritual offerings and services. [They bestow] the supernatural power of unlimited will because their nature is that of supreme freedom. //162//

vāmādīnāṃ purāṇāṃ tu jananī tripurāmbikā //161//

parasvātantryarūpatvād icchāsiddhir maheśvari /

etāḥ sarvopacāreṇa pūjayet tu varānane //162//

Vāmā is one of the three main goddesses surrounding Tripurasundarī: Vāmā, Jyeṣṭhā, and Raudrī. They are called "cities" probably because they are near Tripurasundarī, the "Beautiful [Mistress] of the Three Cities." The Dī, however, says that it is because they are presided over by Kāmeṣvarī, whose nature is that of the three basic energies, *icchā, jñāna,* and *kriyā.*

Then comes the worship in the ninth, central, *cakra*:

In the supreme Sarvānandamaya *cakra*, O Goddess, whose nature is that of the supreme *brahman*, one must worship with all freedom of practice Mahātripurasundarī, [supreme] consciousness, who is both egoity and objectivity. She is the great Kāmakalā. She gives the supernatural power of [attaining], the *vidyā*, the *pīṭhas*, and so forth. //163–164//. [This] goddess, the great *mudrā*, must be worshipped.

sarvānandamaye devi parabrahmātmake pare /

cakre saṃvittirūpā ca mahātripurasundarī //163//

svairācāreṇa saṃpūjyā tvahantedantayoḥ samā /

mahākāmakalārūpā pīṭhavidyādysiddhidā //164//

mahāmudrāmayī devī pūjyā

That the supreme Goddess should be *parabrahman* and consciousness goes without saying. The Dī adds, however, that she is, for the worshipper, the goddess of his own consciousness (*svasaṃviddevatā*), underlining thus the *saṃvidadvaita* (the "nonduality of consciousness") conception of the Trika: that there is only one conscious principle, Śiva, of which the individual consciousnesses of human beings are merely aspects. It is in this respect that she is equally *ahantā* and *idanta*, both the absolute pure I and the multiplicity of the objective world.

Tripurasundarī is also "the great Kāmakalā." This refers to the *kāmakalā* diagram, symbolizing the union of Śiva and Śakti, which we have already seen in chapter 2, *śl.* 21.

She is to be worshipped with all freedom of practice (*svairācāreṇa*), that is, says the Dī, "with elements pleasing to the senses and whose nature is what the worshipper desires," a practice, it adds, characterized by an intense one-pointed mental concentration on the blazing pulsation (*parisphurat paramānusaṃdhāna*) of the supreme. Tantric worship, as we have already seen, implies the total mental and bodily, intensely lived participation of the officiant in the ritual action. The Dī quotes here stanza 74 of the *Vijñānabhairava*: "Wherever the mind of the individual finds satisfaction, on this supreme point the mind is to be firmly concentrated, for the supreme bliss shines intensely there."

The *siddhi* gained here is *prāpti*, the power to attain everything. Here it is the power to realize the nature of the *śrīvidyā*, to reach (symbolically) the four *pīṭhas* of the Śrividyā tradition, and to unite with the four deities, Kāmeśvarī, and so on, all of which gives the adept the power to rest in the supreme, on the plane "beyond the fourth" (*turyātīta*)[49]—and therefore to be omnipotent, like Śiva.

The great *mudrā* is the *yonimudrā*, which is in this *cakra* because it is a triangle, the triangle being the usual symbolic representation of the feminine sexual organ, the *yoni*. We have seen the *yonimudrā* in chapter 1, *śl.* 70b–71a.

> Made up of fifteen [syllables] and as many *tithis*, eternal, she is the ninth supreme Bhairavī //165// [to be worshipped in] each *cakra*, together with the *mudrās* described in the [first chapter] "Encounter in the *cakra*."
>
> *pañcadaśātmikā*
>
> *tattattithimayī nityā navamī bhairavī parā //165//*
>
> *praticakraṃ samudrās tu cakrasaṃketakoditāḥ /*

The Goddess is said to be made up of fifteen syllables, because the *srīvidyā* of fifteen syllables is herself in her mantric aspect. She is also made up of the *tithis*, the fifteen lunar days, because they form together the whole moon, another totality. In fact, the number of the totality (and of the moon) is not fifteen but sixteen. The Dī explains, therefore, that if one adds to the fifteen *tithis* or syllables of the *śrīvidyā* the *ṣrīvidya* as a whole, taken as a unit, one has 15 + 1 = 16. The *mūlavidyā* worshipped in this central triangle is thus seen as made up of her separate syllables plus their ensemble, thus being sixteenfold.

The Goddess is to be worshipped also in the whole *śrīcakra*, since she pervades it entirely.

The worship in the nine *cakras* of the *śrīcakra* ends with another ritual worship:

> The sage must perform a sacrifice to Nityaklinnā, etc., using optional rites, //166// either in the triangle or in the intermediate space of the square.
>
> *nityaklinnādikāś caiva kāmyakarmānusārataḥ* //166//
>
> *caturasrāntarāle vā trikoṇe vā yajet sudhīḥ* /

Nityaklinnā is placed on the left side of the central triangle between two other goddesses, Kāmeśvarī and Bhagamālinī. The other goddesses of the inner retinue of Tripurasundarī (meant by "etc.") are thirteen Nityās.[50] They are to be worshipped either in the central triangle or on the sixteen-petaled lotus, meant here by "the intermediate space of the square."

The use of so-called optional rites (*kāmyakarmaṇi*), that is, rites undertaken to attain a desired object, is normal in the present Tantric context, since the worship of all these deities gives *siddhis*, which are desired (*kāmya*) by the adept. The Dī describes these rites as consisting of "flowers, visualizing meditation [*dhyāna*], syllables, etc., adapted to such optional rites as subjugation, etc." The next stanza is more explicit:

> Having honored the deities with alcohol, pieces of cooked meat, perfumes, and incense, //167// the worship of the *cakra* is thus accomplished. [The officiating adept] must [then] offer the lamp of *kula*, blazing with its own splendor, shining forth internally and externally, O Dear One! //168//
>
> *alinā piśitair gandhair dhūpair ārādhya devatāḥ* //167//
>
> *cakrapūjāṃ vidhāyetthaṃ kuladīpaṃ nivedayet* /
>
> *antarbahirbhāsamānaṃ svaprakāśojjvalaṃ priye* //168//

The term we give here in English as "alcohol" is *hetu*, which means "cause." It is one of the several terms used to mean an alcoholic beverage without mentioning it explicitly.

The offering of lights to the deity is the waving of lights in front of the image, which is a part of all *pūjās* (called *arati*, it is nowadays often its main, if not its sole, part).

This action is here metaphysically interpreted, *kula* being, as we have seen, one of the terms used to mean the body, whether cosmic or human. *Kula*, says the Dī, is "the body made of the thirty-six *tattvas*", in other words, the whole world, which is thus symbolically offered to the Goddess. But the Dī also interprets this as follows: this lamp "is the dynamism of consciousness shining in the lotus of the heart and which, through the senses, shines in the same way in all objects." "This lamp it adds, "shines by its own light, which is the direct intuitive perception of the supreme reality," the act of offering being, for the adept, "the inner quiescent tranquillity [*viśrānti*] in consciousness that he experiences when turning inward."

Now comes the last rite of this *pūjā*, the *japa*.

Japa

The *japa* is the mandatory penultimate act of all *pūjās* (normally, but not here, followed by an offering in the sacrificial fire, a *homa*). It consists of reciting a more or less large number of times the root mantra, the *mūlamantra*, of the deity being worshipped. This is, however, not the case here, for this *japa* is, in fact, a long and complex meditative and yogic practice in which the enunciation (*uccāra*) of the *śrīvidyā*, associated with the ascent of the *kuṇḍalinī*, is accompanied by mental visualizations of elements of the *śrīvidyā* imagined (and, to a certain extent, experienced) as taking place in the yogic body of the adept together with the ascent of *kuṇḍalinī*. We have described its general pattern above in the introduction. Here we will follow, with the help of the Dī, the details of the process as described (or alluded to) in stanzas 169b–189a. (See table 3.1.)

Then, having done the *añjali* with flowers, he must practice *japa* with a composed and steady mind. //169a//

puṣpajlaliṃ tataḥ kṛtvā japaṃ kuryāt samāhitaḥ /

O Great Goddess! [The *japa* consists of] the conjunction of the *cakras* placed one above the other [realized] by the *nāda* in the three *kūṭas* and the threefold *kuṇḍalinī*. //169b–170a//

Table 3.1 The *japa* of the three *kūṭa* of the *śrīvidyā*.

śrīcakra	bodily *cakras*	*kuṇḍalinī*	*Śrividyā*
	dvādaśānta		*unmanā*
			↑
			samanā
			|
			vyāpinī
			|
	↑		*śakti*
			|
			nādānta
			|
			nāda
			|
	brahmarandhra		*nirodhinī*
			|
			ardhacandra
			|
			HRĪM
bindu			*SA KA LA*
central triangle	*bindu*	*saṃhāra*	(*śaktibīja*)
8-angled *cakra*	*bhrūmadhya*	*somakuṇḍalinī*	*samanā*
			↑
			nādānta
↑	*tālu*		*nāda*
		↑	|
			bindu
	viśuddha		*HRĪM*
inner 10-angled			|
cakra		*sthiti*	*HA SA KA HA LA*
external 10-angled		*sūryakuṇḍalinī*	(*kāmarājakūṭa*)
cakra	*anāhata*		*samanā*
14-angled *cakra*			↑
	maṇipūra		*nāda*
			rodhinī
↑	*svadhiṣṭāna*	↑	*ardhacandra*
			bindu
			HRĪM
	mūlādhāra	*sṛṣṭi*	*HA SA KA LA*
aṣṭadalapadma			
ṣoḍaśadalapadma	*viṣu*	*agnikuṇḍalinī*	(*vāgbhava*)
caturasracakra	*akulapadma*		

kūṭatraye mahādevi kuṇḍalītritaye 'pi ca //169//
cakrāṇāṃ pūrvapūrveṣāṃ nādarūpeṇa yojanam /

In these [*kūṭas*] are the phonemes *prāṇa*, *agni*, and *māyā*, followed by the *kalās: bindu, ardhacandra, rodhinī, nāda, nādānta, śakti,* accompanied by *vyāpikā*, *samanā*, and *unmanā*, who are in the *dvādaśānta*, O Dear One. //171// Then, for [the *kūṭa*] whose nature is the root *kuṇḍalinī*, and for the middle one, turned [the first] toward emanation, [the second] toward the resorption of the cosmos, O Maheśvarī! //172// The conjunction [goes on] rising higher and higher only as the subtle *nāda*. In the modified third [*kūṭa*], O Goddess, the twelfth *kalā* [is enunciated]. //173//

teṣu prāṇāgnimāyārṇakalābindvārdhacandrakāḥ //170//
rodhinīnādanādāntāḥ śaktivyāpikayānvitā /
samanā conmanā ceti dvādaśānte sthitā priye //171//
mūlakuṇḍalinīrūpe madhyame ca tataḥ punaḥ /
sṛṣṭyunmukhe ca viśvasya sthitirūpe maheśvari //172//
kevalaṃ nādarūpeṇa uttarottarayojanaṃ /
śabalākārake devi tṛtīye dvādaśī kalā //173//

This first part of the *japa* is to proceed as follows: The adept is to imagine that along his *suṣumnā* are tiered the nine constituent *cakras* of the *śrīcakra* (from its square outside part to the central triangle), each associated with one of the nine *cakras* of his yogic imaginal body, from the *mūlādhāra* to the *dvādaśānta*. Going upward along this axis, the *kuṇḍalinī* is conceived of as being threefold. Its lower part, from *mūlādhāra* to the heart *cakra* (*hṛdaya* or *anāhata*), is the so-called *agnikuṇḍalinī*; it is fiery and associated with emanation, *sṛṣṭi*. Then, from heart to *bhrūmadhya* (the *cakra* between the eyebrows, also called *bindu* or *ājñā*), extends the *sūryakuṇḍalinī*, which is solar and associated with conservation, *sthiti*. Third, from *bhrūmadhya* to *dvādaśānta*, rises the *somakuṇḍalinī*, which is lunar and linked to resorption, *saṃhāra*. This conception of the *kuṇḍalinī* as in three sections that have respectively the nature of fire, sun, and moon is found in several Tantric Śaiva texts. Its point seems to be to give a cosmic dimension to the ascent of the *kuṇḍalinī*.

Now the adept is to imagine that in the *mūlādhāra* lies the first part, or *kūṭa*, of the *ṣrīvidyā*, *HA SA KA LA HRĪṂ*. Then, in the heart *cakra*, is the second *kūṭa*, *HA SA KA HA LA HRĪṂ*; and in the *bhrūmadhyā* is the third *kūṭā*, *SA KA LA HRĪṂ*. The enunciation of these three *HRĪṂ*, like that of all *bījas* ending with *Ṃ* (*bindu*), is deemed (as said in *śl.* 170) to be prolonged by a subtle phonic vibration, the *nāda*, which goes through eight ever subtler phonic stages, the so-called *kalāṣ*, named *ardhacandra*, *rodhinī*, *nāda*, *nādānta*, *śakti*, *vyāpinī*, *samanā*, and *umanā*, with the last, "transmental," *kalā*, which finally dissolves in the silence of the Absolute.

This being so, the *japa* consists, for the officiant, of the mental enunciation (*uccāra*) of the three *kūṭas* of the *śrividyā*, enunciating first their letters, from *SA* or *HA* to the *bindu*, *Ṃ*, then prolonging the *uccāra* of *Ṃ* by the eight *kalās*, from *ardhacandra* to *samanā*, this subtle vibration ascending for the first *kūṭa* from *mūlādhāra* to the heart, for the second *kūṭa* from the heart to the *bhrūmadhya*, and for the third *kūṭa* from *bhrūmadhya* to the *dvādaśānta*, where it reaches its ultimate form, *unmanā*, the "transmental." This it does, however, together with the *unmanās* of the two first *HRĪṂ*, with which it intermingles (this is why it is called "modified" in *ṣl.* 173b). There the phonic vibration unites with and disappears in the Absolute. The *kalās* are said by the YH to number twelve, because one is to add to the eight subtle ones, *ardhacandra* to *unmanā*, the four elements that constitute *HRĪṂ*: *H R Ī + bindu*.

This *japa* is thus not a recitation but a purely mental mantric utterance (*mantroccāra*), conceived by the adept as carrying upward the three parts of the *śrīvidyā*, through the *cakras* of his yogic body united with the constitutive parts of the *śrīcakra*, with the *kuṇḍalinī* and with his mind, to the highest level of sound vibration, where it merges in Mahātripurasundarī, supreme Consciousness. It is a complex, both visual and phonic-mental, process. It is a mental process, we note, that also has a cosmic dimension, since, as it unfolds from distinct syllables to *unmanā*, it includes, with the three *kūṭas*, the whole cosmic process, from emanation to resorption, a process parallel to, isomorphic with, the phonic one, which goes from distinct sound to the silence of the Absolute and, implicitly, from ordinary waking awareness (*jāgrat*) to the supreme nondualistic *turyātīta* state of mind. This *japa*, therefore, if effectively carried out, requires an extremely intense and difficult mental/spiritual exercise in creative imagination.

This, however, is only the first part of the *japa*; three other *japas* are now prescribed.

One must perform the *japa* mentally while meditating on the six-fold emptiness, O Goddess, the five conditions of the mind, and the seven equalizations. //174//

śūnyaṣaṭkaṃ tathā devi hyavasthāpañcakaṃ punaḥ /

viṣuvaṃ saptarūpaṃ ca bhāvayan manasā japet //174//

These entities—the six emptinesses (*śūṇya*), the five states or conditions (*avasthā*) of the mind, and the seven *viṣuvat* (a term we translate as "equalization"), says the Dī, are to be meditatively realized (*bhāvayet*) in the constitutive elements of the *śrīvidyā* of which this is therefore a *japa*—of a particular sort.

Dividing into groups of three [the *kalās* of the *uccāra*] from *agni* to the *dvādaśānta*, O Fair-Faced Woman! one will give birth to the threefold emptiness, each [of the emptinesses] being in the interval between each [of the groups of three], O Dear One! //175// In the supreme abode, beyond the threefold emptiness, one is to meditate on the great emptiness.

agnyādidvādaśānteṣu trīṃstrīṇ tyaktvā varānane /

śūnyatrayaṃ vijānīyād ekaikāntaraḥ priye //175//

śūnyatrayāt pare sthāne mahāśūnyaṃ vibhāvayet /

Although called "threefold" (*śūṇyatrayam*), there are six emptinesses. They are linked to the ascending enunciation (*uccāra*) of *HRĪṂ*—its letters, then its *kalās*—the *śūṇyas* being imagined as nodal points placed on the level of a *kalā* between two others, beginning with the *R* of *HRĪṂ* (called *agni*, since *RA* is the *bīja* of fire) and ending on the level of *unmanā*, which is in the *dvādaśānta*, as shown in table 3.1 above.

The officiating adept is apparently to meditate intensely on these imaginary points. The Dī explains that he is to see in his mind the *śūṇyas* looking like "the multicolored circles adorning the feathers of a peacock," for which it quotes sūtra 32 of the *Vijñānabhairava*: "If one meditates on the five voids [using as support] the multicolored circles adorning the feathers of a peacock, one penetrates in the heart, supreme void."

The Dī also quotes part of stanza 41 of the same text: "he will be absorbed in the marvelous ether of consciousness."

The first line of *śl.* 175 implies that there is a still higher, "emptier" level of emptiness, above the sixth one.

The YH then explains the meditation on the five conditions of the mind, the *avasthas*: waking (*jāgrat*), dream (*svapna*), deep sleep (*suṣupti*), the "fourth" (*turya*) state, and the one "above the fourth" (*turyātīta*):

> The meditative realization of the waking senses, then, [must be done] through the state of waking, //176// in the fire, O Goddess, a state of great wakefulness, together with the two [categories of] faculties.
>
> *prabodhakaraṇasyā 'thā jāgaratvena bhāvanam //176//*
>
> *vahnau devi mahājāgradavasthā tvindriyadvayaiḥ /*

The two categories of faculties are the five organs or faculties of apperception (*jñānendriya* or *buddhīndriya*), sight, hearing, smell, taste, and touch, and the five senses of action (*karmendriya*) corresponding to the functions of speaking, holding, walking, excreting, and copulating. These two categories correspond to two groups of *tattvas* in the classification of the Sāṃkhya, categories that are active in the waking state. A meditative realization, an inner experience of the plane of consciousness corresponding to these sense experiences or activities is probably what the adept is supposed to have in this part of the *japa*.

The meditative realization of the great wakefulness is to take place "in the fire" (*vahnau*), which is to say, the Dī explains, "in the letter *RA* present on the tip of the third *bīja*,"[51] that is, in the *R* of the *HRĪṂ* of the third *kūṭa* of the *śrīvidyā*—something we may find difficult to visualize but which is important, since there is no *japa* without (at least a part of) a mantra.

Since there are five ascending conditions of the mind, the meditative process of the *japa* goes on as follows:

> [Linked] to the internal organs is the dream state revealed by *māyā* //177// in the region of the throat.
>
> *āntaraiḥ karaṇair eva svapno māyāvabodhanaḥ //177//*
>
> *galadeśe*

The state of dream (*svapna*) is defined by the Dī as the condition of the knowing subject (*pramātṛ*)[52] when his mental activity is separated from the senses of action and linked to the internal organs. The internal organ, the *antaḥkaraṇa*, is made up of the three *tattvas* between the senses of apperception and *prakṛti*, namely the mind (*manas*), the principle of the ego (*ahaṃkāra*), and the intellect (*buddhi*). These are "revealed by *māyā* in the region of the heart," which is, says the Dī, by the letter *Ī*[53] of *HRĪṂ* to be felt and meditated as present in the region of the heart, which is the "region of dream" (*svapnasya sthānam*).

> *Suṣupti* is the perception of what was previously dissolved with the dissolution of the domain of the movements of the internal organ. //178// [The meditation bears here] on the preceding phonemes taken in the reverse order. It takes place on the *bindu*, between the eyebrows.
>
> *suṣuptis tu līnapūrvasya vedanam /*
>
> *antaḥkaraṇavṛttīnāṃ layato viṣayasya tu //178//*
>
> *pūrvārṇānāṃ vilomena bhrūmadhye bindusaṃsthitā /*

Suṣupti is the state of deep sleep, where no dream appears. All mental activities stop there, because the movements of the internal organ, the *antaḥkaraṇa*, of which one was conscious in the previous, dream state, have now disappeared. In this state, one is intensely conscious (*parāmṛśyate*) only of one's self (*svātma*) and of happiness (*sukha*), says the Dī.

As for the *japa* to be done here, it would consist of meditating on the syllables of the central *kūṭa* of the *śrīvidyā*, the *śaktibīja*, taking them in reverse order, *LA KA SA*, these phonemes being meditated, visualized as being "on the *bindu* placed on the *hṛllekhā* (on the *Ṃ* of the *HRĪṂ*, that is) which is in the *bhrūmadhyacakra*"—the *HRĪṂ* would thus be imagined as placed there, between the eyebrows. This part of the *japa*, like the others, is a yogic practice based on the structure of the mental image of the yogic body.

> [The meditation] of *turya* is the grouping together there of the half-circle, etc. //179// Being the cause of the manifestation of consciousness, [this state] is knowledge of the nature of the *nāda*.
>
> *turyarūpaṃ tasya cātra vṛttārdhades saṃgrahaḥ //179//*
>
> *caitanyavyaktihetos tu nādarūpasya vedanam /*

Turya, the fourth condition of the mind, is above the three normal states of consciousness, being considered their cause. It is not merely peaceful but dynamic. In its *bhāvanā*, says the Dī, there appears an intense awareness (*parāmarśa*) of the phonic vibration, the *nāda*, of the *śrīvidyā* on the three levels of the *uccāra* following *bindu*: *ardhacandra* (the "half-circle"), *rodhinī*, and *nādānta*, these three *kalās* being considered as together "on the apex of the third *bīja*." What the adept is to realize there, we are told, is the inciting (*kalana*) nature, the dynamism, of the *nāda*, which causes the apparition of a pure consciousness of the self.[54]

> *Turyātīta*, O Dear one, is a state of happiness. It is on the level of *nādānta* and what follows it. //181// In that very place, the awakened must, during the time of *japa*, remember the five conditions of the mind.
>
> *turyātītaṃ sukhasthānaṃ nādāntādisthitaṃ priye //180//*
>
> *atraiva japakāle tu pañcāvasthāḥ smared budhaḥ /*

The Dī defines the essence of the condition of *turyātīta* as supreme bliss transcending word and thought (*manovāgatītaparamānanda*), which is, however, to be experienced on the level of *nādānta, śakti, vyapinī, samanā,* and *unmanā*, which are the "region of happiness" (*sukhasthānam*). This "remembrance"[55] is to take place "in that very place," which (according to the Dī) is to be understood "in the *śaktibīja*," the third *kūṭa* of the *śrīvidyā*. "He must remember" (*smaret*) is taken as the equivalent of *bhavayet*: he must meditate intensely.[56]

Another series of *japa* follows now, that of the seven *viṣuvas*. There is no satisfactory translation of the term *viṣuva* because of our uncertainty about what the term designates. In astronomy, it is the equinox. More generally, it means a central or middle point, a point of equality or equalization, equilibrium. Here it evokes a point of equilibrium or equalization between the *prāṇa*, or *nāda*, of the mantra and some other element brought into play by the *japa*. With each of these *japas*, the adept would experience in mind and body a particular union with the phonic vibration, the *nāda*, of the *śrīvidyā* and would thus progress toward union with the supreme.

> The *viṣuva* named *prāṇa* is the union of breath, the self, and the mind. //181//
>
> *yogaḥ prāṇātmamanasāṃ viṣuvaṃ prāṇasaṃjñakam //181//*

This description of the *prāṇaviṣuva* is clear enough, but neither the YH nor the Dī explains how this union is realized or the role the *vidyā* may play in this practice.

> Knowing that what assumes the form of the self is dissolved in the *nāda* which rises from the [*mūl*]*ādhāra*, conjoining and disjoining

the phonemes of the mantra, O Maheśvarī, //182// [then] perceiving that what has the nature of *nāda*[57] [rises] from the *anāhata* to the ultimate [*cakra*, this is the *mantra*]*viṣuva*.

ādhārotthitanāde tu līnaṃ buddhvātmarūpakam /
saṃyogena viyogena mantrārṇānāṃ maheśvari //182//
anāhatādyādhārāntaṃ nādātmavicintanam /
viṣuvam

"What assumes the form of the self" is the divine Consciousness. This Consciousness, assuming the form of the consciousness of the adept, is to be imagined as dissolved in the phonic vibration, the *nāda*, which rises from the *mūlādhāra* up to the *brahmarandhra*, a movement during which it is associated with the three parts of the *śrīvidyā*, first taken separately, then taken together, and, in this case, considered as rising from the *anāhata*, the *cakra* of the heart, to the highest *cakra*. This is done, says the DĪ, "enunciating up to the heart the *nāda* present on the apex of the *vāgbhava* (the third *kūṭa*) which is in the *mūlādhāra*, and dissolving there. The spiritual experience the adept has by one-pointed attention (*anusaṃdhāna*) is that the real nature of his self is divine; such is the *mantraviṣuva*."

What is called *nāḍīviṣuva* is produced by the phoneme when the twelve *granthis* are pierced inside the *nāḍī* in conjunction with the *nāda*, O Dear One! //183b–184a//

nādasaṃsparśān nāḍīviṣuvam ucyate //183//
dvādaśagranthibhedena varṇād nāḍyantare priye /

The phoneme (*varṇa*), says the DĪ, is the *kāmakalā akṣara*—the letter *Ī*—present on the apex of the three *kūṭas*, the letter *Ī*, that is, of the three *HRĪṂ* of the *śrīvidyā*. This phoneme is to pierce the twelve *granthis*, the "knots," namely the six *cakras*, from *mūlādhāra* to *brahmarandhra* and six intermediary knots, tiered along the *suṣumnā nāḍī*. This ascending movement is associated with the equally ascending subtle phonic vibration, the *nāda*, of the three *HRĪṂ*, as we have seen in the first *japa*. ; It is, in fact, practically the same mental yogic practice, with the same spiritual effect.

Conjunction with the *nāda*, the *praśānta*[*viṣuva*] falls within the range of the appeased senses. //184// One is to meditate the fire, *māyā* and *kalā*, *cetanā*, *ardhacandra*, *rodhinī*, *nāda* and *nādānta* dissolved in *śakti*. //185//

nādayogaḥ praśāntaṃ tu praśāntendriyagocaram //184//

vahniṃ māyāṃ kalāṃ caiva cetanāṃ ardhacandrakam /

rodhinīnādanādāntān śaktau līnāṇ vibhāvayet //185//

"The fire is the letter *RA*, *māyā* is *Ī*, and *kalā* is the half-*kalā* following *SA* placed in the middle of this letter [*Ī*] which has the shape of a line.[58] *Cetanā* is the *bindu* which is the inner impulsion of consciousness [*caitanya*]. As for *ardhacandra*, *rodhinī*, etc., they are to be meditated on, being dissolved in *śakti*, as previously described,"[59] says the Dī. This is, it adds, because the energy here is the energy of the officiant who thus feels appeased as he evokes mentally this ascent of the phonic *kalās* of *HRĪṂ* along the way of the *kuṇḍalinī*.

The *viṣuva* named *śakti* is above her. [It consists of] applying one's thought to the *nāda*. Still above this is the *kālaviṣuva*, which extends up to *unmanā*, O Maheśvarī! //186// The perception of the *nāda* [lasts] *muni*, *candra*, eight and ten *tuṭis*.

viṣuvaṃ śaktisaṃjñaṃ tu tadūrdhvaṃ nādacintanam /

tadūrdhvaṃ kālaviṣuvam unmanāntaṃ maheśvari //186//

municandrāṣṭadaśabhis tuṭibhir nādavedanam

The *śaktiviṣuva* is "above *śakti*" because it is to be meditated as extending up to the *samanā kalā*. The *kālaviṣuva*, the *viṣuva* of time, is still above it, since the adept is to consider its meditation as reaching the supreme level of *unmanā*, which transcends time.

The Dī explains that *muni* means seven, and *candra* means one. If one adds eight and ten, the length of the *uccāra* of the *vidyā* from the *HA* of *HRĪṂ* to *unmanā* would be ten thousand eight hundred seventeen *tuṭis*, a *tuṭi* being an extremely small division of time; it is described in a text quoted by the Dī as a hundredth part of the twinkling of the eye.

The equalization which is the cause of the manifestation of consciousness is called *tattva*[*viṣuva*]. //187//

caitanyavyaktihetuśca viṣuvaṃ tattvasaṃjñakam //187//

This *viṣuva* is described in the Dī as the one-pointed attention (*anusaṃdhāna*) to one's own self resulting from the dissolution of the *nāda* during the length of time described above as counted in *tuṭis*, this being experienced on the level of *unmanā*—an experience of a purely transcendent state of consciousness, the summit of which is reached in the last, supreme *viṣuva*:

> The supreme stage, O Great Goddess, is the beauty of uncreated bliss.
>
> *paraṃ sthānaṃ mahādevi nisargānandasundaram* /

This ultimate stage, says the DĪ, transcends the sound and movement that existed in the five vacuities and in the six preceding *viṣuvas*. Its beauty is "the beauty of the place of rest [*viśrānti*] of the universe," which is the Absolute. It both includes and transcends all forms of bliss. It is the supreme level of the deity that is the cause and origin of all that exists and holds it in herself: it is the supreme Goddess as mistress and place of rest (*viśrānti*) of the world, for, as we may say, all is in God.

The YH concludes the passage on the *japas* as follows:

> Who applies thus his mind during the times [prescribed for] *japa*, O Pārvati! //188// will rapidly obtain all the supernatural powers thanks to your favor.
>
> This being done, he must offer the *japa* to the Goddess in her left hand. //189//
>
> *evaṃ cintayamānasya japakāleṣu pārvati* //188//
>
> *siddhayaḥ sakalās tūrṇaṃ siddhyanti tvatprasādataḥ* /
>
> *evaṃ kṛtvā japaṃ devyā vāmahaste nivedayet* //189//

The symbolical offering of the *japa* (*japanivedana*) into the hand of the deity being worshipped is one of the usual actions of the *pūjā*. It is a mark of respect and devotion. The DĪ, however, true to its nondualist philosophical doctrine, interprets it symbolically.

In this perspective, the *japa* that has just been performed is lived by the officiating adept as bringing about a fusion with the *śrīvidyā* associated with the *kuṇḍalinī*, a power both human and cosmic-divine, and thus as having a transcendental-cosmic dimension. It is a lived experience of the resorption of the cosmos into the deity. Given in the left hand of the Goddess, the *japa* is considered as being offered to the dissolving aspect of the deity. The Goddess holds it and reabsorbs it in herself and, with it, the *sādhaka*, who is thus symbolically liberated.

The last rites of the *pūjā* are now to be performed; first, the ritual libation, *tarpana*:

With the joined thumb and ring finger, he must satiate the deities of the *cakra*.

anāmāṅguṣṭhayogena tarpayec cakradevatāḥ /

The joined thumb and ring finger symbolize the union of Śiva (thumb) and Śakti (ring finger). The offering is to be done to all the deities of the *cakra*. How it is done, and with what consecrated water, is not said. The DĪ gives a metaphysical interpretation of this rite

The oblation to the Goddess follows:

He will offer to the Goddess wine, meat, and fish. //190//

madyaṃ māṃsaṃ tathā matsyaṃ devyai tu vinivedayet //190//

Those are usual Tantric offerings. No sexual practice is prescribed here, as is, however, sometimes the case in the tradition of Tripurā.[60]

He will worship her in the company of heroes devoted to the practices of Kula.

kaulācārasamāyuktair vīrais tu saha pūjayet /

There is no indication that this *pūjā* is a collective worship. It is called *cakrapūjā* because it is done with the *śrīcakra*, not because worshippers are placed in circles. We may therefore believe that this prescription aims merely at excluding the presence of noninitiates: the DĪ says it excludes those who are not perfected (*siddha*).

The *cakrapūjā* of the Yoginīs is to be performed in a special manner under the constellations of *puṣya*, when the sun is dominant, O Parameśvarī! //191// on the birthday of the *guru*, on that of one's own constellation, and also on the eighth and fourteenth lunar days. //192//

puṣyabhedena tu vāre saure ca parameśvari //191//

guror dine svanakṣatre caturdasyaṣṭamiṣu ca /

cakrapūjāṃ viśeṣeṇa yoginīnāṃ samācaret //192//

"In a special manner" (*viśeśena*) is to be understood (says the Dī) as using the sort of "occasional [*naimittika*] rites that would satisfy the group of sixty-four, or other categories of, Yoginīs." This precision is not useless, since the part of the *pūjā* performed in the nine *cakras* of the *śrīcakra* was to be done using "optional" (*kāmya*) rites; see *śl*. 166.[61]

Puṣya is the sixth or seventh lunar day. The day when the sun is dominant would now be Sunday (sun-day).

Since sixty-four crores of very powerful Yoginīs are assembled in this *cakra*, O Beloved of the Heroes! //193// [their worship] is to be performed eight times eight times, without cheating on the expenses.

catuḥṣaṣṭir yataḥ koṭyo yoginīnāṃ mahaujasām /

cakram etat samāśritya saṃsthitā vīravandite //193//

aṣṭāṣṭakaṃ tu kartavyaṃ vittiśāṭhyavivarjitam /

A usual number of Yoginīs is sixty-four. From each of these sixty-four, a crore (ten million) emanate. Surely, they are merely to be mentally evoked, even if imagined as crowding the *śrīcakra*. No indication is given about when and how these sixty-four *pūjās* are to be performed.

The rule to act without cheating, without limiting the expenses, is a generally valid principle, already alluded to in the fourth stanza of the first chapter of the YH. Hindu ritual works on a *do ut des* principle: one cannot expect the deity's favor or generosity if one does not worship with generosity.

[But] you alone it is, Enchantress of the Worlds, who are playing under the guise of these [deities]!

tvam eva tāsāṃ rūpeṇa krīḍase viśvamohinī //194//

As a consequence of this, says the Dī, when one worships all these deities who are but fragments of the Goddess, it is in reality the supreme Goddess who is worshipped.

Who, not knowing the doctrine and practices of Kula or paying respect to the sandals of the guru, penetrates in this doctrine, you will assuredly punish him. //195//

ajṇātvā tu kulācāram ayaṣṭvā gurupādukām /

yo 'smin śāstre parvarteta taṃ tvaṃ pīḍayasi dhruvam //195//

The YH repeats the rule already given in the first chapter that only adepts initiated by a guru of the sect and following its rules of behavior are permitted to study and try to follow its doctrine and practices. The efforts of the uninitiated are necessarily fruitless.

> O Woman of beautiful hips! [the adept] who has thus learned, who follows ceaselessly the rules and behavior of the Kula, having offered us wine and meat changed into something else, //196// must consider carefully the forms of the flow of your expansion which is [in fact] none but You.
>
> *evaṃ jñātvā varārohe kaulācāraparaḥ sadā /*
>
> *āvayoḥ śabalākāraṃ madyaṃ māṃsaṃ nivedya ca //196//*
>
> *tvatprathāprasarākāras tvām eva paribhāvayet /*

The forms taken by the expanding flow of the Goddess are the deities that surround her (the *āvaraṇadevatā*), whose forms, the Dī says, are born from her and who therefore are to be considered as mere forms taken by her: "They are figures born from the playful shining forth [*vilāsa*] of the energy of free consciousness [*vimarśaśakti*] which are to be seen and meditated as being none other than you."

The offerings of alcohol and pieces of meat are "changed into something else," since they are believed to be transformed into ambrosia by the ritual of offering. The Dī quotes here a saying: "Wine is Śiva, meat is Śakti; bliss is said to be liberation."

> You, Goddess who takes on the form you desire, are to be perceived under the aspect of the spiritual master. //197// Having made an offering to the master who is no other than yourself, [the adept] must unite with himself what remains of it.
>
> *tvām icchāvigrahāṃ devīṃ gururūpāṃ vibhāvayet //197//*
>
> *tvanmayasya guroḥ śeṣaṃ nivedyātmani yojayet /*

It seems best here to quote all of Amṛtānanda's commentary:

> The Goddess is embodied in all forms that exist [*viśvarūpa*]. Wishing to spread her grace on the universe, she takes on forms by play [*līlā*]. She assumes thus the form she desires. You only are to be perceived under the aspect of the guru. To this master "who is no

other than yourself," who has your nature [*tvadrūpa*], one must have offered "cause (= wine); then the *sādhaka* will unite with himself this offering: what remains, that is, of what he first offered to the deity and to the master. Which is to say that the *sādhaka*, insofar as he has absorbed this remain, will be united, fused [*samarasī bhavati*] with the one and the other.

O Great Goddess! the *bali* is to be offered, using "cause," to myself who am the Guardian of the Field and to Baṭuka who is the self of the Yoginīs. //198b–199a//

yoginīnāṃ mahādevi baṭukāyātmarūpiṇe //198//

kṣetrāṇāṃ pataye mahyaṃ baliṃ kurvīta hetunā /

The rite of *bali* is one of the last parts of the *pūjā*. It is given here a metaphysical dimension underscored in the Dī, which says that the inner nature of Baṭuka is the vibration (*spanda*) of the supreme bliss, which is the self of the Yoginīs.

As for Kṣetrapāla, the "Guardian of the (sacrificial) Field," the "field," it says, is the body. It is, therefore, in the mind (*manasi*) to the guardian of the body and in reality to Bhairava that the *bali* is given. The Dī concludes: "It is by appeasing the movement of the *prāṇa* and *apāna* breaths and by annihilating the threefold[62] differentiation, and with the thought 'I am Śiva,' that one offers the inner *bali*."

Divinized by the *pūjā*, the *sādhaka* may henceforth act freely:

Ceaselessly drinking, devouring, and rejecting, acting on his own of his own free will, //199// realizing meditatively the unity of subject and object, the [adept] will remain in happiness.

nityaṃ piban vaman khādan svvecchācāraparaḥ svayam //199//
ahantedantayor aikyaṃ bhāvayan viharet sukham /

This drinking, devouring, and rejecting may be taken literally as referring to daily life. The Dī, however, understands it as drinking and eating the ritual offerings while rejecting them mentally.

Acting of one's own free will is explained as considering that whatever the *sādhaka* wishes, he must consider permitted. To realize the unity of I (*ahanta*, I-ness) and this (*idantā*, objectivity) is to realize the truth of nonduality.

Amṛtānanda quotes a stanza of the *Vijñānabhairava* which we may attempt to render as follows: "Because of the blossoming of the bliss arising from the pleasure of eating and drinking, one is to fuse mentally with the perfection of this joy; one will then identify with the supreme bliss."

The YH concludes the *pūjāsaṃketa*, saying:

> This divine and excellent threefold practice has been told to you. //200//
> It is to be kept carefully hidden, as one does one's secret parts, O Dear One! Neither to a frivolous being nor to one who merely desires knowledge is it to be revealed, O Perfect One. //201// One must not, in contradiction to the rules, entrust it to unbelievers, O Maheśvarī!
>
> *etat te kathitaṃ divyaṃ saṃketatrayam uttamam //200//*
>
> *gopanīyaṃ prayatnena svaguhyam iva suvrate /*
>
> *cumbake jñānalubdhe ca na prakāśyaṃ tvayānaghe //201//*
>
> *anyāyena na dātavyaṃ nāstikāṇāṃ maheśvari /*

This prescription was already formulated in the first chapter, 1.4.

> I am thus ordered by You who are the form taken by my own will, O Mistress! //202//
>
> *evaṃ tvayāham ājñapto madicchārūpayā prabho //202//*

Bhairava, the supreme God, a form of Śiva, appears here as both dominant, since the Goddess is the form taken by his will, and subordinated, since he is ordered by the Goddess to question her. We may see this as expressing the contradiction between the metaphysical principle that the supreme transcending reality is the male Śiva and the fact that theologically, the Goddess, Śakti, is the supreme deity. She is supreme, but Śiva is metaphysically above her. We must not forget that the Tantras were composed by men.

> Who will give [this teaching] contrary to the rules will surely perish.
>
> Who understands [this] practice will become dear to the Yoginīs. //203//
>
> Receptacle of the fruits of all desires, he will obtain all the fruits he wishes for.

anyāyena tu yo dadyāt sa pareto bhaviṣyati /
saṃketaṃ yo vijānāti yoginīnāṃ bhavet priyaḥ //203//
sarvepṣitaphalāvāptiḥ sarvakāmaphalāśrayaḥ /

The Yoginīs, "rays of light of the supreme Consciousness," says the Dī, have a particular connection (*yoga*) with the supreme Śiva, the master of all powers. The adept who follows this teaching, helped by the Yoginīs, "will therefore become the supreme Śiva," omnipotent and omniscient.

The statement that the adept will enjoy all the fruits he desires may come as a surprise to the reader who has seen that all the practices propounded in this Tantra were deemed to lead the adept to liberation. This, however, is normal in a Tantric context. The Tantric liberation in life—which can be reached, in principle, by using the means of this world, notably *kāma*, passion—gives, in fact, both *mukti* and *bhukti*, liberation and rewards. This is liberation from the fetters of this world but also magical domination over the world thanks to the possession of supernatural powers, *siddhis*.

The Śrīvidyā's initiated adept permitted to perform a *pūjā* is a *sādhaka*: one who possesses *siddhis*. He is usually considered a *bubhukṣu*, a being "desirous of *bhukti*," of worldly and otherworldly rewards, that is, rather than a *mumukṣu*,[63] a seeker of liberation. The *tāntrika*, we might say, is not of this world but in this world, which he has not left but transcends and dominates. This is what the YH offers.

The YH concludes:

What is visible everywhere, O Goddess, how can the sage not turn his thought toward it? //204//

yato 'pi dṛśyate devi kathaṃ vidvān na cintayet //204//

Śiva's—or the Goddess's—omnipresence is surely visible, understandable, by the sage if he follows the YH's teaching. Amṛtānanda concludes his commentary: "O Mother! your nature, which Śiva did not expose clearly because it is very secret, has been explained at the request of the Master"—that is, by the YH.

We hope that the reader will have found this text illuminating and that our attempt at an explanation has been useful.We would conclude in the traditional Sanskrit way—as Amṛtānanda has done in the Dīpikā—by saying, "be indulgent to us for that," *no kṣamasva tat.*

Notes

INTRODUCTION

1. There is also a very important, and still very active, Buddhist Tantric domain, sharing many traits with Hindu Tantra but very different in practice and notions.
2. The world is traditionally considered as threefold: sky, air, and earth. This is an ancient Indian notion. There are also other threefold cosmic divisions.
3. Or rather, in the present case, *mūlavidyā,* since the goddess is feminine. A *vidyā* is a feminine mantra—the mantra, that is, of a female deity. Mantra/*vidyā* and deity are, in fact, identical.
4. For the reader who might be surprised by the shift in Sanskrit terms from *i* to *ai* (*Śiva* to *Śaiva, Tripura* to *Traipura*), let us explain that in Sanskrit, the adjectival form of a verbal or nominal root is made by adding an *a*, hence *tri* + *a* = *trai.*
5. Though very often called "Mother," the Hindu goddess in her various forms and names, is not a "mother-goddess." She has no children (or, at any rate, does not give birth to them normally). Tripurasundarī has Bhairava as a consort but is not married to him.
6. There are *ardhanārī*, half-female, half-male images of this divine pair.
7. On this group of deities, see David Kinsley, Tantric Visions of the Divine: The Ten Mahāvidyās (Berkeley: University of California Press, 1997).
8. This observance consisted for the practitioner in wandering while carrying a skull-topped staff and an alms bowl fashioned of a human cranium.
9. The best description of the *āmnāya* system and, more generally, of the Śaiva traditions is that of Alexis Sanderson, "Śaivism and the Tantric Traditions," in Stewart Sutherland et al., eds, *The World's Religions* (London: Routledge, 1981), pp. 606–704.
10. On the *pīṭhas*, see note 22 of chapter 1 below.

11. This tradition has been studied by Douglas R. Brooks, notably in Auspicious Wisdom: The Texts and Traditions of Śrīvidyā, Śākta Tantrism in South India (Albany: SUNY Press, 1992).
12. There is Brooks's study quoted above and also his *The Secret of the Three Cities. An Introduction to Hindu Śākta Tantrism* (Chicago: University of Chicago Press, 1990). Though informative, these two books do not cover the vast area of texts of the Tripurā tradition of the *dakṣiṇāmnāya.*
13. Edited and translated by Arthur Avalon in the *Tantrik Texts,* first published in 1922 (reprint Madras: Ganesh & Co., 1953).
14. The *Subhagodaya* and the *Subhagodayavāsanā* of Śivānanda or the *Jñānadīpavimarśinī* of Vidyānanda, for instance.
15. This was done by Pdt. V. V. Dvivedi in the introduction (in Hindi) of his edition of the YH. The hypothesis does not lack probability. Abhinavagupta mentions central India (*madhyadeśa*) as the seat of all the Śaiva treatises (*niḥśeṣaśāstrasadanam*). This remains to be proved.
16. The Pratyabhijñā (the "Recognition"), one of the philosophical systems of Kashmirian nondualist shaivism, was propounded first by Somānanda (c. 900–950), then by his disciple Utpaladeva, whose work was commented on and expanded by Abhinavagupta. It is one of the most remarkable Indian philosophical systems. Its main contention is that liberation is gained by the recognition (*pratyabhijñā*) of the identity of the human self (*ātman*) and the supreme Lord, Śiva. The "transpersonal" self thus realized contains the totality of subjective and objective phenomena in a nondualistic synthesis where all distinctions disappear in the fullness of the Absolute. A concise and clear presentation of the Pratyabhijñā was made by Kṣemarāja in the *Pratyabhijñāhrdaya.* It is translated into English by Jaideva Singh, Pratyabhijñāhṛdayam, Sanskrit text with English translation and notes (Delhi: Motilal Banarsidass, 1963).
17. It has not been translated into English. Bhāskararāya wrote a short and useful treatise on the *śrīvidyā,* the *Varivasyārahasya.* It was edited with an English translation in the Adyar Library Series, no. 28 (1948). I translated Amṛtānanda's *Dīpikā* together with the YH in *Le coeur de la Yoginī:* Yoginīhṛdaya *avec le commentaire* Dīpikā *d'Amṛtānanda* (Paris: Collège de France, 1994)
18. A typical, though extreme, case of this is Pāṇini's Sanskrit grammar, the *Aṣṭādhyāy,* which is entirely cryptic. Its first sutra is: *vṛddhirādaic*...
19. On these two forms, see below.
20. Other Śaiva traditions have a goddess as their main deity, such as the Kubjikā tradition or the Krama, with Kālī. The Śaiva nondualist Kashmirian system of the Trika has three supreme goddesses: Parā, Parāparā, and Aparā. We may underscore here the fact that with very few exceptions, the Tantric traditions whose main deity is a goddess nevertheless hold the male divine form of the deity, usually Śiva/Bhairava, as metaphysically higher. Tantras, we must not forget, were composed by male brahmins; their extolling of the goddess or of

feminine powers were (to quote an American anthropologist) "male constructions of femaleness."

21. The *mātṛkās* are either seven, the *saptamātṛkā*, or eight (*aṣṭamātṛkā* or *matāṣṭaka*). The number eight is important in Tantric texts. Eight times eight is the (theoretical) number of Bhairava Tantras. Sixty-four is also four times sixteen, which is an important lunar number, the number of fullness. Sixteen is also the number of the Nityās, the first of which is Tripurasundarī (see YH 3.113); and the name of the VM/NṢĀ, *Nityāṣoḍaśikārṇava*, means "The Ocean of the Sixteen Nityās."
22. A *crore* (*koṭi*) is ten million.
23. On the Śaiva nondualist conceptions of the heart, see Paul Eduardo Muller-Ortega, The Triadic Heart of Śiva (Albany: SUNY Press, 1989).
24. But a light that is consciousness, a conscious light.
25. We say "manifested" rather than "created," for in a nondualist system, the deity does not create outwardly the world; she manifests, causes to appear outwardly (though in herself), the cosmos, which is in seed in herself. There is no *fiat* taking place at the beginning of time; creation as manifestation is being eternally, perpetually manifested by the godhead who pervades and animates it—otherwise, it would disappear.
26. Indian philosophical systems, like the classical Western (Greek) philosophies, are not abstract theoretical constructions but ways of life, traditions to live by.
27. *Bhāvanā* is a very important practice in the universe of Tantra. The term is derived from the causative form of the Sanskrit verbal root *BHU*, to cause to exist (*bhāvyate*). It designates a practice consisting of evoking mentally the image of a deity with the same precision as a concrete image or creating, by calling it intensely to mind, any image, vision, or thought, thus identifying the meditating person with the subject or theme being meditated. It differs from *dhyāna* in its intensity and identifying power and in the fact that it creates its object, which is not necessarily the case in *dhyāna*. Its role is fundamental in Tantric mental practices, spiritual life, and ritual. As is well known, in Tantrism, *dhyāna* designates meditation but also, and more important, the mental visualization of a deity as described in stanzas of ritual manuals called *dhyānaślokas*.
28. *Uccāra* is an utterance of a mantra that is both an enunciation and an upward thrust of the phonic subtle sound, the *nāda*, of the mantra in the body of the mantrin. This ascending phonic movement is often associated with the ascent of *kuṇḍalinī* along the *suṣumnā*; it is more a yogic practice than a verbal enunciation. This is, notably, the case of the *japa* of the *śrīvidyā* described in the third chapter (*śl.* 169–188) of the YH.
29. On the levels of *vāc*, see chapter 2, *śl.* 63, and n. 25 ad loc.
30. See the commentary and notes to *śl.* 1.57.
31. The *uddhāra* of a mantra is the ritual procedure by which one "extracts" (*ud-DHṚĪ*) its constituent syllables from the ensemble of the Sanskrit

alphabet, this being displayed, according to particular rules, on a consecrated surface or placed in a particular order in a diagram called *prastāra* ("display") or *gahvara* ("cavern" or "hiding place"). This permits revealing the composition of the mantra only to initiates who know how to "extract" the syllables thus hidden. The *uddhāra* can also consist of listing the syllables of a mantra, giving them conventional, theoretically secret names, or by alluding esoterically to them.

32. There are, in fact, various other forms, made of three clusters but of varying length, quoted notably in Purṇānanda's *Śrītattvacintāmaṇi*.
33. On this important term, see YH 1.67 and its commentary.
34. The basic work on the *kāmakalā* is Puṇyānanda's *Kāmakalāvilāsa*, which was edited and translated by Arthur Avalon in 1922 (reprint Madras: Ganesh & Co., 1953). A careful and interesting study of this diagram is found in chapter 4 of David G. White's *Kiss of the Yoginī: "Tantric Sex" in Its South Asian Contexts* (Chicago: University of Chicago Press, 2003).
35. *Nirīkṣaṇa*, also called *dṛṣṭipāta* ("the casting of a glance"), as a means to influence, harm, or else help spiritually, plays an important role in Indian religious or magic practice. The compassionate glance of the guru helps his disciple.
36. Hindu rites are traditionally divided into three classes. *Nitya*, "regular," are daily and mandatory rites; their performance does not bring any merit, but not to perform them is a fault. The *naimittika*, "occasional," rites are obligatory but are to be performed on particular prescribed occasions; they bring merit. *Kāmya*, "optional," rites are undertaken to attain desired aims; mantric rites are *kāmya*, as are, of course, all "magical" rites.
37. On the practice and spirit of the Tantric Śaiva worship, see Richard H. Davis, Ritual in an Oscillating Universe: Worshipping Śiva in Medieval India (Princeton, N.J.: Princeton University Press), especially the chapter titled "Becoming a Śiva." This book is a study of dualist shaivism, for which only ritual liberates one from the fetters of this world, a conception opposed to that of nondualist shaivism and therefore of the YH. The rites are, however, generally the same.
38. It is mentioned by Abhinavagupta in the *Tantrāloka* and in Tantras of the Kubjikāmata.
39. There are traditionally eight main *siddhis* always quoted, beginning with *aṇimā*, the power to become as small as an atom (*aṇu*). The others are *laghimā*, to be light; *mahimā*, being large; *prāpti*, to obtain all; *prakāmya*, being irresistible; *īśitva*, domination; *vaśitva*, subjugation; and *yatakāmavaśayitā*, to be able to go to whatever place one wishes. A ninth *siddhi*, *garimā*, to become heavy, is sometimes added.
40. On this center of the yogic body, situated twelve finger-breadths above the head, see chapter 3.49.
41. See note 17 above.

CHAPTER 1

1. There are innumerable instances both in the past and in the present of the narrow relationship between economics and religion in India. The large Hindu temples are very rich, and some rites are very costly, so much so that temple priests today are sometimes not fully initiated because they cannot afford the financial cost of a *dīkṣā*.
2. The Dī glosses *saṃketa* by several words, among which is *samaya*, which means not only agreement but also a conventional rule or practice or an observance.
3. A triangle apex downward is the usual symbol of the *yoni*, the feminine sexual organ, which is also called *janmasthāna*, the place of birth.
4. On these notions, see the commentary below on *śl.* 40.
5. The text has *ātmanā*, a dual form, meaning two *ātmans*. But the Dī interprets this as referring to the "four *ātmans*," four aspects of the Absolute Self, a notion found in some Upaniṣads (see, for instance, the Ātmopaniṣad). These *ātmans* are: *ātman*, the Absolute, the Brahman; *antarātman*, the inner self who enjoys the world; *parāmātman*, the supreme Self, the level of the subtle living creature (*ṣūkṣmajīva*); and *jñānātman*, which is the Brahman as nonseparate from the living being (*jīvābhinna*).
6. There is no sanskrit term for religion, a notion that is foreign to traditional India. For Hindus, the *dharma* regulates the social and what we would call the religious aspect of their life.
7. Their names are given in chapter 2, *śl.* 3–5.
8. *Pramā* or *pramāna* means, in fact, measure: the subject "measures" the world, which is the work of *māyā*, a word whose root is *MĀ*, to measure.
9. *Citkalā* could be more precisely translated as a limiting dynamism, for *kalā*, in shaivism, is a limiting form of energy or power to act, a dividing or parceling energy.
10. The Sanskrit *śaktyādi* could also be understood as "the first (*ādi*), which is *śakti*" (this is how Bhāskarāya understands it). There are, in any case, not ten but nine letters between *YA* and *KSA*; the exact meaning of this passage is therefore uncertain.
11. The forty-nine phonemes of the Sanskrit alphabet are, in their traditional order (the *varṇasamāmnāya*): sixteen "vowels," from *A* to the aspirate *visarga*; then twenty-five consonants, in five groups (*varga*) of five, classified according to their places of articulation, from the throat to the lips (guttural, palatal, cerebral, dental, labial), ordered in each group according to their phonetic characteristics (voiced, voiceless, aspirate, nasal); then four "semivowels," *YA*, *RA*, *LA*, *VA*; then three sibilants; and finally, the aspirate *HA*, to which is added the consonantal group *KṢA*, so as to have fifty letters. The reader will note that the Sanskrit alphabet is not in a complete phonetic disorder, as is our own, but

is shown (for more than two thousand years) in a logical and phonologically grounded order, an order that European linguists discovered only about two hundred years ago.

12. The name *krodhīśa* is given to *KA* because, in the ritual placing (*nyāsa*) on the body of the fifty Rudras (called *śrīkaṇṭhādinyāsa*), which is done together with the fifty letters of the alphabet, the Rudra Krodhīśa is to be placed with *KA*.
13. Those are twelve *tattvas* corresponding to the mind and the senses of human beings.
14. On the *kāmakalā*, see note 34 in the introduction, above. We shall come back to the subject later (chapter 2, *śl.* 21). For a theoretical and well-informed study of the subject, see David G. White, "Transformations of the Art of Love: Kāmakalā Practice in Hindu Tantric and Kaula Traditions," History of Religions *38* (November 1998): 172–198, or his book, *Kiss of the Yoginī: "Tantric Sex" in Its South Asian Contexts* (Chicago:University of Chicago Press, 2003).
15. A *mora* (*mātra*) is a prosodic instant. It is defined in traditional Indian phonetics as the length of time required to pronounce a short vowel.
16. To associate a particular visual aspect to the infinitely subtle planes of phonic energy of the *kalās* may seem surprising. These are, however, traditional notions. They are shown on the table of the *japa* of the *śrīvidyā* at the end of the Adyar edition and English translation of Bhāskararāya's *Varivasyāprakāśa* (Adyar, 1948).
17. The term thus translated (in fact, mistranslated) is *vapus*, which means shape, appearance, or body but not an ordinary body—a beautiful one, the body or apparition of a deity. It evokes, too, the essence of something, notably when it is contemplated in deep meditation (*bḥavanā*)or in mystical absorption (*samāveśa*).
18. The term used is *aṅkuśa*, which means hook or curb and also oblique. The meaning here is "oblique," referring to the left, oblique line of the triangle.
19. There is no satisfactory translation of the term *vaikharī*, which evokes the notion of spreading out (·*vi*) and is generally understood as evoking the external, concrete, perceptible dispersion of articulate speech, as opposed to the subtle concentration, and of the preceding stages of the word. In Indian thought, the less concrete, the briefest, the inaudible, is always the better or the best; the manifest, the concrete, the audible, is considered the lowest.
20. The complex and interesting process of apparition or spreading out of the Word, from *parā* to *vaikharī*, both as a cosmic process and as the process of apparition of speech and consciousness in humans, was described notably in Abhinavagupta's *Parātrīṣikāvivaraṇa* and in the third chapter of his great Tantric work, the *Tantrāloka*. There is no easily readable English translation of the first work and none of the second. The subject was studied and described by A. Padoux in *Vāc: The Concept of the Word in Selected Hindu Tantras* (Albany: SUNY Press, 1990; Delhi, 1992). The theory of the levels of *vāc* (without *parā*) was

originally put forward by the philosopher-grammarian Bhartṛhari (5th c. a.d.) in his treatise "On the Sentence and the Word," *Vākyapadīya*, a difficult work, part of which can be read in an English translation.

21. The term rendered in English by "manifesting" is *bhāsanā*, from the verbal root *BHĀS*, to shine, to be bright, which is used because in such systems as that of Tripurā, the manifestation of the cosmos (in fact, all manifestation) is conceived as a shining forth, a luminous manifestation, *ābhāsa*. This is an essential notion of the Pratyabhijñā philosophy, explained at length by Utpaladeva and Abhinavagupta.
22. The *pīṭhas* are seats or places of power sacred to the Goddess. They are usually said to number fifty-one, being the places of the Indian subcontinent where pieces from the dismembered body of Satī, Śiva's consort, fell as he roamed with it after she died following Dakṣa's sacrifice. Their numbers, however, vary. The oldest traditions have only four (or five); of those mentioned here, the principal is Oḍḍiyāna, even when, as here, it is not mentioned first. Kāmarūpa's *tattva* is the earth. It is a yellow square. Geographically, it is Kamākhya, in Assam. Pūrṇagiri's *tattva* is air. It is gray, shaped as a circle with six *bindus* inside. It is difficult to locate in the Indian subcontinent. Jālandhara's *tattva* is water. It is white, shaped as a half-moon. It would be in the present region of Jullundur, in the Punjab. Oḍḍiyāna's is fire, red, triangular. It is identified with the valley of Swat, now in Pakistan. On the colors attributed to the elements, see T. Goudriaan, *Māyā Divine and Human* (Delhi: Motilal Banarsidass, 1978), chap. 4. The *pīṭhās* are here manifestations of the Goddess. They are also places where esoteric doctrines were revealed—hence the use of the word *piṭha* for particular traditions or ritual practices (e.g., Mantrapīṭha and Vidyāpīṭhā to designate two divisions of the Bhairavatantras). The *pīṭhas* are also considered aspects or forms of energy corresponding to planes of the yogic imaginary body, as is the case here.
23. Some Śaiva texts say: "The *pīṭha* is Śakti, the *liṅga* is Śiva."
24. In many Tantras, notably those of the Trika, the best *liṅga* is said to be the *tūra*, a human skull decorated with incisions.
25. See the commentary above on *śl.* 40, on the theory of the four levels of the word.
26. *Spanda* is the primary subtle vibration that animates the eternal dynamism of the supreme deity and pervades and animates the cosmos. *Spanda* is one of the fundamental notions of the Kashmirian nondualist shaivism. It was expounded in the *Spandakārikā* deemed to have been composed by Utpaladeva (10th c.). On this important system, see Mark S. G. Dyczkowski, *The Stanzas on Vibration* (Albany: SUNY Press, 1992).
27. The repartition of items into a certain number of parts to which is added another part made of the totality of these parts is quite frequent in India, especially the division into 3 + 1: three parts plus the whole. This is what we have here. The

śrīvidyā is also sometimes described in this way: its three parts taken separately, then taken as a whole, which is sometimes called *turīyavidyā*, the fourth *vidyā*.

28. The theory of the *avasthās* (also called *sthāna*) goes back to the early Upaniṣads, notably the Maitri, where the fourth is described as *acittaṃ cittamadhyastham acintyam*, a thoughtless unthinkable present in thought: it is a condition of pure consciousness (*caitanyamātravṛtti*), says the Dī. *Jagrat* is the waking state; *svapna*, which more specifically means dream, is the state of sleep, whereas *suṣupti* is deep, dreamless sleep. The state «"above the fourth" (*turiyātīta*, a more recent notion) is described in the Dī as a transcendent state (*atītarūpam*) of consciousness of the Self. It is the «"unsurpassed" (*anuttara*), the absolute, «"light of all lights" (to quote the Mundaka Upaniṣad II.2,10), which, though transcendent, is present as their self (*ātman*) in all living creatures.
29. The *Pratyabhijñāhṛdaya*, by Kṣemarāja (11th c.), a disciple of Abhinavagupta, is a short philosophical treatise describing the main traits of the Pratyabhijñā system. It has been translated into English by Jaideva Singh (Delhi, 1963); see introduction, note 16, above. It is not a difficult text and is well worth reading. The Dī on *śl*. 50 is rich and interesting. It is unfortunately too long to be translated here.
30. The term we translate by triangular is *śṛṅgāṭa*, which is the nut of the water chestnut, the which is triangular in shape. *Śṛṅgāṭa* is often used to mean a triangle or something triangular or threefold.
31. As mentioned in the introduction above, Kāmeśvarī (with Kāmeśvara) can, along with Tripurasundarī (with Bhairava), be considered the chief deities of the *dakṣiṇāmnāya*. The coincidence of two, male and female, figures underlines the twofold though nondual nature of the supreme deity. This character is sometimes iconographically shown in images of Kāmaśvara and Kāmeśvarī as one bisexual *ardhanari* (half-female) figure—see, for instance, Ajit Mookerjee, *Kuṇḍalinī* (London: Thames & Hudson, 1982), plate X).
32. The energies are four when a supreme one, the Peaceful, *śāntā*,, or Ambikā, the Mother, is added to the basic three.
33. The expression we translate as "embodied as the *śrīcakra*" is *śrīcakravapuṣā*, "having the *śrīcakra* as body" (*vapuḥ*). This last word means form, figure, beauty, beautiful appearance, or a form one discovers in meditation, rather than a concrete body. It is therefore sometimes translated as essence, cosmic, beautiful form or presence. The *śrīcakra* is in effect viewed as a cosmic embodiment of the Goddess, not as a concrete body or form.
34. In the nondualist Śaiva systems—the Trika or Pratyabhijñā, especially—the supreme godhead is described as being inseparably light (conscious light) and reflective awareness (*vimarśa*), *prakāśa* being masculine, Śiva, and *vimarśa* feminine, Śakti. *Vimarśa* (a term found in the Dī but not in the YH) designates the consciousness or awareness one has of what is being perceived or experienced, contributing in this respect to the autonomy and total freedom of

consciousness. This is why the supreme deity is free and active, not unmovable as in the Vedānta; this is one of the points on which Vedānta and Tantra differ.

35. The Goddess, says the DĪ, transforms herself really into the world, as milk becomes curd. This point is also one of the main differences between the Tantric views and those of the Vedānta.
36. This sort of interpretation, called *nirukta*, goes back to Vedic times. It is sometimes falsely called etymology and then criticized as fanciful, but it is not an etymology. It is an imaginative way to enlarge the semantic field, the aura of meanings, of a word by associating it with other verbal roots, as shown here.
37. These actions are *avahāna*, inviting the deity to come; *sthāpana*, fixing it in the icon; *saṃnidhāna*; and, finally, *saṃnirodhāna*, detaining it there.
38. We write Mudrā when referring to the goddesses so-called and *mudrā* when referring to the notion or to the hand gesture, it being understood that they are perceived by the YH and the DĪ as being simultaneously both deity and gesture.
39. *Kṣobha*—which may be translated as effervescence—is, among Trika authors such as Abhinavagupta, the state of consciousness in which the cosmic manifestation appears, perturbing by its diversity the original quiescence of the Absolute. This role of *kṣobha* is also found in other traditions, such as the *Viṣṇupurāṇa*, I.2.29–31.
40. Such doors here are symbolical, since one does not enter a *śrīcakra*. But when a *cakra* or yantra drawn on the ground is large, as is the case in various rituals, the officiant can actually enter or leave it using these doors.
41. In the third chapter (*śl.* 127), these *kalās* or "vowels" are called *vāyu*, or winds, that is, vital forces, *prāṇas*.
42. See chapter 3, *śl.* 126–128.
43. On *kṣobha*, see note 39, above.
44. The number of *cakras* varies according to traditions. In the Tripurā tradition, they number nine, corresponding to the nine divisions of the *śrīcakra*. There are also secondary centers (*adhāra*, *śūnya*, *vyoman*, *bindu*, etc.), the number and places of which in the imaginal yogic body vary also according to traditions.
45. On the *āyudhas* of deities, see chapter 3, commentary on *śl.* 159, and n. 15.
46. *Khe* is the locative form of *kha*: "in *kha*."
47. *Bhūtraya:* not because there are three earths but because the outer part of the *cakra*, called *bhūgṛha*, "house of the earth," is encircled by three lines.

CHAPTER 2

1. This, we may note, is a case in which mantra and deity are indistinguishable.
2. A *vyāpakanyāsa*, a diffusive or spreading placing of a mantra on the body, is normally made with the two hands over the whole body or on a whole part of it, the power thus placed being deemed to pervade the whole region thus submitted to the power of the mantra. In the present case, the *mūlavidyā* would

pervade the whole body of the adept with the power of the Goddess. Although it is mantric, this practice is therefore entirely mental. For the performer, however, it is a total—both mental and bodily—experience.

3. These nine centers of the yogic body with their presiding deities are enumerated in *śl.* 25–27a of chapter 1; see above.
4. On the term *uddhāra*, "extraction" of the letters of a mantra, see above, note 11.
5. *Saṃghaṭṭa* means coming together and also rubbing, interacting. It therefore has a sexual connotation, hence its use to denote the union of Śiva and Śakti.
6. "Indra, thanks to his magical powers [*māyābhiḥ*], takes on diverse forms" (Ṛgveda, VI.47.18). See also the *Bṛhadāraṇyaka Upaniṣad* II.5.19.
7. On the planes of the Word (*vāc*), from *parā* to *vaikharī*, see our commentary above on chapter 1, *śl.* 36–40.
8. Amṛtānanda says, in fact, "the fourth mantra," the totality of the *śrividyā* being taken as a fourth element made up of the three *kūṭas*: 3 + 1 = 4.
9. *Visarga* means emission. In the phonematic emanation system of the nondualist Śaiva traditions, *visarga*, as the last "vowel," preceding the consonants in the traditional order of the Sanskrit alphabet, is deemed to "emit" them.
10. Sun, Moon, and Fire (Sūrya, Soma, and Agni) are the three astral luminaries (*dhāman, dhamatraya*) of the Śaiva traditions. They are usually conceived as three concentric discs visualized on top of one another. Their symbolic meanings or correspondences are often mentioned. They are homologized with various powers: the three *guṇas*, yogic *nāḍīs*, etc. *Dhāman*, a locus of light or glory, is the place where a deity or power is present, manifesting itself luminously. The indologist Jan Gonda defined it as "a holder or container of numinous potency."
11. On the theory and symbolic meaning of the *kāmakalā*, the reader is referred to Puṇyānandanātha's *Kāmakalāvilāsa*, edited, translated, and with commentary by Arthur Avalon, a study first published in 1922. This diagram was especially studied by David G. White in *Kiss of the Yoginī: "Tantric Sex" in Its South Asian Contexts* (Chicago: University of Chicago Press, 2003).
12. *Bhāva* has, in fact, many meanings: it may mean natural, simple, but also conjectural or meditative, etc. Since it is to be attained by meditating intensely (*bhāvayan*), "a meaning attained by meditation" could perhaps be a likely rendering of the term.
13. See Arthur Avalon's edition and English translation of this work, published in the Tantrik Texts series (Madras: Ganesh & Co., 1953).
14. The YH takes over the notion, expounded notably by Abhinavagupta, that there is a thirty-seventh *tattva*, called *paraśiva*, which is "emptier than empty" (*śunyātiśūnya*) and represents Śiva as identical with and inseparable from the universe. Still higher, there is, for Abhinavagupta, a thirty-eighth *tattva*, which is unlimited and is taught mainly for meditation (see *Tantrāloka* beginning at 11.22).

15. On the intense identifying form of meditation called *bhāvanā*, see note 27 of the Introduction, above.
16. The cosmology of the YH is, as in all Tantric texts, that of the Sāṃkhya, for which the constituting elements of the cosmos are the twenty-five *tattvas*, "realities," going from *puruṣa*, the Lord, to the earth (*pṛthivī*), to which are added, above *puruṣa*, from five to eleven other *tattvas* corresponding to higher planes of the godhead. The subtle elements (*tanmātra*) are, in descending order, sound, contact, form, taste, and smell; the gross ones (*bhūta*) are ether, air, fire, water, and earth.
17. *Pralayākalā* is to be understood as "without *kalā*, etc., thanks to the *prayala*"; they are subjects, that is, who will survive the next *pralaya* (the end of the cosmos) because they have not burned away all their karma. The *vijṇānakalas* are "without *kalā* [and other fetters] thanks to their discriminative knowledge." The *sakalā*, "associated with [the *tattva*] *kalā*," which is the lowest of the *kañcukas* (the cuirasses which imprison the soul), are submitted to all possible fetters and limitation. The YH and its commentary mention here three *pramātṛ* only, although there is, in all Śaiva systems, a hierarchy of seven *pramātṛ* (the term is variously translated as subject, conscious or experiencing subject, or experiencer, no translation being very satisfactory) going from Śiva, the highest, to the *sakala*, The three quoted here are the three lowest ones. The other, higher ones are, after Śiva, the *Mantramaheśvaras*, Great Lords of the Mantras, the *Mantreśvaras*, Lords of Mantras, and the *Mantras*.
18. *Nigarbha*: Bhāskararāya, in his commentary (*Setubandha*, p. 155), explains this rather unusual term, saying that *nigarbha* is as if entirely in a womb (*nitaraṃ garbhe*), thus completely secret (*rahasyottama*). Jayaratha, in another text, says that it is an inner (*āntaratayā*) experience of the pure Self (even if it is differentiated into master, disciple, etc.).
19. The moon has fifteen "sections" (*kalā*) or digits (*tithi*) for its half-month but sixteen if one counts the *āmāvasya*, the night of the new moon; see note 26 below.
20. The term *gaṇeṣatva* is to be taken as "the state of mistress [*īśatva*] of the troup [*gaṇa*]" of deities, not as "having the nature of Gaṇeśas." These deities are to be placed by *nyāsa* on the body of the officiant of the *pūjā* which we will see in chapter 3, *śl.*14–21.
21. See note 9, above.
22. The nine *grahas* are: Sun, Moon, Venus, Mercury, Mars, Jupiter, and Saturn, to which are added Rāhu and Ketu, heavenly bodies that are favorable or dangerous. The Grahas, "Seizers," are also a category of demons that "seize" human beings, especially women and children. Their worship, the *grahapūjā*, aims at pacifying them, stopping their dangerous action.
23. The *nakṣatras* are the lunar mansions, the constellations through which the moon passes. They are both divisions of the ecliptic and goddesses. Like the Grahas, they have influences, either bad or good, on humans.
24. These are the sixteen vowels; the five groups of consonants; the four semivowels *YA*, *RA*, *LA*, and *VA*; the sibilants *ŚA*, *ṢA*, *SA*); and *ḤA*.

25. The theory of the levels of the Word was first propounded by the grammarian-philosopher Bhartṛhari (5th c.), for whom there were only three levels. Later on, Tantric authors, notably Abhinavagupta, added a fourth (or, rather, a first) transcendent, supreme, *parā* level, considered the basis of the three others, those through which the word first appears in consciousness, then becomes subtly formulated, then is fully manifested as speech, these three stages being also the stages of the manifestation of the cosmos. On the subject, see A. Padoux, *Vāc: The Concept of the Word in Selected Hindu Tantras* (Albany: SUNY Press, 1990; Delhi, 1992), pp. 166–222.
26. The lunar month has thirty days, called *tithi*. It is also considered to be divided (for the half-month) into sixteen *kalās*, the fifteen days, plus the so-called *amākalā*, which is the *amāvasya*, the night of the new moon during which sun and moon are supposed to be together; this *kalā* is deemed invisible and immortal. The division of the supreme reality into sixteen goes back to ancient, even to Vedic, times; see the Bṛhadāraṇyaka Upaniṣad, I.5, 14–15, on the division of Prajāpâti into sixteen parts.
27. As we have seen in the first chapter (1.25), there are in this system two lotuses with a thousand petals, one at the base, the other at the summit of the course of the *kuṇḍalinī*.
28. Chāndogya Upaniṣad 6.8, 7.
29. The term *pratīti* is often used in the DĪ in the sense of an intuitive nondiscursive comprehension of the reality. It is defined notably as *pramātṛviśrānti*, that is, repose, meditative contemplation, spiritual absorption in the supremely conscious. The Goddess is here defined as such insofar as she must be understood by the adept in this way, in her cosmic glory, through a mystical experience.
30. On the *kalās* of *HRĪṂ*, see chapter 1, the commentary on stanzas 25–35, above.
31. *Mahāprayojanam*, that is to say, a very high use, a very prominent goal: the realization of the highest meaning, liberation, the union with Śiva. See also the commentary on stanza 5, Chapter 1, above.
32. On the Ḍākinīs and the bodily elements, see the commentary on stanzas 60 and 61, above.

CHAPTER 3

1. We have already seen *nyāsas* in chapters 1 and 2. It consists of the ritual placing (or imposition) of mantras on the body or on some support. It is done by uttering (and/or evoking mentally) a mantra while placing it where needed with a particular hand gesture, a *mudrā*. The effect of the placing is sometimes conceived of as extending pervasively on a whole part of the body; this is called a *vyāpakanyāsa* (usually done with both hands; see chapter 2, note 2). Such is the case here for the lines of the square that form the outer limit of the *śrīcakra*. For a thorough overview of the subject of *nyāsa* as expounded in Sanskrit texts, see A. Padoux, *Tantric Mantras* (London and New York: Routledge, 2011), pp. 54–80.

2. The division of a category of subjects or objects into three groups—highest, middling, inferior (*uttama, madhyama, adama*) or supreme, supreme-nonsupreme, nonsupreme (*para, parāpara, apara*)—is usual in Indian philosophy and metaphysics.
3. The term *sādhaka* is seldom used in the YH, but only an adept who has received the *sādhaka* (or *nirvāṇa*) *dīkṣā* (initiation) has the formal capacity (*adhikāra*) to perform the ritual. The adept, here as in the preceding chapters, is therefore a *sādhaka*.
4. The planets (called *graha*) include, in addition to fourteen heavenly bodies, Sun, Moon, etc., Rahu and Ketu, which are two lunar nodes. *Grahas*, as their name shows (it means "seizer"), are powers that can magically "seize," that is, influence, human beings. Different sorts of demons or evil supernatural beings are also called *graha*.
5. The twenty-seven *nakṣatras* were already mentioned in chapter 2, *śl.* 58b–60a.
6. When considered as numbering seven, this group of Yoginīs includes Yākinī.
7. The episode is described in several Purāṇas.
8. The *pīṭhanyāsa* would thus be performed uttering a mantra such as "*AIṂ HRĪṂ ŚRĪṂ AṂ Kāmarūpāya namaḥ*" on the head, for the first *pīṭha* and the phoneme *A*.
9. The *siddhis*, supernatural powers, are also minor goddesses, Yoginīs. We therefore sometimes refer to them as Siddhis. Their number is not the same in all texts. Their list, however, usually begins with *aṇimā*, the power to be as small as an atom (*aṇu*). The usual number of *siddhis* is eight. They are *aṇimā*, *laghimā* (to become light), *garimā* (to become heavy), *mahimā* (greatness), *prāpti* (to obtain what one wishes), *prakāmya* (to be irresistible), *īśitva* or *īśitā* (domination), and *vaśitva* (to subjugate). To this canonical list is sometimes added *śānti* (pacification) or even other ones, The Dī lists ten *siddhis*. See *śl.* 115.
10. This translates *vyāpakatvena* as "pervasively."
11. The term *vyoman* designates the inner "space" of the mystical heart (also called *kha*, a term that refers to the central void of the axle of a wheel and, by extension, the void of the heart). It is therefore also the highest level of consciousness. There are sometimes several *vyomans* that are centers of the yogic body. See above, chapter 1, the commentary on *śl.* 62.
12. The Dī gives the names of these fourteen energies and the names of the series of twice ten (Sarvasiddhipradā, Sarvajñā,...) ones. We will meet them again later, starting at *śl.* 115.
13. The term used to mean southeast is *agni*, fire, because Agni, the god of the sacrificial fire, presides over this direction of space.
14. On the yogic imaginal body, see the introduction, above.
15. The so-called weapons (*āyudha*) are the objects that the deities hold in their hands. They are not always arms but different tools or symbols. Tripurasundarī (or Kāmeśvara/Kāmeśvarī) holds the elephant goad (*āṅkuśa*), the noose (*pāśa*),

a bow (*dhanuś*), and arrows (*bāṇa*). *Āyudhas* are also deities and are then shown in human form, each carrying one of the weapons. They are then part of the deity's retinue (*āvaraṇadevatā*).

16. These deities are often shown in "half-woman" (*ardhanarī*) form, both male and female, the male aspect forming the right half of the image, the female the left half.
17. Her mantra, the *śrīvidyā*, is similarly the *mūlamantra* of this tradition.
18. The *āvaraṇadevatā*, "surrounding deities," are those forming the retinue of a main deity. They are usually disposed around her or him in concentric circles—a "mandalic" pattern, as one often says.
19. The number and the names of the Mātṛkās vary according to traditions and texts, the first being often Brahmī/Brahmanī. They are enumerated and described in *śl.*116–123 for their worship.
20. The Dī explains: "that is to say, on the forehead."
21. On the absolute as inseparably Light and Act of Consciousness, (*prakāśavimarśamaya*), see the Introduction.
22. A *bali* is a ritual offering to a deity, notably, in a Śaiva context, to Yoginī, or to Baṭuka, and Kṣetrapāla, both often seen as forms of Bhairava. It may consist of food, various beverages, or ingredients. It sometimes includes an animal sacrifice.
23. The term "ray" (*marīci*), or "ray of consciousness" (*cinmarīci*), is used for the Yoginīs and also for the sense organs, which underlines the luminous and conscious character of these deities with which the sense organs are sometimes identified.
24. *AU* is the central part of *SAUḤ*, the *bījamantra* of Parā, the supreme goddess of the Trika.
25. The secret place (*guhya*) is "the place between the anus and the male organ" (the perineum), says the Dī. By face (*mukha*), one is to understand the forehead.
26. The six *aṅgas* are, in fact, not the limbs (which is the usual meaning of *aṅga*) of a deity but attributes, perfections, or powers of a deity. They number six: *hṛdaya* (heart), *śiras* (head), *śikhā* (tuft), *kavaca* or *varman* (cuirass), *astra* (weapon), and *netra* (eye). They play a role in ritual, being imposed (*nyāsa*) by their mantras.
27. *Arghya* usually consists of water specially prepared, mixed with various substances, and accompanied by a mantra. One traditionally distinguishes between ordinary or common *arghya* (*sāmānārghya*) and special *arghya* (*viśeṣārghya*). The latter is used for particular deities or specific rites. In Tantric rites, *arghya* may include blood, different bodily fluids or excretions, or other "transgressive" elements. *Arghya* is one of the ritual "services" (*upacāra*) presented to a deity during worship. Here the *arghya* prescribed is the common one.
28. We have not found any information on these deities.
29. The composite phoneme *KṢA* is, as we have seen, often added to the forty-nine letters (ending with the aspirate *HA*) in order to have fifty letters. The so-called Vedic *Ḷ* is sometimes also added in order to have fifty-one letters.

30. The sequences of Sanskrit letters given here are not arbitrary; they follow the traditional grammatical order (the *varṇasamāmnāya*) of the Sanskrit alphabet.
31. The term *madya* may refer to different alcoholic beverages, but when several different terms are used, *madya* tends to designate wine (made with grape juice).
32. *Vauṣaṭ* is one of the exclamations, the *jātis*, added at the end of a mantra to adapt it to different uses. *Jātis* are of Vedic origin. They are six in number: *namaḥ, svāhā, vauṣaṭ, hūṃ, vaṣaṭ*, and *phaṭ*.
33. See YH 1.34.
34. In the Pratyabhijṇā system, the *ahantā* is the I-ness, the conscious perceiving subject, the state of being "I," as opposed to all that constitutes the objectivity, the objective world, the "this-ness" (*idantā*).
35. This rather obscure list of elements includes all the "realities" (*tattva*), or principles, constituting the cosmic manifestation. Each of them is considered here as corresponding to a section of the *śrīcakra:* the fourfold inner organ corresponds to the central triangle; *avyakta, ahaṃkāra*, and the five *tanmātra* to the eight-triangle *cakra*; and so forth, down to the sixteen "evolutes" (*buddhi, ahaṃkāra*, the senses, and the elements) corresponding to the sixteen-petaled lotus.
36. We write "sacrifice" because the Sanskrit verb used here (for metrical reasons) is *yajet*. It refers, however, to the usual Tantric *pūjā*.
37. Many different terms are used for ritual alcoholic beverages, the most usual being *hetu* and *kāraṇa*, which both mean "cause."
38. There are sixteen when one adds to the fifteen lunar days the *amāvasya*, the night when sun and moon are deemed to coincide and which is invisible. These days are also called *kalas*, "portions." As for the *śrīvidyā*, it numbers sixteen syllables when the *vidyā* as a whole is added to its fifteen constitutive letters. Sixteen is a lunar number. It is also the number of divisions of Prajāpati or of the Puruṣa, since the Veda.
39. A general rule in Tantric worship is that the aspect of the deity to be worshipped (usually to be visualized) is to be adapted to the aim of the ritual: a fearful form, for a "cruel" (*krura*) rite, a peaceful one for an appeasing one, and so forth, the shape, clothes, ornaments, color, etc., of the deity being different in each case.
40. The term *matuluṅga* is variously translated as "wild lemon" or (in the Monier-Williams Sanskrit-English dictionary) as "horn-apple."
41. In the traditional Sanskrit grammar, the "vowels" (*svara*) are considered male and active, as seeds (*bīja*), whereas the consonants (*vyañjana*) are deemed to be feminine and inactive by themselves; they are *yonis* (wombs). In the traditional Indian view, the role of the womb is passive, as a mere receptacle of the male seed. (We put "vowels" in quotes because the sixteen *svaras* include two diphthongs and two accessory signs—*bindu* and *anusvara*—which are not grammatically vowels.)

42. See our commentary on chapter 1, *śl.* 42, above.
43. A lunar month is made up of thirty lunar days; half of it (waxing or decreasing) lasts fifteen lunar days, to which is traditionally added the *āmavasya*, the day of the new moon, which makes sixteen.
44. *Bhūtalipi* is often translated as "demon-writing" (in the Monier-Williams Sanskrit-English dictionary, for instance). But this is a misnomer, its different groups of phonemes being associated with the gross elements (*bhūta*) of the cosmos, an association mentioned in the Dī. The *bhūtalipi* is made up of forty-two letters only, from *A* to *SA*, ventilated into nine groups (*varga*) of vowels, diphthongs, and semivowels, then of consonants ending with the sibilants, the last of which is *SA*. In spite of its being called a writing, *lipi*, its uses seem more oral and metaphysical than concrete; here we are on the plane of *madhyamā*, a subtle, nonmanifested level of the Word (*vāc*).
45. The names of the different categories of Yoginīs of the Tripurā tradition are given above in the explanation of *śl.* 90 of this chapter.
46. On *bhāvanā*, see chapter 2, note 12 above.
47. This conception of *kula* will be seen again with stanza 168.
48. See chapter 1, *śl.* 41–43, and chapter 1, note 22.
49. On the five conditions or states (*avasthā*) of the mind, from waking (*jāgrat*) to *turyātīta*, see chapter 1, *śl.* 49, above.
50. The Nityās as quoted in the YH number sixteen (see *śl.* 112b–113a). They include Nityā, Kāmeśvarī, and Bhagamālinī, mentioned here first, followed by the thirteen others.
51. *RA* is traditionally the *bīja* of fire (*agnibīja*), *LA* is that of water, etc
52. On the notions of *pramātṛ*, *prameya*, and *pramāna*, see chapter 1, *śl.* 13, above.
53. *Māyā* often designates *HRĪṂ*. The *Ī* here is the *Ī* of the *śaktikūṭa*.
54. Other Tantric Śaiva texts give different definitions of *turya*.
55. *Smaraṇa* (or *smṛti*) has an important role in nondualist shaivism, for, in joining the past to the present, it abolishes time. (An analogous role is given to memory by Marcel Proust in *Time Regained*.)
56. In Śaiva philosophy, remembrance or memory (*smṛti*, *snaraṇa*) is an important state of consciousness, since in remembrance, consciousness, turning back upon itself and desisting from the perception of new objects, recalls those previously perceived and rests within itself in a subtle state. Also, connecting time past with time present, memory transcends time and thus opens the way to the Absolute.
57. We have translated *mantrātmā* in this way, but *ātmā* does not, in fact, add anything to *ṇada*. *Rūpa* at the end of a word often does not convey any special meaning.
58. This refers to the curved shape of the letter *Ī* in *devanāgari* script.
59. In the commentary to YH 1.29–30.

60. The so-called *pañcamakāra* is a modern notion. Older texts mention as Tantric offerings only wine, meat, and sex (*madya, māṃsa, mithuna*), a triad, incidentally, already mentioned in Manu's Laws as involving no fault (*na doṣaḥ*).
61. *Naimittika* rites are obligatory; they must be performed, but not every day, only on particular occasions or at particular times of the year, such as the *parvans*, or in special cases, such as initiation (*dīkṣā*), rites of installation (*pratiṣṭha*) etc., and, of course, on the occasions mentioned here.
62. The traditional triad of knower, known, and knowledge, which is taken to refer to the totality of the world.
63. In Tantric texts, the category of *mumukṣu* includes women and children.

Glossary

Sanskrit terms whose meanings are customarily well known (*Brahman, liṅga, māyā, mudrā, śakti*, for instance) are not included here. All terms are listed in the index.

adhvan: path, way, both of cosmic manifestation and to be followed to reach liberation.

ājñā cakra: the *cakra* between the eyebrows where the adept receives the command (*ājñā*) of his guru.

akula: a name of the Absolute in the Kaula systems.

āmnāya: transmission, of which there are four in the Kula tradition.

amṛta: nectar of immortality, ambrosia.

anāhata: "unstruck"; the most subtle, totally inaudible aspect of *nāda*, deemed to underlie all audible sounds.

ānanda: bliss; not to be confused with pleasure (*sukhā*).

ardhacandra: crescent moon; one of the divisions (*kalā*) of the utterance (*uccāra*) of *OṂ*.

arghya: untranslatable; the liquid offering to the deity done during worship and of which the worshipper is to partake; consists usually of water (or other fluid), mixed with various substances; the two sort of *arghya* are ordinary (*sāmānya*) and special (*viśeṣa*).

artha: meaning; also object.

āsana: throne of a deity.

ātman: the human self or the Absolute divine Self (there is also a system of four *ātmans*, four aspects of the absolute Self).

avasthā: the five states or conditions of the spirit—waking, sleep, deep dreamless sleep, the fourth, and above the fourth.

āveśa: possession or absorption.

āyudha: "weapon"; the name for the different instruments or objects a deity holds in his or her hands.

bali: offering to a deity or to ancestors.

bhāvanā: intense creative and identifying meditation.

bhukti: mundane or supramundane joys or rewards.

bhūta: gross elements, the five lowest *tattvas*.

bīja bījamantra: seed, seed mantra; always monosyllabic.

bindu: dot, drop.

brahmarandhra: the opening of Brahmā, the thousand-petaled lotus on the top of the head.

cakreśvarī: the mistress (the presiding deity) of a *cakra*.

cit: consciousness.

citta: mind.

dakṣiṇa: right, the right side of a figure; a category of Tantras as opposed to Tantras "of the left," *vāma*, those of the right being seen as more staid than those of the left.

darśana: view, viewpoint; the main philosophical systems of Hinduism notably described and classified from the point of view of Śaṅkara's Vedānta in Mādhava's *Sarvadarśanasaṃgraha*.

dhāman: "splendor"; luminary, place of light, of which there are three cosmic ones: Sun (*sūrya*), Moon (*candra*), and Fire (*agni*), often mentioned in ritual; also forms of power present in the yogic body.

dhātu: constituent element of the body, traditionally seven in number—lymph, blood, flesh, bone, fat, marrow, and semen.

dhvani: general term for sounds of all kinds; sometimes a subtle form of sound.

dhyāna: meditation, visualization.

dhyānaśloka: stanza of visualization of a deity or mantra.

dīkṣā: initiation in a particular Tantric tradition; not to be confused with the *upanayana*, the initiation of boys of the three higher *varṇas* (Brahmin, Kṣatrya, Vaiśya).

dvādaśānta: the *cakra* twelve finger's breadths above the head, the highest point reached by the ascending *kuṇḍalinī*.

granthi: "knot"; a name for the *cakras* of the yogic body.

guṇa: quality, property, notably the three qualities that pervade all the *tattvas*—*sattva*, *rajas*, and *tamas*.

hṛd hṛdaya: the heart, especially as a mystical center; name of a *cakra*.

icchā (*icchāśakti*): will, the power of will, of the deity; the highest of Śiva's three basic powers.

jāgrat: waking, one of the five *avasthas*.

japa: ritual recitation of a mantra.

jīvanmukta: liberated in this life; *jīvanmukti* is the state of liberation in this life.

jñāna: knowledge, gnosis.

jñānaśakti: the power of knowledge, the second of the three powers through which Śiva manifests the cosmos.

kalā: limited power to act; usually the first evolute of *māyā*; *kalās* are phonic subdivisions of mantras, notably of the subtle *uccāra* of *bījamantras* ending with *Ṃ*.

kāmakalā: a ritual diagram symbolizing the sexual union of Śiva and Śakti.

kapāla: skull (worn by a yogi); *kāpālika* is a skull-bearing ascetic.

karaśuddhi: purification of the hands (before a ritual action).

kaula, kaulika: "of the Kaula" ensemble of traditions.

kha: inner void (like the central void for the axis of a wheel).

khecara: moving in space or the void; *khecarī* is she who moves in space or the void; a class of Yoginīs; also a very high spiritual state where one moves freely in the space of pure (divine) Consciousness.

kriyāśakti: energy or power of action, the third (after *icchā* and *jñāna*) power of Śiva when manifesting the cosmos.

kṣobha, kṣobhana: agitation, effervescence, perturbation; a creative divine (or human) state of agitation, appearing also in creative imagination, sensual pleasure, or aesthetic enjoyment.

kula: family or clan; a name first used for the clans of Yoginīs; also the name of the main nondualist Śaiva ensemble of traditions, divided into four "transmissions" (*āmnāya*); in these traditions, also used for the highest—but not transcendent—divine plane; also used for the human body seen as a microcosm.

kulācāra, kaulācāra: the correct behavior according to the Kaula.

kuṇḍalinī: "she who is coiled"; the divine *śakti* as present in the yogic body and active in the cosmos.

līlā: the divine cosmic "play."

mātṛ mātṛkā: mother; name used for the eight Mothers, Brāhmī, etc.; also used for the phonemes of the alphabet, seen as aspects of *vāc* when they are placed on the body by *nyāsa*, for instance.

mūlādhāra (*cakra*): "the root support"; the bodily *cakra* on the level of the perineum where the *kuṇḍalinī* lies coiled

mūlamantra: root mantra, the main mantra of a male deity or power.

mūlavidyā: root mantra of a female deity or power.

nāda: subtle phonic vibration.

nāḍi: channel of the yogic body of which there are seventy-two thousand in the human body.

nirīkṣaṇa: rite of gazing, this gaze being considered as powerful; the gaze of the guru saves, for it is charged with the grace of God (*anugraha*).

pīṭha: seats or places of power of the Goddess; there are four main *pīṭhas* considered as the sources of the Śrīvidyā doctrine—Kāmarūpa, Pūrṇagiri, Jālandhara, Oḍḍiyāna.

prakāṣa: light; in nondualistic shaivism, the supreme godhead is *prakāśa*, pure light that is absolute Consciousness by which it manifests the world; it is also *vimarśa*, the free consciousness of that state of freedom.

pramātṛ: "experiencer"; the subject that perceives the object (*prameya*) and judges according to criteria (*pramāṇa*).

prāṇa: breath, vital energy; a generic term for all the breaths, respiratory or vital; different *prāṇas* have different functions.

pūrṇa pūrṇatā: fullness, plenitude of being.

puryaṣṭaka: "the eight in the body"; the subtle transmigrating body.

śabda: sound, one of the five subtle elements (*tattvas*).

sādhaka: initiated adept, looking for or possessing *siddhis*.

samāveśa: complete absorption in the divine.

siddhi: supernatural or magic power.

spanda: "vibration"; the subtle vibration of the divinity that pervades and animates the cosmos.

sṛṣṭi sthiṭi saṃhāra: the cyclical cosmic ensemble of emanation (*sṛṣṭi*), continuation or preservation (*sthiti*), and destruction or resorption (*saṃhāra*) of the cosmos going on eternally from age (*yuga*) to age.

śūṇya: void.

suṣumnā: the main channel (*nāḍī*) of the yogic body; a vertical axis going from the lowest *cakra* to the *brahmarandhra* or *dvādaśānta*.

suṣupti: dreamless sleep.

svapna: sleep (including dreaming).

turya: the fourth state or condition of the spirit.

turyātīta: the state above the fourth.

uccāra: utterance of a mantra; upward movement of *prāṇa*.

uddhāra: the rite of "extraction" of a mantra, giving its phonetic composition.

ullāsa: splendor, shining forth, especially that of the godhead in its cosmic action bringing forth the universe as a shining forth of light.

unmanā: the transmental.

vāmā: left, oblique; see *dakṣiṇa*.

vīra: hero, a fully initiated adept, able to meet and unite sexually with Yoginīs.

visarga: emission; the name of the letter of the Sanskrit alphabet transcribed as *Ḥ*.

vimarśa: the consciousness aspect of the supreme godhead who is both *prakāśa* (pure light) and *vimarṣa*.

yoni: the female sexual organ, graphically shown as a triangle point downward.

Bibliography

With only a few exceptions, this bibliography is limited to works in English and excludes works meant for a limited scholarly readership.

TEXTS

Abhinavagupta. There are Italian translations but no English translations of Abhinavagupta's great treatise, the *Tantrāloka*, or of his very interesting work, the *Parāttriśikāvivaraṇa*, on which, however, see Bettina Baümer's study listed below.

Kāmakalāvilāsa by Punyānanda with the Commentary of Natanānandanātha, translated with commentary by Arthur Avalon in *Tantrik Texts*. Madras: Ganesh & Co., 1958.

Kṣemarāja. *Pratyabhijñāhrdayam*, Saṃskṛta text, English translation and notes by Jaideva Singh. Delhi: Motilal Banarsidass, 1963.

Lakshmī Tantra: A Pāñcarātra Text, translation and notes by Sanjukta Gupta. Leiden: E. J. Brill, 1972.

Muktananda (Swami). *Play of Consciousness (Chitshaktivilas)*. South Fallsburg N.Y.: SYDA Foundation, 1978.

The Serpent Power, Being the Shat-chakra-nirūpana and Pādukapañchaka, translated from the Sanskrit, with introduction and commentary by Arthur Avalon. Madras: Ganesh & Co., 1953.

The Stanzas on Vibration: The Spandakārikā with Four Commentaries, translated with an introduction and exposition by Mark. S. G. Dyczkowski. Albany: State University of New York Press, 1992.

Tantrarājatantra: A Short Analysis, by Sir John Woodroffe. Madras: Ganesh & Co., 1954.

Utpaladeva. *Sivastrotrāvalī of Utpaladeva: A Mystical Hymn of Kashmir*, exposition by Swami Lakshman Joo, transcribed and edited by Ashok Kaul New Delhi: D. K. Printworld, 2008.

Vijñānabhairava, or Divine Consciousnesss: A Treasury of 112 Types of Yoga, translation by Jaideva Singh. Delhi: Motilal Banarsidass, 1979.

STUDIES

These are in addition to the studies referred to in the notes.

Baümer, Bettina. *Abhinavagupta's Hermeneutics of the Absolute, Anuttaraprakriyā: An Interpretation of His Parātrīśikā Vivaraṇa*. New Delhi: D. K. Printworld, 2011.

Brooks, Douglas. *The Secret of the Three Cities: An Introduction to Hindu Śākta Tantrism* Chicago: University of Chicago Press, 1990.

Dyczkowski, Mark S. G. *A Journey in the World of the Tantras*. Varanasi: Indica Books, 2004.

Flood, Gavin. *Body and Cosmology in Kashmir Śaivism*. San Francisco: Mellon Research University Press, 1993.

———. *The Tantric Body: The Secret Tradition of Hindu Religion*. London: I. B. Tauris, 2005.

Fürlinger, Ernst. *The Touch of Śakti: A Study in Non-Dualistic Trika Śaivism of Kashmir*. New Delhi: D. K. Printworld, 2009.

Harper, Katherine Anne, and Robert L. Brown, eds. *The Roots of Tantra*. Albany: State University of New York Press, 2002.

Hawley, John Stratton, and Donna Marie Wullf, eds. *Devī, Goddess of India*. Berkeley: University of California Press, 1996.

Kinsley, David. *Tantric Visions of the Divine Feminine: The Ten Mahāvidyās*. Berkeley: University of California Press, 1997.

Muller-Ortega, Paul Eduardo. *The Triadic Heart of Śiva*. Albany: SUNY Press, 1989.

Silburn, Lilian. *Kuṇḍalinī: The Energy of the Depths*. Albany: State University of New York Press, 1988.

White, David Gordon. *Kiss of the Yoginī: "Tantric Sex" in Its South Asian Contexts* Chicago: University of Chicago Press, 2003.

Index